T0171339

The City

Cook

Big City, Small Kitchen
Limitless Ingredients, No Time

More than 90 recipes so delicious
you'll want to toss your takeout menus

Kate McDonough

with photographs by Mark Dichter

Simon & Schuster
New York   London   Toronto   Sydney

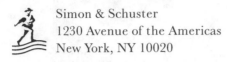 Simon & Schuster
1230 Avenue of the Americas
New York, NY 10020

First Simon & Schuster hardcover edition November 2010

SIMON & SCHUSTER and colophon are registered trademarks of
Simon & Schuster, Inc.

The City Cook with city skyline logo is a registered trademark of The City Cook, Inc.

For information about special discounts for bulk purchases,
please contact Simon & Schuster Special Sales at 1-866-506-1949 or
business@simonandschuster.com.

The Simon & Schuster Speakers Bureau can bring authors to your live event.
For more information or to book an event contact the Simon & Schuster Speakers Bureau
at 1-866-248-3049 or visit our website at www.simonspeakers.com.

Designed by Nancy Singer

Manufactured in the United States of America

10 9 8 7 6 5 4 3 2 1

Library of Congress Cataloging-in-Publication Data

McDonough, Kate.
   The city cook : big city, small kitchen, limitless ingredients, no time : more than
90 recipes so delicious you'll want to toss your takeout menus / by Kate McDonough ;
with photographs by Mark Dichter.
       p. cm.
1. Cookery. 2. Cookery, International. 3. Quick and easy cookery. I. Title.
   TX714.M3824 2010
   641.5'55—dc22   2010018758

ISBN 978-1-4391-7200-1

For my Mark. Life with you is a continuous feast.

For starters, learn how to cook.
—U.S. poet laureate Charles Simic when asked
how people can become happy

Contents

Preface

This book is for the new cook with her first apartment who wants the satisfaction, control, and creativity of home cooking.

It's for the urban explorer who has learned the pleasures of adventurous eating from visits to ethnic and stylish restaurants and wants to replicate his favorite dishes at home.

It's for those who cook to support local farmers and improve our food supply.

This book is for parents who want to not only feed their children well but also teach them about the flavors, traditions, value, and health of home cooking.

It's for the weekend host who wants to break bread with friends and family at home and have the food be as good as the company.

This book is in praise of the grocers, farmers, butchers, cheese mongers, fishmongers, bakers, spice merchants, market organizers, CSA volunteers, urban gardeners, salami makers, tomato growers, pickle guys, and others who bring us the best ingredients in the world.

Above all, it's a book for home cooks—regardless of where you may live.

Part 1

City Cooking: A Primer

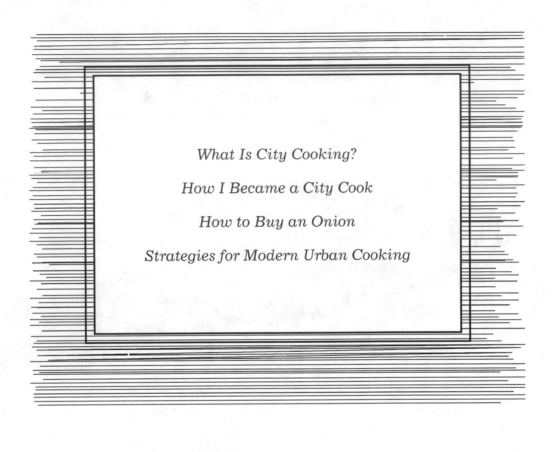

Cooking in the City

What Is City Cooking?

City cooking celebrates the flavors that come from our small urban kitchens. We cook with ingredients from downtown farmers' markets, small grocers, community supported agriculture deliveries, and neighborhood merchants.

Our kitchens are small and space is precious. We often take public transit to work. Many of us live close enough to our neighbors to be welcomed home in the evening by the aromas of their dinners. More than half of Americans now live in cities, and for those of us who do, there is an adjacency to our lives that affects what we eat and how we cook.

City cooking means finding a way to put daily home cooking into our always busy, often stressed, urban lives. Days start early and go late. Subways are delayed, and umbrellas are forgotten. Dogs need to be walked. But we're determined to make dinner instead of having it delivered.

City cooking is about knowing how you want to eat every day and cooking your own meals with flavor and with confidence. We cook for our health, our budgets, and the pleasures of good food. And we want the satisfaction of making our own meals and of time spent in the kitchen with our families and our friends.

Should we still eat in great restaurants? Absolutely. Our chefs delight, inspire, and motivate us. Likewise, we shouldn't abandon the convenience of takeout meals. I would feel very hard done by if I were never again to have sushi from my favorite neighborhood Japanese restaurant or couldn't comfort a winter cold with a container of hot matzo ball soup from a much-loved deli. But living in a city shouldn't mean we eat out or carry-in because we have no other options.

It is impossible to think about being in an urban kitchen without celebrating the changes that are now transforming how we cook and eat at home. Influenced by chefs, food writers, urban farmers, environmentalists, and other activists, efforts are being made to improve and protect the quality of our food because home cooks are demanding better ingredients, improved sustainability of our food supply, and, yes, more satisfying flavor.

This food revolution is under way in cities across America. Urban farmers' markets are held every day throughout the year. Community supported agriculture lets us give direct financial support to local farms in return for a share of the crops. Regional specialties, often made by the same methods for generations, are increasingly available. Beekeepers are harvesting honey on the rooftops of city apartment and office buildings. New rivals are challenging large supermarket chains as the small neighborhood market returns to viability and popularity.

Finally, our cities are sophisticated global tables, inspired by the ethnic cuisines of our immigrant forebears and strengthened by our own regional cooking. Because we have access to many of the best ingredients in the world, home cooking makes the city kitchen a delicious destination.

How I Became a City Cook

I first learned to cook because I couldn't afford to eat in restaurants. I was working long hours plus going to school, first in Boston and then in New York. My apartments were always small; my kitchens even smaller. My first kitchen was so tiny that I could pivot on one foot to reach my stove, sink, and refrigerator. But these were welcoming havens as I would come home hungry after a long day, craving both the meal I would prepare and the satisfaction of domesticity. As I chopped and stirred, I would play back my day in my head and begin to relax. Or maybe I would watch the news or invite a friend to join me for supper, making my little kitchen a homey refuge.

The first meals I made were simple, barely spiced, and made from ingredients I could afford. Chicken. Canned tuna. Pasta. Salad. As my career moved ahead, I began to have business lunches and dinners in restaurants—good restaurants, including some of the best in New York City. It was from those meals that I began to develop my palate. I learned why pasta was cooked *al dente*. And duck left rare. I lost the ability to eat bottled salad dressings and began to taste the difference between food cooked in olive oil and that cooked in butter. I discovered the delicacy of raw fish and the power of chiles.

For a few years my job required me to travel. I had never been overseas, and my journeys to Asia, Europe, and the Middle East were both palate and life changing. My work required keeping project diaries, but I filled the margins with the details of what I ate.

I wanted to find a way to take all these eating experiences and bring them into my daily life, so I began to take cooking lessons. At first, too afraid to pick up a knife in public, I only took classes where I could watch. But soon I was joining others in learning how to sauté a steak, peel a tomato, bone a chicken breast, and reduce a cream sauce. When on vacation I would seek out local cooking classes. I once took a small ship through the Greek islands and pestered the captain until he let me spend time in the boat's galley; I was determined to find out how the cook made such wonderful and authentic meals in such a tiny space.

After I had learned some of the basics of cooking, I began to take individual classes on subjects in which I felt particularly unskilled, such as cooking fish and shellfish and making pies and tarts. Finally, for a milestone birthday, I gave myself a work sabbatical and spent three months at New York's French Culinary Institute.

But the way I really learned was by cooking every day. On weekends I'd explore New York's neighborhoods, food market by food market, from pickle stores and bakeries on the Lower East Side, to pasta makers in Brooklyn's Williamsburg. Visits to Greek markets in Astoria, mozzarella mongers in the Bronx, and sidewalk fish stands in Chinatown taught me that some of the best ingredients in the world were in my city and that these merchants would provide the means for me to cook well.

How to Buy an Onion

I discovered that I wasn't the only one cooking at home. New York's restaurants were crowded, but so were its food markets. On a visit to the produce aisle of Fairway, an iconic, busy New York grocer on upper Broadway in Manhattan, I met a woman who was lamenting the overwhelming selection of onions. The week before Thanksgiving, she held a shopping list that filled a large sheet of paper. But the onions left her stumped, and thus discouraged. She had the bravery to take on a multicourse holiday meal but was derailed by a vegetable.

I started talking with friends and colleagues about their cooking triumphs and failures, and I found that most were baffled by the basics. They have stacks of cookbooks and cooking magazines and piles of Internet recipe printouts but are intimidated when buying ingredients. They want to keep versatile foods on hand to make a meal after a long day but don't know how to stock a pantry. They have wacky kitchen gadgets but never bought a chef's knife. They know it's easy to broil a luxurious veal chop but would prefer a less costly London broil, pork loin, or tilapia fillet. They visit farmers' markets but are overwhelmed by the choices and go home clutching only a jar of jam.

I saw that many want help in planning meals, buying ingredients, and fitting cooking into already overcommitted daily lives. To share the strategies I learned, I created TheCityCook.com and wrote this book.

Strategies for Modern Urban Cooking

The City Cook became a place to show how home cooking can be put into a busy urban life. There I share tips about how and where to buy great ingredients. And I share the recipes I have developed over my years of cooking—recipes that work for weekday cooking when you come home late and hungry and don't have time to shop, along with recipes for holiday cooking and entertaining in a small urban home.

Here I've developed and adapted recipes that I hope you will enjoy and make part of your regular menus. But even more, it's my wish that you will use these recipes to help you cook the way you like to eat. You may substitute cilantro for basil or reduce or increase the amount of heat in a dish—the point is to make these recipes yours.

Most of all I hope this book gives you more confidence in the kitchen. If I've learned anything from my years of being a home cook despite having a busy life, it's that we will cook more if we don't feel discouraged when facing the task of making dinner. And we'll cook more if our meals are satisfying to eat.

The Strategies

- While it may seem a cliché, it is true that the best food is made with great ingredients cooked simply.
- Knowing how to buy ingredients is as important as knowing how to cook them.
- Cook what you want to eat and follow your own palate. If you prefer certain flavors, spices, ethnic dishes, or ingredients for reasons of health or politics, then these should be the foundation of your home cooking.
- Learn how to shop at farmers' markets, food co-ops, and community supported agriculture programs; don't hesitate to ask local artisans for advice. It will not only get you better ingredients; the more we support local farmers and producers, the better our food supply will become in the long run.
- City living lets us shop daily which lets us cook from the ingredients up. If you begin with what's in season and what's local, you will get the best flavors.
- Stock your pantry. This includes your refrigerator and freezer. If you keep certain ingredients on hand, you can buy fresh food on your way home from work and have all you need for a stress-free weekday dinner.
- Learn to shop from specialty merchants, such as cheese mongers, fish stores, and butchers, who can teach you about their products and how to cook with them. Many of these specialists now also sell online (I've included many of my favorites

in the back of the book) so you can supplement the markets where you live with products sold by the best food merchants in the country.

- Equip your city kitchen with the best-quality pots, pans, knives, and tools you can afford. Resist buying too many gadgets that will fill up your precious storage space. For example, you can make any meal with only three knives—chef's, serrated (for bread and tomatoes), and paring. Learn how to sharpen and hone them yourself, and your cooking will improve.

- Develop your own recipe repertoire. Your grandmother could make her perfect potato gratin or tomato sauce because she cooked it once a week for forty years. Same thing for chefs: they practice a dish dozens of times before it appears on a menu. While making new recipes is always fun, having a core list of dishes that are "yours" will make you a more confident cook. Before you know it, friends will be asking you to make your special short ribs or guacamole or lamb curry.

- Get educated about the changes taking place in our food culture. Learn the language of today's ingredients: organic, local, artisanal, sustainable. Our food merchants will sell us what we want to buy, but to do so, we need to know what we want. (See the Glossary on page 263 to get started.)

The best thing you can do is just cook. Cook for yourself and cook for others. Take risks. You'll make mistakes—we all do—but it's only dinner. And tomorrow you can try again.

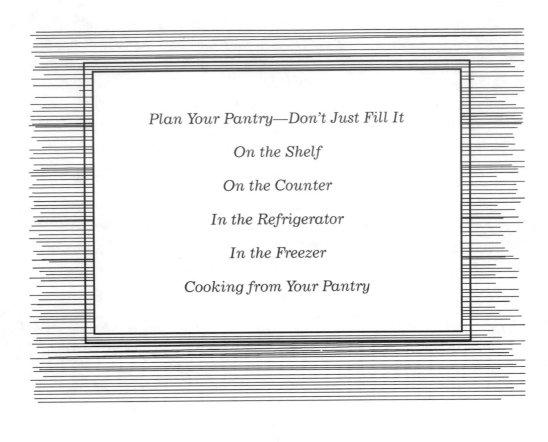

Plan Your Pantry—Don't Just Fill It

On the Shelf

On the Counter

In the Refrigerator

In the Freezer

Cooking from Your Pantry

The City Pantry

The notion of a pantry may seem a bit old-fashioned if it conjures an image of a small room off the kitchen with shelves lined with canned goods. In an apartment or a small city house where space is precious, such an arrangement is rarely possible.

But a pantry doesn't have to be a place. Instead think of it as a strategy based on planning ahead. Stocking a pantry simply means keeping core ingredients on hand. Some pantry items are kept on a shelf, but many will be in your freezer and refrigerator.

A well-stocked city pantry gives us flexibility. We can buy fresh produce, meat, poultry, or fish and know that at home we have ingredients to turn them into dinner. Sometimes the pantry can even generate the entire meal. Just don't overbuy or you'll waste space and money and lose focus.

Finally, a pantry is about convenience. Who wants to hunt for a decent bottle of olive oil for salad dressing on the way home from work? Plus, if you stock in advance, you'll have the chance to buy the best quality at the best prices.

Plan Your Pantry—Don't Just Fill It

We've all done it: bought something exotic, like a jar of tomato jam or lemon-flavored olive oil, thinking it will give us options. It won't. Unless these are favorite flavors, they'll only take up space before you someday toss them out. Instead, before stocking your pantry, take a frank look at how you cook and how you prefer to eat. For example, if you are a vegetarian or a vegan, include items like vegetable stock and more dried and canned legumes. If you primarily cook Asian foods, keep hoisin sauce and rice vinegar. Some important foods, like the small bottle of ketchup I keep on hand for a favorite meatloaf recipe, may be used infrequently. As you make your pantry your own, you'll gradually figure out which items are essential.

But don't be too spare: a well-edited pantry can add easy versatility to everyday cooking. For example, a jar of harissa, the spicy red pepper paste popular in North African cuisine, can become an easy rub to add flavor to pan-grilled shrimp or lamb chops and make a pan of plain couscous far more interesting.

If there's an ingredient you won't use often but still want on hand, buy the smallest size. I know it may seem more cost-effective to buy bigger, but if you don't use it often, it will only go bad and where's the cost savings in that? Plus smaller sizes are easier to store.

For spices that can fade in flavor, write the purchase date on the label or bottom of the jar. The same goes for anything you put in the freezer. That way you'll know for sure if something is past its prime.

Keep a small pad of paper in the kitchen so that when you use the last of an essential item or when a bottle or jar is nearly empty, you can make a note. Then the next time you're shopping at your favorite market, replace it.

What's essential to one home cook is useless to another. This list can get you started but add and delete for yourself.

On the Shelf

- Oils: extra virgin olive oil, canola oil or other light vegetable oil, peanut oil for deep frying
- Vinegars: red wine vinegar, white wine or Champagne vinegar, other vinegars such as cider, sherry, balsamic
- Soy sauce or tamari
- Tabasco or other favorite hot sauce
- Honey
- Worcestershire sauce
- Dried herbs and spices: black peppercorns, cinnamon, paprika (hot, sweet, Basque espelette), red pepper flakes, oregano, chili powder, bay leaves, cumin (ground), cayenne pepper, dry mustard
- Salt: fine grain, kosher, sea salt
- Canned vegetables: chickpeas, black beans, cannellini beans, artichoke hearts, whole San Marzano tomatoes, canned cherry tomatoes, tomato paste (can or tube)
- Canned tuna, sardines, and anchovies
- Rice: long-grain, Arborio, basmati, brown, specialty rices such as red Bhutanese
- Dried pasta: spaghetti, cut short pieces such as ziti or rigatoni, tiny pastas such as orzo or ditali for pilaf or soup
- Boxed chicken stock and vegetable stock
- Grains: bulgur, couscous, Israeli couscous, quinoa, farro, barley
- Nuts: walnuts, almonds (pine nuts are in the freezer)
- Asian ingredients: fish sauce, oyster sauce, rice vinegar, sesame oil, wasabi (powder or paste)
- Harissa
- Jar of salsa or piquillo peppers

- Flour: unbleached all-purpose white, whole wheat, rye
- Sugar: white, light brown, confectioners'
- Cornstarch
- Baking soda
- Baking powder
- Cornmeal
- Cocoa (Dutch process)
- Vanilla (extract, not flavoring)

TIP: Freeze nuts if you're not going to use them quickly. Otherwise they can become rancid.

TIP: Don't buy oils too far in advance as they can lose flavor or spoil. Same goes for buying large amounts of them because by the time you get to the bottom, the oil may have gone bad, and any cost savings from buying a big quantity will be lost.

On the Counter

My apartment doesn't have a cellar or garage, so to store my aromatic vegetables I keep a small supply on hand in a large ceramic bowl on the counter (out of the sun if you have a windowed kitchen).

- Whole ginger
- Jalapeño peppers
- Garlic
- Shallots
- Onions: yellow and red
- Tomatoes

TIP: Tomatoes should not be refrigerated but instead stored on the counter, out of the sun, at room temperature. The chill of refrigeration breaks down the sugar in tomatoes, making them mealy and tasteless.

In the Refrigerator

- Dijon mustard (I like the one by Maille)
- Eggs (large is the usual size in recipes)

- Mayonnaise (regular or reduced fat)
- Ketchup
- Olives (black cured in oil and green in brine)
- Cornichons
- Capers (in brine and in salt)
- Parmesan cheese (a chunk kept wrapped in plastic wrap and foil)
- Another versatile cheese such as goat cheese or feta
- Bacon or pancetta
- Carrots
- Celery
- Lemons
- Limes
- Parsley (flat-leaf)
- Thyme, rosemary, cilantro, other fresh herbs
- Milk, half-and-half or light cream
- Anchovy paste (in a tube)
- Tomato paste (in a tube)
- Dry white wine (for cooking and a glass for the cook)

TIP: While it's true that Parmesan is always best grated just before you use it, a large amount can be inconvenient to grate by hand at the last minute. So if you use Parmesan often, grind a piece in a food processor and refrigerate it in a plastic container; it will keep its good flavor for at least a week.

In the Freezer

- Pine nuts (I use these costly nuts in small amounts and they can easily spoil)
- Butter (unsalted)
- Panko (Japanese bread crumbs; I store leftovers in the freezer after I've opened the package)
- Peas
- Pearl onions
- Artichoke hearts
- Spinach
- Puff pastry dough (Pepperidge Farm or Dufour)
- Bread crumbs (homemade by grinding pieces of stale bread in the food processor)

- Chicken and/or vegetable stocks (either made by you or small amounts of leftover boxed stock)
- Vanilla ice cream
- Martini glasses

TIP: If you use boxed stock and have some left over, pour it into a small plastic container and freeze it. For convenient small portions, pour it into an ice cube tray and when fully frozen, transfer the cubes to a large plastic freezer bag.

TIP: Melt vanilla ice cream for an instant crème anglaise to dress up a bakery-bought brownie or simple baked apple.

TIP: Chilled martini glasses will have a pretty frosted finish and help keep a just-made cocktail icy cold.

Cooking from Your Pantry

Most of us don't think about what we'll make for dinner until the end of the day. If you have a well-stocked pantry, you can stop at a fish store on the way home from work and buy a pound of wild shrimp, and without buying anything else, you'll have options for cooking them. For example:

- Peel, clean, and dust the shrimp with cornmeal to which you've added a pinch of cayenne pepper. Do a quick sauté in a nonstick pan with a tiny bit of olive oil, cooking until golden, then place on top of salad greens, or
- Rub with a little spicy harissa, broil for 2 minutes a side, and serve with quick-cooked couscous, or
- Sauté in a little olive oil, minced garlic, and a pinch of red pepper flakes until the garlic is golden and the shrimp is just opaque. Add a small can of Italian cherry tomatoes and quartered (defrosted) frozen artichoke hearts and simmer for 10 minutes to get the raw taste out of the tomatoes. Serve with rigatoni.

So with a pound of shrimp you have three ways to make a quick dinner. But you only have these options if your pantry already contains cornmeal, cayenne pepper, harissa, couscous, olive oil, garlic, red pepper flakes, canned tomatoes, rigatoni, and frozen artichoke hearts.

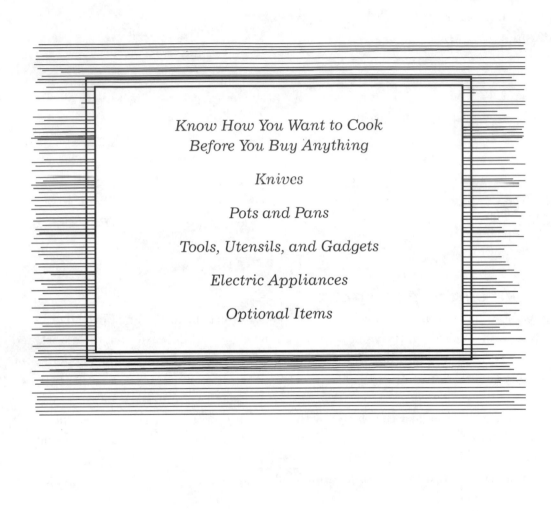

*Know How You Want to Cook
Before You Buy Anything*

Knives

Pots and Pans

Tools, Utensils, and Gadgets

Electric Appliances

Optional Items

Equipping a City Kitchen

While city kitchens are often small and short on space, the fact is that you could have acres of counters and not be a better cook. I've been in neighborhood restaurant kitchens and ship galleys and watched extraordinary meals coming from well-organized but tiny places. I've been in McMansions where the stoves are never used. So space is no guarantee of better cooking.

In fact, it can get in the way. The four square feet of workspace I was assigned when I attended culinary school was enough for a 15- by 20-inch cutting board, a metal garbage bowl, and a place for that day's tools. Still, I was physically exhausted by the end of the day from pacing across the kitchen classroom to the sinks, stoves, and refrigerators that we all shared. My tired legs reminded me that small is better.

But when it comes to storing kitchen tools, limited space can be frustrating. If you're like me, I could own the entire contents of a cookware store and still want more. But I've learned that having no place to keep something forces you to be disciplined—own less, choose carefully, and buy the best quality you can afford.

This applies to every piece of kitchen equipment: knives, pots, pans, appliances, and gadgets.

Know How You Want to Cook Before You Buy Anything

You could ask a dozen home cooks which tools they can't live without and get twelve different answers. That's because the equipment we need depends upon how we cook: A wok is a necessity for someone who does lots of stir-fries. For someone else it could be a vegetable steamer or a pasta pot. My list would include a favorite sauté pan, my enameled cast-iron Dutch oven for making stews, a colander to drain pasta and rinse vegetables, and an instant-read thermometer for checking meats and poultry.

If we have the right tools, we will get better results. Plus you may try new dishes if you don't have to compromise on your equipment. You really can't make a soufflé without a soufflé dish; a nonstick pan is essential for omelets; and a pair of tongs will give you precision when turning anything that's being browned or broiled, without piercing the surface. And the first time you cook with a sharp, well-balanced chef's knife is simply a revelation.

If you've developed your kitchen tool kit gradually over the years, give yourself the gift of taking inventory. Notice the items you use daily versus rarely. Have your knives sharpened by a professional or buy a knife stone and sharpen them yourself. If your most often-used tools are beat up or could use an update, consider a few replacements. And before you go cookware shopping, make sure you do the equivalent of eating lunch before grocery shopping: check your kitchen for storage space to make sure you don't buy anything you a) won't use often and b) don't have room for.

Here are what I think are the basic tools and equipment for a small kitchen.

Knives

Owning good knives is probably the single most important investment you can make to become a better cook. And there's almost nothing you can't do as long as you have the holy trinity: a chef's knife, a paring knife, and one with a serrated edge.

- **Chef's knife.** Also called a cook's knife, this comes in lengths from 4.5 to 12 inches, but the most typical are 8, 9, and 10 inches. Which you choose depends upon the size of your hand and how the knife feels in terms of weight and balance. If you could only have one knife in your kitchen, this would be it. Buy one you love, keep it sharp, store it carefully, always wash it by hand, and use it for everything.
- **Paring knife.** These are used for trimming and other detail work. The blades range from 2.5 to 4.5 inches; if you're only going to have one, 3 to 3.5 inches makes sense.
- **Serrated knife.** The most common serrated knife is a bread knife but others include small tomato knives. A 7- or 8-inch serrated knife can serve multiple purposes and is a very useful tool for cutting anything that has a resistant surface, such as artichokes or angel food cake.
- **Honing steel.** This is a rod of steel that's used to realign the edge of your knives in between sharpenings. A knife's blade may still be sharp, but with use, it develops tiny burrs, invisible to the eye, that need to be rubbed back into alignment. By passing a knife's blade along a honing steel several times while alternating the side of the blade, the edge returns to its best sharpness.

Most of the time you only need to hone a knife's blade every three to five times you use it. Doing so not only will keep your knife's edge but also allow you to put off sharpening (which actually wears down the metal on the blade) to only once a year or so, adding to the life of your knife.

Once you have these basics, you can add to your collection those that make specific kitchen jobs easier. These include:

- **Boning knife.** The flexible blade makes it good for filleting fish and deboning poultry.
- **Scissors.** For trimming vegetables, snipping herbs, or cutting up a chicken.
- **Slicing knife.** For slicing roasts.
- **Cheese knives.** There are different kinds for different cheeses—one cuts soft cheese, such as Brie, without damaging the rind; another peels off thin slices from a medium-hard cheese like Gouda. My favorite is shaped like an arrowhead with a short point and is best for chipping off chunks from Parmesan and aged Pecorino.
- **Mandoline.** This slicing tool is very useful for salads and essential for dishes such as potatoes Anna, fennel slaw, and other recipes that require thin, uniform slices. Mandolines come in fancy professional models and smaller, less costly ones with ceramic blades. These are quite sharp, so if you're at all clumsy (as I am), also buy a mesh glove to protect your fingers when slicing. They're sold in the cutlery department alongside knives.

Always buy the best-quality knives you can afford and then take care of them. Good knives are an investment that will last for many years and will help you become a better and happier cook.

Pots and Pans

Pots and pans are awkward to store, and since most city kitchens have limited space, we need to choose wisely. What most cooks eventually figure out is that there are the essentials and then there are the extras.

When buying cookware, resist the lure of those preselected sets. The price may seem compelling, but I promise you that at least one piece will end up never used. Instead buy exactly what you need, and you'll get more value and have less to store.

I prefer stainless-steel-clad aluminum saucepans and either stainless-clad or cast-iron skillets and always choose ones that can be used in the oven as well. However, I also have one nonstick frying pan for eggs, crêpes, and omelets. My favorite is a 10-inch Swiss Diamond, but whatever kind of nonstick pan you choose, periodically check its surface for wear and replace it as soon as you see surface corruption.

For everything else, there are several good manufacturers. My personal favorites are All-Clad for sauté and saucepans, Lodge for cast iron, Le Creuset for enameled cast iron, and Pillivuyt or Emile Henry for ovenproof porcelain. Pyrex is also an excellent choice for baking dishes, loaf pans, and pie plates.

Unless there's a dish you make frequently that requires a specific pan, such as paella, be sure that each piece you buy gives you multiple uses. For instance, a ceramic rectangular pan can be used to roast a small chicken, make lasagna and gratins, and bake fish with tomatoes. A soufflé dish can also be used for baking bread pudding or a casserole and is pretty enough to be a salad bowl. A loaf pan is perfect for meatloaf, banana bread, and vegetable pâté.

Here are the basics:

- **Saucepans with covers.** 1 quart and 3 or 4 quart.
- **Sauté pan with a cover.** 4 quart (approximately 3 inches deep with straight sides, 10½ inches in diameter). I use this pan more than anything else in my kitchen. It has a surface like a skillet; it takes a cover; the straight sides help reduce sauces; it's deep enough to poach or steam in; you can fill it to the rim with spinach; and you can start something in it on top of the stove and finish it in the oven.
- **Skillets.** 7 and 12 inches (with handles that can go into a hot oven) in either stainless-steel-clad aluminum or cast iron. A 12-inch skillet can take the place of both a sauté pan and a small roasting pan—it's extremely versatile except that it doesn't take a cover. Also a 10- or 12-inch nonstick skillet for eggs, omelets, and sautéing without added fat.
- **Cast-iron grill pan.** 10 to 12 inches, with grill ribs. Great for stovetop grilling of steaks, chops, fish, vegetables, and even stone fruit such as peaches. This pan can easily end up as one of your favorite pieces because it adds big versatility to the smallest kitchen.

TIP: A square grill pan more easily accommodates foods than a round one.

- **Pasta pot (7 to 8 quarts) with insert and cover.** This pot can double as a stockpot, and with the insert can also serve as a steamer for vegetables or fish.
- **Enameled cast-iron French or Dutch oven.** 6 to 10 quarts. Get one big enough to be versatile but small enough for the size of your household. These pots are very heavy, so buy one you can lift safely when it's full and hot from the oven.

- **Porcelain or ceramic ovenproof rectangular pans.** Approximately 1 to 3 quarts, about 8 by 12 inches, small enough to bake a gratin or apple crisp but big enough to roast a small chicken.
- **Rimmed sheet pans (also called jelly-roll pans).** Approximately 12 by 18 inches (called a half-sheet pan) and smaller at about 12 by 9 inches (a quarter-sheet pan), these can be among the most used in your kitchen. For more than baking cookies, this pan is perfect for roasting vegetables or meats, browning bones for stock, slow cooking tomatoes, and much more. You can even put a rack on it and roast a turkey. Buy a good one so that it doesn't warp when it gets hot.
- **Teakettle.** I think it's prudent to have one with a whistle.

Depending on how you cook, there are other pans you may consider essential. These include: roasting pan, wok, a big stockpot, cast-iron griddle (larger than a grill pan and with both smooth and ribbed surface), loaf pan, soufflé dish, or tagine.

As with knives, always buy the best quality you can afford and select pieces that you love and think are beautiful. It will only make you enjoy your cooking even more.

Tools, Utensils, and Gadgets

While we can make most meals with only a good knife, a wooden spoon, and a set of tongs, there are other essential tools that should be in any kitchen. After that it's up to you to resist the lure of the kitchen gadget. You know what I'm talking about—the garlic peeler, the strawberry huller, the little articulated metal juicer shaped like a wedge of lemon. I won't tell you to avoid gadget temptation because it's so much fun, but before you fill your precious drawer space with tools you'll rarely use, buy the essentials.

- **Tongs.** Metal with a spring action that lets the tongs work either open or closed.
- **Wooden spoons and spatulas.** Have as many as you have room for and try not to wash them in the dishwasher so that they last longer.
- **Spatulas.** Made from silicone for use in hot pans.
- **Microplane zester.** For grating cheese, lemon zest, chocolate, garlic, ginger.
- **Box grater.** For grating cheese, vegetables.
- **Metal spoons with long handles (including a ladle).** For soups, sauces, risottos, and basting.
- **Instant-read thermometer.** There's no other way to know if a roast is properly done.

- **Whisks.** Two sizes—4 to 6 inches for salad dressings, 8 to 12 inches for whisking sauce, pudding, mayonnaise, and eggs.
- **Vegetable peeler.**
- **Can opener.** Mechanical or electric (I love my Zyliss mechanical opener).
- **Wooden juice reamer.** One of my favorite kitchen tools, a reamer makes it easy to produce fresh citrus juice by hand. If you don't need a large quantity of juice, it's faster than pulling out an electric juicer.
- **Colander and strainer.** One large and one medium; big enough for draining boiled pasta or grains or vegetables and for rinsing fruits and vegetables. Also one small with a fine mesh to strain lemon juice or brewed tea.
- **Ice cream scoop.** Get the kind with a spring action and you can use it for making meatballs, scooping cookie dough, and other kinds of mounds.
- **Spider.** Used in Asian and Italian cooking, this is essentially a sieve on a handle.
- **Corkscrew.**
- **Bottle opener.** Sometimes called a church key.
- **Pliers.** For pulling bones out of fish, plus they're handy for fixing things in your apartment.
- **Little bowls.** To premeasure ingredients in a recipe-saving and timesaving step called *mise en place* (see page 43). Six-ounce Pyrex cups are perfect but any little bowls will do.
- **Metal dry measuring cups.** ¼-, ⅓-, ½-, and 1-cup measures.
- **Glass liquid measuring cups.** 1 cup, 4 cups. Ones by Pyrex are excellent.
- **Salad spinner.**
- **Pepper mill.** Get a good one that lets you adjust the milling as fine or coarse as you like it. I love my aluminum Perfex, made for decades in the same factory in Saint-Etienne, France. It costs more, but you'll use it happily and forever.
- **Saltcellar.** A little dish to hold cooking salt, leaving the saltshaker for the dinner table.
- **Butcher's twine.** Heavy-duty cotton string used to tie the legs of a whole chicken, tie up a roast, hold a bunch of asparagus together, or package a cheesecloth square of herbs. Make sure the string is 100% cotton or else it will melt in the oven.
- **Parchment paper.** Safely coated with silicone so it won't burn at high temperatures, this versatile paper can be used to create an envelope in which to steam fish, line a sheet pan for roasting vegetables, or even make a little pastry bag. Once you start using it, you'll use it often. It's usually sold in supermarkets alongside waxed paper (which is not the same thing) and aluminum foil, or in cookware stores.

- **Mixing bowls.** For assembling recipes, two or three glass or metal bowls are very useful. One can be a countertop garbage holder while you prep ingredients.

TIP: Dry and liquid measuring cups are not interchangeable. Dry and liquid ingredients must be measured in a proper cup to avoid getting the wrong amount. One cup flour is not the same as one cup water.

Electric Appliances

- **Coffee grinder.** I have two: one for coffee beans and a second for grinding spices.
- **Coffeemaker.** I have been a devotee of my nonelectric Chemex drip coffeemaker for decades, but most people I know prefer an electric coffeemaker.
- **Immersion blender.** For some home cooks, this tool plus a blender means they don't need a food processor.
- **Blender.**
- **Food processor.**
- **Handheld mixer or stand mixer.**
- **Toaster oven.** It's more energy efficient than your oven and many do much more than make toast.
- **Slow cooker.** Some consider this irrelevant; for others it's essential.
- **Pressure cooker.** Same as for slow cookers.

Optional Items

These are utensils and tools that are personal favorites, are needed for certain types of cooking, or may be otherwise idiosyncratic to you. But resist stocking up on gadgets you'll rarely use; you'll only fill up precious drawer space.

- **Garlic press.** Favorite of some cooks but scorned by others because it crushes the garlic.
- **Wine and Champagne stoppers.**
- **Bulb baster.** For turkeys, other roasts. I also use mine to help make tarte Tatin, pulling the caramelized sugar up from the bottom of the pan to baste the apples.

- **Oven thermometer.** If you have any doubt about how accurate your oven is (most are not—mine consistently runs 25°F hot), an oven thermometer, which usually costs less than $10, will let you know for sure.
- **Canning tools.** These include a large metal pot with a cover, a rack, large tongs for removing the hot jars, and all those jars, lids, and covers.
- **Rolling pin.** I love my heavy wooden one that I just rub with a little flour to make it nonstick, but the new silicone ones are also popular. Regardless which you choose, get one with some heft to help do the work.
- **Pastry brush.** To add an egg wash, brush off excess flour or cornmeal, brush melted butter or oil on roasting poultry, add an herbed oil to fish, or glaze a rack of ribs with barbecue sauce. It doesn't have to be fancy—an inexpensive paintbrush works perfectly.

It's Not the Cooking. It's the Shopping.

Ten Tips for Buying the Best Ingredients

*How to Buy Ingredients First and
Then Set a Menu*

How to Cook from the Ingredients Up

Your cooking can only be as good as the ingredients you use. Our best chefs know this and spend as much time sourcing and choosing ingredients as they do cooking.

Likewise for us—the most important part of home cooking is not the making but the planning and the buying of ingredients. We have access to thousands of recipes, including the few more in this book I've added to the recipe universe. But once we know the food we want to cook, set a grocery budget, and have some self-awareness about our skill level, then comes the point at which many of us get flummoxed: planning a menu and buying groceries.

It's Not the Cooking. It's the Shopping.

Who hasn't finished a long and busy day and, faced with the dilemma of what to make for dinner, given up and reached for the phone? Choosing what to cook can sometimes be just one too many decisions for the day. But with a little forward thinking, a stocked pantry, and a regular repertoire of familiar meals, everyday cooking can be a reward and not a burden.

Begin with a menu plan. At some point once a week think about your upcoming schedule and where and when you'll be having your meals. Include lunches packed for work or school, breakfasts, and end-of-day meals that can be made in less than an hour. Sketch out a week's menu and then take an inventory of ingredients in your refrigerator and freezer.

Get in the habit of making repeats. My mother, who made a satisfying and special dinner every night for my dad, brothers, and me, had a schedule of menus that she kept in rotation. We had fish every Friday, roast beef or chicken every Saturday, and once a week a vegetarian dinner. The familiarity was comforting for us as we each had our favorite dishes, but I now know it also made her life far easier.

Make a shopping list, then a shopping plan. Decide which ingredients you need to buy, where are the best places to get them, and when can you get the shopping done. This may mean combining a weekly online grocery order with Saturday morning at the farmers' market and a couple of lunchtime errands to buy fresh fish or chicken in your work neighborhood, stashing the bags in your office refrigerator until the end of the workday. The trick is to integrate regular grocery shopping into your normal routine—then it won't be burdensome.

Keep replenishing your pantry. We all have days when we have neither the time to shop nor the state of mind to even think about cooking until we get home exhausted and hungry. With the right items always on hand (see page 13 for pantry cooking), you can make a satisfying meal that will be much better than that day-old burrito from the steam table at the deli.

The same lessons apply to weekend cooking, making food for friends and family, and those big special events like holiday meals: come up with a plan, make a menu, reread recipes to make sure you have every ingredient on hand and to remind you of essential prep work (such as an overnight marinade), and then shop in advance.

It also comes down to this: as you watch your favorite TV chef pull together a tempting meal, appreciate that what you're watching is the last 10% of the whole process. If the preceding 90%—the planning, shopping, cleaning, and prepping—isn't done well, that last 10% won't really matter.

Ten Tips for Buying the Best Ingredients

This is important: if you become a better grocery shopper, you will become a better cook.

Think about the big difference a small detail can make. Using salted instead of unsalted butter will change a sweet dessert. Grilling a shoulder cut of meat as you would a steak will produce a tough result; likewise make a stew from a rib-eye and it will be tasteless. Maple-flavored bacon will add an odd cast to spaghetti carbonara. An underripe peach will make a far less flavorful peach cobbler than one that is juicy with sweetness.

Likewise, our ingredients can take a meal from good to great. A midwinter tomato will make a tasteless gazpacho, but come August, a local beefsteak can make this summer soup a miracle. So here are ten easy ways to immediately make you a better shopper.

Pay attention to the calendar. Buy foods that are in season because this is when they taste the best and cost the least. If you live in a northern climate and you're craving raspberries in February, you'll be better off buying frozen than fresh. Or better yet, cook with citrus, which is at its bright, big-flavored peak in midwinter.

Make a list. I'm always amazed how few people I see in the market with a grocery list. Maybe they have a better memory than I, but it's more likely that there's no cooking plan. On your shopping list make a note of the dishes you're planning to make in case you need to make substitutions (see below).

Be flexible. You may head to the market to buy asparagus, but if it looks stringy and the zucchini is deep green and beautiful, switch your vegetables.

Take lessons from your grocery stores. Pay attention to what's being featured. In-season foods tend to be front-and-center because these are the items that your grocer can get the most easily and at the best price.

Shop at multiple places. I know this can add to shopping time, but specialists almost always have better quality, more choices, and better prices. This means buying whole grains and dried legumes in bulk from a natural-food store, meat from a butcher, fish from a fishmonger, and produce from a farmers' market. Our ethnic markets—especially ones in ethnic neighborhoods—can be the best source for variety and also price.

Stock your pantry. If you keep a supply of your core ingredients (see page 9) on hand, it will take significant pressure off your grocery buying. You won't need to shop for every item in a recipe, which will save you time and money.

Ask questions. Food merchants are almost always knowledgeable and proud to help educate you. I've learned my best meat-cooking tips from butchers, and I was given my favorite fish recipe (page 198) by Dorian Mecir, owner of Dorian's Seafood in New York City. But I've also learned about pâtés and rillettes, how cheeses are stored, choosing spices, how to use leaf lard in a pie crust, and much more from the hard-working people who bring us our food. So ask.

Use your senses. Look at, touch, and smell the food you're buying. Fresh fish isn't "fishy"— it smells like the sea. Fruits and vegetables should be free of bruises or signs of decay. A ripe cantaloupe will have a sweet perfumed aroma. Vegetables should be firm.

Learn the language. Food buying now has its own jargon and much of it is confusing. You're sure to encounter such terms as organic, free-range, hormone-free, local, wild, farmed, sustainable, conventional, vegetarian, or vegan. Learn what they mean and watch to see how they're applied to the food you're buying. They can change the nutrition, cost, and flavor, and once you know what's what, you can make an informed choice. (See the Glossary, page 263.)

Read labels. Anything that's packaged usually has labeling, including nutrients, calories, expiration dates, and where the food comes from. But fresh foods also come with some of the same details, especially where the food is from. Take a look at the signage above each produce bin or ask your butcher or fishmonger.

How to Buy Ingredients First and Then Set a Menu

One of my most memorable cooking experiences came in a class taught by Italian cookbook author and teacher Marcella Hazan. She was in New York City promoting one of her books and agreed to teach two sessions at The French Culinary Institute. I already owned her books and considered *The Classic Italian Cookbook* essential. But that class with Signora Hazan taught me lessons that changed forever how I cooked by awakening me to the importance of cooking from the ingredients up.

As the class began, about a dozen of us took our places and were handed a menu and recipes for the dishes we would make together. The kitchen assistants began to bring in the ingredients but there was some confusion. Signora Hazan explained: she had frustrated the class organizers because she refused to tell them what we would be making until that day. Instead she insisted on going to the markets to choose the ingredients based on what was fresh and in season. Only then would she set the menu and present the recipes.

Before us were boxes of small, briny clams, tiny green zucchini, deep purple eggplants, thick-skinned lemons and thin-skinned seedless cucumbers, boxes of Carnaroli rice, and snowy white halibut fillets. Over the next four hours we would blister-roast the eggplant, make a salad of paper-thin slices of lemon and cucumbers, pan-sear the halibut, and steam clams and diced zucchini in a perfect risotto.

It was a meal Signora Hazan could not have planned before she went to that morning's market. The flavors were so perfect because each ingredient was uncompromised. I finally understood what it means to cook from the ingredients up.

Most of us don't have the time or patience to shop every day, but the principles still work. Cook with what's in season, be open to changing your menu based on what you see at the market, and let yourself be inspired by what looks best.

Grocery Shopping Strategies

*Shopping at Farmers'
Markets and Greenmarkets*

*Alternative Food Sources:
Community Supported Agriculture,
Urban Farms, and Food Co-ops*

Be a Brilliant Food Shopper

I've tried to convince you that your cooking can be only as good as your ingredients. Being educated, mindful, and tactical when buying groceries can result in lower costs, less stress, and much better flavor. It's also fun to know where to find the freshest fish, the sweetest peaches, and the hottest chiles. Just because we buy groceries often—sometimes every day—doesn't mean we should be any less strategic when we go food shopping than when we make major household purchases.

One of the biggest advantages of city grocery shopping is that we have choices. Although this may mean a subway trip or a quick drive into a different neighborhood for a special ingredient or product from a skilled artisan, the journey is usually worth it.

In my years of exploring food neighborhoods, I've learned a few lessons on how to be a successful food shopper. The best place to start is at your local markets.

Grocery Shopping Strategies

Move beyond the supermarket. Our big markets can be convenient, but most cities also have specialists who can customize your purchase and usually have more and better choices. They include butchers, charcuteries, fish stores, cheese shops, bakeries, and ethnic markets.

You don't need to spend a lot to buy from a specialist. A butcher will be happy to sell you a single chicken breast.

Specialists love to give advice. Ask your fishmonger for cooking tips, ask your cheese shop for a taste before buying, or ask your baker when the loaves come out of the oven. Most artisans share a single characteristic: pride in the work they do every day and the quality of the foods they offer. They will welcome your questions.

Specialty stores can often be a better value. If you plan your food shopping in advance, including restocking your pantry, it's easier to make a detour to stores where you can get better prices than at the supermarket. This is particularly the case when buying grains and dried legumes in bulk, or allergen-free foods from natural-food markets, or ethnic ingredients sold in their own ethnic neighborhood.

Shop in other neighborhoods. Some urban neighborhoods have very expensive food stores, but a few blocks can make a big difference in price and selection. Go explore.

Bring a shopping list but be flexible. Go into a store with a plan but also look to see what seems special or new.

Ask for what you don't see. Merchants want to sell what you want to buy. If you have a favorite market where you would regularly buy a certain overlooked item, you're probably not the only one. Speak to the owner or the manager and ask if they'll stock it for you.

Try not to shop at peak time. For busy people this can be unavoidable but anticipate that a very busy store is not only more stressful but also the merchants have less time to spend with you.

Call ahead. If you've only bought groceries in a supermarket, you may not know you can place an order with a butcher or fish store by phone and then pick it up when it's convenient for you. Some will also deliver for free or a small fee that's probably less than the cost of you going to pick up your order. Also, if you're not sure of what or how much to buy, you can call and get advice. These services are particularly helpful when you're making a special meal, like a Thanksgiving turkey.

Buying fish on a hot day? Ask the fishmonger for a chill pack or a little plastic bag of ice to keep your purchase cold until you get home.

Shop like Europeans. In most European cities, food stores are open into the early evening for customers who shop daily for that night's dinner. Most food stores in U.S. cities are also open late, giving you the same option.

Shop in pieces. This means buying supermarket staples every couple of weeks, meat once a week from the butcher, produce at your weekly farmers' market, and fish on the day you'll cook it. It may seem like more work, but if you plan ahead and coordinate the shopping with other errands, it will give you better choices. It may also save you money because you'll only buy what you need.

Shop near work. I first did this when I lived in a city neighborhood that was a food desert. There were many more options in my office neighborhood, so either at lunchtime or on my way home from work, I'd grocery shop, stashing perishables in the office refrigerator. Then every couple of weeks I'd do a major grocery purchase and have it delivered. Even if you have great food stores in your home neighborhood, your work neighborhood may give you alternatives.

Shop online. Many U.S. cities have at least one food merchant that offers the option of placing your order online and having it delivered. Experiment with the food, price, and service quality of online groceries and decide for yourself which ingredients are best to buy this way. For example, you can get household goods, canned foods, and bulk items from an online merchant and then purchase fresh produce and fish as you need them.

Shopping at Farmers' Markets and Greenmarkets

Across the country, urban farmstands have become essential institutions. With established locations and schedules, area farmers bring local produce, meat, fish, and artisanal foods to city home cooks.

But farmers' market shopping can be a challenge because unlike at a grocery store, we can't be sure what will be for sale. It's easy to be seduced by the gorgeous produce or the chance to buy organic leaf lard to make end-of-summer fruit pies, only to get home having spent a lot of money with no plan for how to make meals out of what we've bought.

I've developed a few shopping strategies that can help you get the most enjoyment from shopping and the best meals from your favorite farmers' markets.

Go prepared to shop. Bring your own bags, wear comfortable shoes, and keep your hands free by stashing your money and phone in your pocket. I also suggest you leave your dog at home; markets are busy places and most people are looking at the food and not the dog at their feet.

Arrive early or go late. The best items are often in short supply and will sell out first. So take a tip from local chefs who always shop the market just as it opens. Going early is also a good idea when the weather is hot because fragile produce can wilt under summer's sun. Alternatively, at the end of the day, farmers may discount prices because they don't want to bring anything home.

Before buying anything, *walk around to see what's available* and what appeals to you. Then make a mental list of how many meals you'll be making in the week ahead. It's usually not a good idea to buy produce for more than a week in advance because it will spoil (exceptions are things like garlic, onions, root vegetables, apples, and other more sturdy items). Sketch out a mental plan of vegetable sides, fruits, ingredients for baking, lunch items and so on, and then do a quick hit list of what to buy.

Form an image of your finished meal and think in terms of serving sizes. Here are a few rules of thumb:

- Buy two or three small potatoes per person.
- Leafy greens, such as spinach, cook down significantly, so you may need to buy as much as two pounds to produce two servings.
- Use your hand to grab and measure a serving size of green beans or asparagus.
- A half pound of fish or boneless meat is two servings. If the meat has bones, buy more; if in doubt, tell the merchant how many servings you need.
- Mushrooms also reduce when they cook so buy three or four times the volume you'll want to see on your plate. If you're using them raw in a salad, remember to choose attractive ones that will be appealing when sliced and added to salad greens.
- Vegetables that you will cook and then purée—such as butternut squash or beets—should be bought in the same size/amounts as the final dish. In other words, a quarter pound beets will produce about a quarter pound purée. But buy extra to have leftovers after doing all that work.
- A large head of lettuce will produce about four servings of salad.

Store your produce once you get it home. You can wash and carefully dry salad greens before you refrigerate them, but rinsing most other fruits and vegetables will shorten their shelf life. Instead wash as you use them.

Do not refrigerate tomatoes. The chill causes the flesh to become mealy and lose flavor. Instead just leave them on a kitchen counter, preferably out of the sun.

Buy meats and poultry both to cook soon and freeze for later. If you're in doubt about the upcoming week's schedule and what you'll need for meals, remember you can change your mind and just transfer that heritage breed chicken to the freezer.

When you buy cheese, protect it from refrigerator odors by wrapping it in plastic or aluminum foil. If you don't use the cheese immediately, rewrap it every couple of days in case moisture has collected inside the wrapping.

Be flexible. You may head to the market in search of basil to make a supply of pesto. If you arrive to find gorgeous garlic scapes, or spring onions, or arugula, change your main pesto ingredient. You can get basil another time.

Be adventuresome. Try something unfamiliar and then figure out what to do with it. You can ask the farmer or other customers nearby for tips, or you can find a recipe later. Sometimes the best way to learn about an ingredient is to cook it as simply as possible the first time. This way you learn its flavor, texture, and how it responds to heat, steam, and so on.

Remember the basics. Greenmarkets are wonderful places to get many core ingredients: herbs, shallots, garlic, onions, and eggs. Their local freshness can make a big difference in all of our cooking.

What can I do with this? This is the question that chefs ask when they walk the markets. In a kind of that-moment brainstorming, you can ask yourself the same thing when you see a pile of celery (make a celery salad with a Roquefort dressing), beets (cold borscht), lettuce (risotto with lettuce and peas), eggplant (ratatouille), tomatoes (fresh pasta sauce or sliced with fresh mozzarella), kale (cook and use as a pizza topping, with fresh ricotta), beans (serve with a room-temperature roast leg of lamb). You get the idea. Isolate the ingredient in your mind and think about how to showcase it. Then buy enough to make that dish.

Do you have storage room? Buy extra and do some freezing or canning. This is particularly tempting when we can get local fruit or tomatoes at an excellent price.

If you're buying fish, try to buy it last because it is so fragile. If your favorite fish guy sells out fast, go ahead and buy while it's still available but always ask for a little bag of ice to keep the fish chilled while you continue to shop.

Watch for high prices versus value prices. Some farmers' markets are the place to find unusual or scarce ingredients—like baby turnips or unusual herbs or the first sour cherries of the season. But the precious can also be expensive. What I do is treat myself to small amounts of things I love but are more costly; for example, I'll buy a quarter pound baby salad greens and add them to a less expensive head of Boston lettuce. On *value-priced foods*, which are usually those at their peak season, I'll buy lots and just enjoy the bounty. For example, during the first two weeks of September I make something with local tomatoes just about every day.

Finally, talk to the farmers. The people who bring you these wonderful ingredients are proud of what they do and love to talk about how things are grown and how to cook them. Over time you'll also find that you'll get to know the farmers, which only makes the experience of market shopping more gratifying. We connect not just through the food but also as people with a shared mission: to eat better.

Alternative Food Sources: Community Supported Agriculture, Urban Farms, and Food Co-ops

Increasingly, there are alternatives to shopping at supermarkets and neighborhood grocery stores. This is because home cooks are seeking locally grown ingredients, direct relationships with farmers, better prices, and food that has been produced with regard for the environment.

The three primary alternatives to large-scale and national grocery production and distribution are community supported agriculture, urban farming, and food co-ops.

Community Supported Agriculture

CSA, as it's commonly known, creates direct relationships between consumers and local farmers. Typically a nonprofit organization, such as a church or community group, does the matchmaking and paperwork, making it possible for individual consumers to buy—in advance—a season's worth of produce directly from a local farmer. In exchange, a small family farm knows it has a reliable market and receives income ahead of the harvest, helping the farmer plant crops for the year.

Each CSA is different in its terms, arrangements, and prices. Some offer shares in different sizes to accommodate the wide variety of households found in any city, from large families to singles. Some let you pay by credit card. A few have fancy websites. As with food co-ops, all require some of your time volunteered to help run the distribution.

Once a week, the farm delivers produce and sometimes also eggs, poultry, meat, dairy products, honey, and other organic items to a depot-like location where CSA members pick up that week's supply. What you receive will depend upon what's in season, the weather, and the type of share you've purchased at the start of the season. For example, you may have only signed up for vegetables, or maybe also fruit, eggs, or dairy products.

The concept first appeared in the U.S. in the mid-1980s at a Massachusetts apple farm, and today across the country thousands of CSAs match home cooks and farmers. It may have started in a rural setting, but today's CSA is decidedly urban. It's now a familiar sight to see a farm truck double-parked in busy traffic as volunteers unload crates of just-picked organic fruits and vegetables and other foods to be brought home to city kitchens.

Urban Farms

While some city dwellers have backyards or outdoor spaces for growing their own food, most of us do not. As more of us want control over where our food comes from, and also to pay more sweat equity than cash for our ingredients, urban farming may be the answer. It's not only being done on a grow-your-own and feed-yourself basis, but also on a large scale, as one of agriculture's most promising new answers to the growing demand for locally grown food.

In cities where space can seem precious and unavailable, proponents of urban farming are finding unexpected locations. Some urban gardens are planted in schoolyards, on the grounds of hospitals, or at community centers and churches. Others have been created on river barges, in abandoned lots, and as "vertical farms" on city rooftops.

Sometimes local government is a facilitator. For example, in Seattle, the Department of Neighborhoods, in conjunction with a nonprofit trust, operates what are called "P-Patch" community gardens where any resident can pay a modest annual fee and get a small plot of land—plus support and advice for becoming an urban farmer. These P-Patch gardens are hugely popular and make it possible for more than 2,000 households to cultivate over twenty acres of land across Seattle's neighborhoods.

And in Washington, DC, and Chicago, local government has encouraged urban farming—including rooftop gardens—by giving tax incentives to property owners.

Urban gardens can feed the families that do the planting and harvesting, plus in many cases, the gardens also grow foods donated to food banks and urban feeding programs. The gardens create an affordable source of good ingredients grown with small carbon footprints since the distance from the garden to the city dinner table is short. There is the added reward of improving environmental sustainability, creating jobs, and creating a hyper-local source of food.

Food Co-ops

Food co-ops are voluntary, member-run cooperative grocery stores that range in size from small to huge. The largest food co-op in the country is PCC Natural Markets in Seattle, Washington, which began in 1953 when fifteen families organized a food-buying club. Today it has more than 40,000 members and nine stores. But cities across the country, as well as many small and rural communities, have different kinds of food co-ops.

Some are organized simply as buying clubs. Others have a food or nutritional or political point of view. For example, many co-ops sell only organic foods. Others are strictly vegetarian. Still others are fully stocked and full-service markets that rival

Whole Foods—in quality and selection, but not in price: a hallmark of food co-ops is value because while they are run as businesses, they don't need to make a profit. When you become a member, you pay a membership fee plus you must volunteer a few hours a month working at the co-op stocking shelves, sweeping floors, or working the cash register. Because members do most, if not all, of the work, it means better prices for everyone. Members usually also have a say in which items are sold at the co-op.

See page 261 for organizations that have more information about community supported agriculture, urban gardens, and food co-ops.

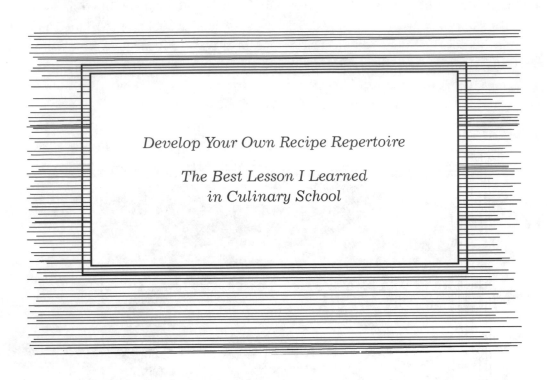

Develop Your Own Recipe Repertoire

The Best Lesson I Learned
in Culinary School

Making It Work in Your Own City Kitchen

When I first started to cook, it wasn't for lifestyle or politics or health. I wasn't trying to be social or clever, nor was it a hobby. There was no epiphany that made me start buying cookbooks or collecting wooden spoons. For that matter, there was no Food Network nor celebrity chefs nor blogs by butchers. I was just trying to make dinner on a small budget in an even smaller kitchen. And I loved to eat.

Let's be practical: How can we make the leap from ambition (so many recipes, so little time) to competency? And as much as we want to make a successful spaghetti sauce or shrimp masala, what we also want is that calm and pleasure that comes from knowing what we're doing.

I think one of the biggest challenges of being a home cook in a big city is that any night of the week we can go to a restaurant—a fancy one or a little neighborhood place—and we can eat anything we want. Since it's a fantasy to think we can replicate all those tempting choices in our own kitchens, the next best thing is to make our own cooking good enough (and less costly, more healthy, and more flavorful) to compete with our local restaurants' variety.

So before we get to the recipes, I want to share with you two core practices that our best cooks—both professional chefs and professional grandmothers—know but you may not. The first has to do with what to cook; the second, how to cook. Adopt them both into your cooking and you will become a better and happier cook. Really.

Develop Your Own Recipe Repertoire

When a restaurant creates a new dish, it's practiced dozens of times before it goes on the menu. Once the recipe is nailed down, the kitchen establishes protocols to make sure there's no variance in its cooking. That's why you can go to a favorite restaurant and order the same dish time after time, and it always tastes exactly as you remember.

Likewise, when your grandmother repeatedly makes the same spaghetti sauce or lamb curry, it's not unlike professional dancers whose legs memorize choreography. She can't *not* make it perfectly.

Compare this to what you do when you cast about for ideas for what to make for dinner. You scan the Web or cookbooks and choose a recipe to make for the first time. Yet there's no way you can gauge the results because the recipe is, at least in your hands, untested. You aren't sure of the flavor or texture and maybe halfway through you're asking yourself, "Is this what it's supposed to look like? Taste like?" Then there are the variables: weather (ever try to make pie dough on a hot, humid day?), having all the right ingredients, or the distraction of having had a bad day at the office or a sick child. The task of making dinner becomes stressful.

I love to make new dishes and do so often, knowing it's how to discover new favorites or to satisfy a craving. Plus, it can be lots of fun. But most of the time, relief, certainty, and satiation only come from having a repertoire of practiced meals.

A repertoire is like a restaurant's menu: a set of regular dishes plus the occasional "special." It needn't be a strict schedule of fish on Fridays or chicken every Sunday. Instead it's knowing you have a dozen or so go-to meals that you love to cook and love to eat.

This idea needn't contradict the practice of cooking from the ingredients up. The two concepts are totally compatible because what will emerge are favorite dishes that in practiced hands (yours) can be adjusted according to what's in season, what looks best, and what's on sale.

I'll give you two other arguments for having your own kitchen menu. First, it reduces the surprise factor: you get to know exactly how to cook a three-pound roast to medium-rare, that it's four minutes in the steamer for the asparagus, that a pound and a quarter of salmon is perfect for your family's dinner. By having fewer surprises, you'll get a very steady hand, and you'll be more confident.

The other benefit has to do with all the planning and shopping I've been talking about. If you work with a regular bunch of recipes, you can zip through a farmers' market on your lunch hour or stop at a grocer's on the way home from work and you won't need an app on your phone to tell you what you need to buy to make dinner. You can see beautiful bay scallops on sale and scan your mental recipe database and know a) how much to buy and b) how you'll cook them.

So how do you create your own kitchen menu? There's some trial and error, but here's how to start.

- Devise five weekday dinner menus. Include main courses and sides, plus salads and vegetables that you can revise throughout the year as in-season foods change. Choose dishes that you can mix and match and include at least one easy pantry dinner and two desserts. If you bring your lunch to work, include recipes that make good leftovers.

- If you tend to cook more on weekends, add three or four weekend meals: snacks, dinners, breakfasts, and lunches. This is where to put a curry or lamb stew.
- Create one or two showstopping entertaining dinners. Include something impressive, something that's in the "comfort food" category, a signature beverage or cocktail, and some special treats. This could be your signature chocolate chip cookies, or your "famous" Super Bowl turkey chili, or the chicken soup that gets delivered to sick friends.

The ingredients for these meals should become the basis for what's in your pantry. With your kitchen menu as your culinary foundation, you will be free to let the recipe and market muses inspire you to try new dishes—as if you were a chef adding your own "specials."

The Best Lesson I Learned in Culinary School

My first hours in culinary school were a big letdown. I was eager to turn up the cuffs of my new white chef jacket and start making sauces. But instead there were six hours of kitchen safety, food handling, and sanitation.

But soon we got to unpack our knives and set up our workstations. Ringing the room were shelves filled with huge jars of spices, bins of flour and sugar, large plastic bottles of oils and vinegars, and to the side, stacks of metal bowls and cookware, scrubbed clean but still wet from their last washing.

And then there were the little plastic cups. Hundreds of little plastic cups that were like the ones that sometimes come with takeout sushi. These were for the *mise en place*.

Mise en place. It means "putting in place." The term originated in a French culinary tradition that dates back to the nineteenth century when Escoffier, the great chef and writer, modernized the restaurant kitchen with what came to be known as the brigade system. In its simplest form, the brigade sets up kitchens with specialists, each working a single job at a single station. All day someone just makes salads, or grills meat, or makes pastry. The kitchen brigade's specialists are akin to those of the military, adding a discipline that makes it possible for kitchens to produce more, with better results. At its core, *mise en place* means a chef must have all the ingredients measured out and all the tools at hand before cooking begins.

So why is this a big deal? And what about all those little cups?

In home kitchens *mise en place* means you know what you're about to do and you're ready. You've read your recipe (twice). You've pulled out every pot, pan, and knife you'll need. The oven has been preheated. The big pot of water is already coming to a boil. You've gathered all your ingredients and measured them out right down to the smallest pinch of salt or quarter teaspoon of vanilla—that's what the little cups are for. And you've done all this before you begin any cooking.

Mise en place is the essence of thirty-minute meals. It's how restaurants can plate forty servings of striped bass in parchment paper in less than three hours. It's how television chefs demonstrate a complex recipe in a six-minute segment. And for home cooks like you and me, *mise en place* is how we can make the most extraordinary Slow Roast of Pork (page 174) without forgetting to add the thyme or discovering halfway through cooking that we didn't buy any red wine for the final braising.

Without *mise en place,* you'll be trying to score the skin of your pork roast while at the same time pulling out the roasting pan and digging through your jumble of spices to find the peppercorns to refill your pepper mill. And if you're distracted with pots, pans, and peppercorns, you can't possibly be properly stuffing and tying the roast to make it ready for the five hours of slow roasting that's to follow.

Most important, *mise en place* means you have focus. And focus produces better cooking. This is what all professional kitchens know but most home kitchens do not. Those little plastic cups transformed the way I cook and became a symbol of the biggest value I received for my culinary school tuition check.

Today when I cook in my city kitchen, instead of using little plastic cups I use a combination of six-ounce Pyrex cups, small white ceramic ramekins, and tiny open-mouthed glass jars that I rescued from a friend's trash when she brought home a souvenir sampler of caviar from a trip to Russia. Placing all these little empty containers on my kitchen counter as I begin to cook is now as automatic for me as it is to swipe my chef's knife over a honing steel. I then reread the recipe and measure out every single ingredient before I start any cooking. I mince the garlic, dice the onion, sift and measure the flour, pull leaves of rosemary from their sprigs, and fill those little jars that once held caviar with teaspoons of spices, extracts, or hot sauce. It's all part of the preparation, of my *mise en place*. And once done, I can begin to cook.

In my pre–culinary school years of cooking, I was already focused, if only because I was so insecure despite my big ambition. But then I'd see these TV chefs stop mid-recipe to start cutting oranges in half to squeeze a cup of fresh juice or detour to a pantry to retrieve a forgotten ingredient. Where I'd be beleaguered, for them it always seemed so casual, so easy. In fact, it's not. But as I learned in culinary school, if you do your *mise en place*, it can be.

And even if it's not easier, your cooking will be better. I promise.

Part 2

Recipes

This is how I cook. I love big flavors and complexity, but I also want to taste the ingredients. I am mindful of healthful eating but also want to experience all the wonderful flavors possible in today's global kitchen. In other words, I have no fear of butter, but I usually use olive oil instead.

The food I cook has been influenced by a combination of palate, appetite, skill, and the food cooked by others, both pros and home cooks. These recipes include some that I regularly cook for weekday meals, but also ones that I make for company. I've created my own repertoire of everyday and weekend dishes, but if you eat at my table you'll find I also make dishes that I've learned from the masters—Julia Child's *Boeuf Bourguignon*, Marcella Hazan's *Ossobuco*, Barbara Kafka's Chicken Soup, and my aunt Mary's cabbage pierogies.

I live in New York, a city fed at an international table, and I've often had a taste in a restaurant either here at home or when I've traveled and then strived to re-create it in my own kitchen. Now that I write a cooking website it means I'm more attentive to the food media—both entertainers and serious journalists—and it all influences what and how I cook. But so do my roots: I grew up in a small town where we had both Japanese and Middle Eastern neighbors, and my family was a melting pot of western and eastern Europeans. It is no wonder that my palate is eclectic.

As I've strived to make cooking part of my daily life, it's meant creating and refining recipes that I can rely on and can afford to make often. This means I can afford to buy the ingredients, I can afford the time to make them, and I can afford the calories. That's why you'll find here an emphasis on less expensive cuts of meat (pork tenderloin, hanger steak), more fruit than chocolate in the desserts, a big nod to Mediterranean grains and pastas, and more recipes in the vegetable section than in any other.

I've also adapted recipes from greats like Jacques Pépin (using his port pan sauce on duck instead of pork), Nobu Matsuhisa (making black cod with miso in an hour instead of two days), and Thomas Keller (using his method for roasting beets).

I make no assumptions about your skills, nor your level of enthusiasm for cooking. I've included simple but big-flavored ways to make Weeknight Roast Chicken-in-Parts, as well as recipes like Whole Fish Baked in a Salt Crust and Bloody Mary Sorbet with Crab Salad Brioche that may seem like showpieces but in fact are easy in a small city kitchen. Having a core of practiced and reliable dishes lets me cook and eat well all the time and makes me confident and proud to cook for others.

I'm sharing these recipes with the hope that they will do the same for you.

Hors d'Oeuvres and Starters

The starter is always my favorite part of the meal. It's when our appetites are most eager and flavors most anticipated. Sometimes the beginning is just a tease, a taste that creates expectations for what will follow, or a salty contrast to a chilled apéritif. But other starters like a hearty soup or a rich, briny seafood salad can double as the main event.

Baked Potato Chips

Smoked Trout Pâté

Genovese Minestrone with Spinach Pesto

Fried Stuffed Green Olives

Slow-Cooker Pea Soup with Pork Three Ways

Poached Pears with Parmesan Foam

Eleven Easy No-Cook Hors d'Oeuvres

Warm Bacon-Wrapped Dates Stuffed with Blue Cheese

Roasted Red Peppers with Feta

Bloody Mary Sorbet with Crab Salad Brioche

Cheddar Wafers

Baked Potato Chips

These baked chips are an almost-guilt-free treat for your guests. Or for you. It's best to use a mandoline or Japanese slicer to produce uniform and extremely thin slices. Aim for long, large slices and avoid cutting the potato at its width.

The other two tools you'll need are a pastry brush for the olive oil and parchment paper to line the rimmed sheet pan. Without the parchment paper, there's no amount of oil that will prevent them from sticking (and it makes cleanup easy afterward).

Peeled potatoes quickly darken. Usually you prevent this by putting them in a bowl of water, but if you do that here, you'll have to dry each slice before baking. Instead work quickly and only prepare as many slices as you can fit on your pan at once. If you have two sheet pans, you can bake both at the same time.

You can experiment with added flavors. Add a tiny whisper of cayenne pepper or cumin to the salt, or rub each raw slice with a piece of cut garlic before brushing with oil. You can also make this recipe using sweet potatoes.

Makes about 24 chips, depending upon the size of the potatoes

2 large russet potatoes, often called baking potatoes (choose long and even shapes for attractive slices)

¼ cup extra virgin olive oil

Sea salt

Preheat the oven to 375°F. Line a sheet pan with parchment paper.

Wash or peel the potatoes. Using a mandoline or ceramic slicer, cut the potatoes lengthwise into very thin (about 1/16-inch) slices. Place the potato slices on the parchment-lined sheet pan, and using a pastry brush, brush the top of each with enough olive oil to coat but not soak the slice. Sprinkle with sea salt.

Bake for about 20 minutes total. About halfway through, rotate the pan to help the slices cook evenly. If you're baking two sheets at once, put one in the upper third of the oven and the other in the lower third and reverse their positions halfway through.

Watch during the last 10 minutes to make sure you don't overbake. The goal is to have golden brown, crispy slices. You may need to take a few slices out of the oven early, leaving others to cook a bit longer.

Transfer the chips to a rack to cool. If you don't eat them all immediately, they can be stored in an airtight container for a few days.

Smoked Trout Pâté

You can make this pâté with any smoked oily fish. Trout is usually the easiest to find, but if you can find smoked bluefish, use that instead of the trout because its strong flavor combines well with the other ingredients. For those not familiar with prepared horseradish, it's sold in refrigerated jars, often near a grocer's dairy case; if you have a choice between red horseradish, which is tinted with beet juice, or plain white, choose the white.

This spread is nice on small squares of toasted bread, crackers, croutons, or thin slices of seedless English cucumber.

Makes 2 cups or enough for about 40 cucumber rounds

8 ounces smoked trout or bluefish, skin removed and discarded

One 8-ounce package regular or reduced-fat cream cheese, at room temperature

1½ teaspoons prepared white horseradish

1½ teaspoons fresh lemon juice

Optional: 2 to 4 drops Tabasco or other hot sauce

2 tablespoons tiny capers, drained

Break up the fish into pieces and place in a food processor equipped with a steel blade. Add the cream cheese and pulse until the fish and cream cheese are combined. Add the horseradish and lemon juice and pulse to combine. Taste and adjust the seasoning, adding more lemon juice or horseradish if necessary. Add the Tabasco if desired. Add the capers and pulse a few more times until they are mixed throughout.

Spread on crackers, pieces of toasted bread, or thin slices of seedless English cucumbers or use as a dip with crudités. The pâté can be made a day in advance and stored covered in the refrigerator. Just bring it to room temperature when you're ready to serve so that it's easy to spread.

Genovese Minestrone with Spinach Pesto

This classic vegetable soup can be made with homemade or store-bought beef or chicken stock. What makes it reminiscent of the Italian city of Genoa is the addition of a spoonful of pesto, which in this case is made with spinach instead of basil. While you could use basil pesto, keep in mind that basil has a stronger flavor, so you can use a bit less.

I like to cook small pasta separately and add it to the hot soup just before serving. Precooked brown or white rice would also be a nice addition.

Serves 4

¼ cup extra virgin olive oil

1 clove garlic, finely minced

1 small to medium yellow onion, finely chopped

1 leek, white and tender green parts only, diced; rinse very carefully before using

1 tablespoon minced fresh flat-leaf parsley

1 teaspoon fresh thyme leaves, minced

Salt

1 tablespoon tomato paste

One 14-ounce can peeled whole tomatoes with their juice, preferably San Marzano, squished in your hand into small pieces (If you want the tomato pieces to stay noticeable in the soup, cut into bigger chunks before adding instead of crushing.)

2 stalks celery, finely diced

2 carrots, peeled and cut into ½-inch dice

2 medium Yukon Gold, Red Bliss or 1 large baking potato, peeled and cut into ½-inch dice

One 10-ounce package frozen green beans; choose cut or French cut, already sliced into thin strips

1 cup canned red kidney beans or chickpeas, drained and rinsed

6 cups homemade or good-quality boxed beef or chicken stock

Freshly ground black pepper

1 cup dried small pasta, such as ditali or tiny shells

Spinach Pesto (recipe follows)

Optional: ½ cup grated Parmesan cheese

In a large stock or soup pot, heat the olive oil until it shimmers. Add the garlic, onion, leek, parsley, thyme, and a generous pinch of salt. Cook over medium heat until the onion is transparent and soft.

Add the tomato paste, tomatoes, celery, carrots, potatoes, green beans, and kidney beans and stir to combine. Add the stock and several grinds of fresh pepper.

Bring to a boil, then reduce to a simmer. Cover the pot, leaving a bit of an opening so that the soup simmers without cooking off too much liquid. Simmer for about 1 hour.

When ready to serve, cook the pasta separately in salted water according to the package instructions. Add the cooked pasta to the soup.

Taste and adjust the seasoning, remembering that the pesto and grated cheese will both add salt to the soup.

Serve with a spoonful of pesto, and if you like, a sprinkling of grated cheese.

> **TIP:** If the tomatoes are canned with a sprig of basil, discard the basil before using them.

Spinach Pesto

While this pesto is a flavorful addition to this vegetable soup, it's also wonderful tossed on any pasta as an alternative to a traditional basil pesto.

Makes about 1 cup

One 10-ounce package frozen chopped spinach, defrosted and completely drained (squeeze out any excess water with your hands)

1 teaspoon dried or 1 tablespoon minced fresh basil

3 cloves garlic, finely minced

1 tablespoon minced fresh parsley

¼ cup extra virgin olive oil

2 tablespoons unsalted butter, at room temperature

¼ cup grated Parmesan cheese

Combine all the ingredients in a food processor and pulse until it forms a paste. You may need to use a spatula to wipe down the sides of the processor to keep all the ingredients combined.

TIP: When making pesto, I usually begin by letting the machine mince the garlic before adding the other ingredients. This saves me the step of mincing the garlic by hand. If you put the whole cloves in with all the other ingredients, you won't get as fine a mince.

Union Square Greenmarket
New York, New York

Serving Hors d'Oeuvres

I think the point of food with cocktails (I'm using this term to mean a beverage before dinner, alcoholic or not, mixed or not, shaken or stirred) is to have a little mouth thing going on. Something salty to make the drink even more pleasant. A tiny taste of anticipation. But it's not dinner.

Still, there is a middle ground between a bowl of peanuts and a groaning sideboard. From years of entertaining at home, here are my operating principles:

- Consider the entire meal when planning hors d'oeuvres. If the meal is rich and complex, go easy on the flavor and the quantity of the finger food. If you want to start with something substantial, like an antipasto platter, lighten up the meal that's to follow.
- Avoid finger food that is messy. No one wants to deal with sticky fingers and teeth issues when they're guests in someone's home.
- Some hors d'oeuvres may need little plates and forks. All will need napkins.
- Cheese and crackers will absolutely wreck an appetite. It's just too much fat and carbs. Your guests will eat everything and then hate you afterward.
- Salty flavors are best with cocktails.
- Make hors d'oeuvres that can be eaten in one bite and plan on three per person.
- Be generous with bowls of olives and nuts and provide a little dish for pits and shells.
- Avoid snacks with really strong flavors, like those wasabi peas. I love them but they are so pungent that I will treat my drink as if it's Gatorade—not a good thing if I'm drinking Grey Goose.
- You don't need to set up an entire bar or get engaged in making mixed drinks unless it's part of your event (like serving margaritas at a Cinco de Mayo dinner). While I will offer to pull out my martini shaker, most people are happy with a glass of wine or Champagne, or if you know your friends well enough, a bowl of ice and a bottle of their brand of Scotch. Always have some sparkling water and fruit juice, plus a dish of lemon and lime wedges, for those who either don't drink alcohol or aren't that night.
- Regardless of what you serve, it is most important to make your guests feel comfortable and attended to. So offer a drink, a nibble to help anticipate dinner, and your warmest welcome.

Fried Stuffed Green Olives

I first tasted fried stuffed olives at lunch at a tiny neighborhood restaurant in Assisi on my first trip to Italy. Six large, crispy olives arrived on a small plate lined with a paper napkin. I wasn't prepared for the flavor: a remarkable combination of salt, heat, spicy sausage, and oiliness. It was perfect.

The inconvenience of this recipe is that the olives really need to be fried just before they're served, because they're best when still very warm. Your guests may miss you during cocktails, but when they taste these olives, they'll readily forgive your absence.

Because the cavity in the pitted olive is small, you'll have more luck stuffing them if you use a pastry bag with a small tip. You can also use a plastic food storage bag with one corner snipped off.

This recipe makes enough stuffing for about 60 olives, which is more than I usually make at one time. I either refrigerate what's left over and add it the next day to scrambled eggs, or I sauté it to top pasta or steamed vegetables, with a sprinkle of bread crumbs to finish. Sometimes I cook it and eat it right out of the pan as a small treat for the cook.

Makes 30 olives

2 tablespoons unsalted butter

4 ounces sweet Italian sausage, removed from its casing

4 ounces lean ground veal

½ cup dry white wine

½ cup chicken stock

1 cup fine dry unflavored bread crumbs (store bought is fine)

2 large eggs

1 tablespoon chopped fresh parsley

½ teaspoon salt

Freshly ground black pepper

30 pitted large green olives

Flour for dredging, about 2 cups

Canola or olive oil for frying

In a skillet, melt the butter over medium heat. Combine the sausage and veal and add to the melted butter. Lightly brown the meat just enough to cook it through. Don't overcook.

Add the wine and continue to cook over medium heat until the liquid evaporates. Add the chicken stock and simmer until most of the liquid has reduced and the mixture is soft, about 5 minutes. Remove from the heat and let cool for about 5 minutes.

Transfer the cooked meat to a food processor. Add 2 tablespoons of the bread crumbs, 1 egg, the parsley, salt, and several grinds of pepper. Pulse until the mixture becomes a coarse paste.

Rinse the olives and dry completely with a paper towel. Using a small spoon, a pastry bag with a tip, or a plastic storage bag with a clipped-off corner, fill each olive with about 1 teaspoon of the meat mixture. Don't overfill the cavity.

Set up an assembly line of 3 shallow bowls to prepare the olives for frying: put flour in the first, the remaining egg in the second, and the remaining bread crumbs in the third. Mix the egg with a fork and add about 1 tablespoon water to dilute it. Dredge each olive in the flour, dip it in the beaten egg, and then roll in the bread crumbs, shaking off any excess.

Heat ½ inch of oil in a large skillet or sauté pan over medium-high heat until hot but not smoking. Add the breaded olives and sauté until crispy and golden brown, about 10 minutes. Transfer first to a paper towel and then to a serving plate.

Serve immediately while hot.

TIP: If you can't find large pitted olives, buy large ones that are stuffed with pimentos; remove those and discard. Don't try to pit the olives yourself because you won't be able to create a sufficient cavity for the filling.

Slow-Cooker Pea Soup with Pork Three Ways

This recipe was shared with me by my friend Greg Socha who makes this soup in a slow cooker on cold winter weekends. By adding three types of pork—bacon, ham hocks, and sausage—a classic pea soup becomes something more substantial, rich, and flavorful.

Lots of bacon does not deliver a greasy soup. This recipe makes a large quantity, and the bacon, which offers a richer flavor than the cream or butter you find in many soups, is the primary source of fat.

This makes a perfect winter supper when served with chunks of bread or large croutons. Make croutons by broiling thick slices of fresh or day-old bread that have been brushed with olive oil and sprinkled with grated cheese until the cheese melts and begins to brown. We've included instructions for making this soup both in a soup pot on top of the stove and in a slow cooker. It tastes just as good either way.

Makes 6 generous servings

One 15-ounce bag dried split green peas, equivalent to about 2 cups

8 to 12 ounces sliced bacon; smoked uncured or applewood-smoked bacon are both good choices

1 medium yellow onion, chopped

8 to 12 ounces andouille sausage, cut into ¾-inch pieces

2 cloves garlic, thinly sliced

1 pound Yukon Gold potatoes, peeled and cut into 1-inch chunks

12 ounces carrots, peeled and cut into 1-inch pieces (about 1½ cups)

4 stalks celery, cut into 2-inch pieces

6 cups chicken stock (boxed stock is excellent for this)

2 large, meaty ham hocks

Bouquet garni: 2 bay leaves, 5 sprigs fresh thyme, and 5 sage leaves wrapped in a small piece of cheesecloth, and tied into a little sack with a piece of cotton string

In a Stovetop Soup Pot

Pour the peas into a bowl and pick through them to remove any debris or stones. Rinse the peas several times using cool water, draining in a fine sieve or colander.

Cut the bacon into 1-inch pieces and place them in a large soup pot over medium heat. Cook until the pieces have begun to get soft and translucent and fat is collecting in the pot but do not brown the bacon. Add the onion and cook until the onion softens and becomes translucent, about 2 minutes. Add the sausage and cook until the surface begins to brown just slightly, about 2 minutes. Add the garlic, potatoes, carrots, and celery. Stir to coat and cook until the garlic becomes fragrant, about 1 minute. Add the split peas, stock, ham hocks, and *bouquet garni*. Do not add salt; other ingredients will add enough.

Bring to a boil and then reduce to a low simmer. Cover and cook over low heat for 2 hours, stirring occasionally. When the vegetables have become very soft and the peas have broken down, remove the ham hocks, sausage, and *bouquet garni* from the soup. Discard the *bouquet garni*.

When the ham hocks have cooled enough to handle, remove any bits of meat (discarding the skin, fat, gristle, and bones) and set aside with the sausage pieces.

Using a handheld blender, a blender, or a food processor, purée the soup until it becomes completely smooth and thick. Return the meat to the soup and stir to combine.

The soup can be served immediately, or store refrigerated for up to 3 days and then reheated when ready to serve.

In a Slow Cooker

Pour the peas into a bowl and pick through them to remove any debris or stones. Rinse the peas several times using cool water, draining in a fine sieve or colander. Cut the bacon into 1-inch pieces.

Place all the ingredients in a large slow cooker and cook on high for 5 to 7 hours, stirring occasionally. When the vegetables have become very soft and the peas have broken down, remove the ham hocks, sausage, and *bouquet garni* from the soup. Proceed as directed for soup on the stovetop.

> **TIP:** Instead of using cheesecloth for the *bouquet garni*, you can tie the herbs between 2 pieces of celery with a piece of string.

Poached Pears with Parmesan Foam

I created this recipe from my memory of a dish I tried at a restaurant in Parma, Italy, the name of which I've sadly long forgotten.

The restaurant called it foam, but it's really more like a thick home-churned butter with the taste of Parmesan. The flavor is as rich as that of a piece of cheese, so serve small portions. This is certainly a fine first course, but I also like it as a riff on a cheese course instead of dessert.

Makes enough foam for 6 pears plus leftovers

Parmesan Foam (recipe follows)

1 lemon

3 cups red wine (always cook with a wine that is also good enough to drink; Pinot Noir, Syrah, or Zinfandel would be good choices here)

3 cups water

2 cups sugar

1 cinnamon stick

6 Anjou or Bosc pears, peeled but left whole with the stem attached

Make the Parmesan foam.

Use a vegetable peeler to remove the rind from the lemon, then squeeze it to produce 2 to 3 tablespoons juice.

In a large saucepan, combine the wine, water, sugar, lemon rind, lemon juice, and cinnamon stick. Bring to a boil, stirring to dissolve the sugar.

Add the pears to the poaching liquid and reduce the heat for a gentle simmer. If the pears are not completely submerged, turn them over occasionally while they poach.

Cook for 30 to 45 minutes. The cooking time will vary depending on the size and ripeness of your pears. The pears are done when tender and easily pierced with a paring knife.

Remove the pears from the heat and let cool in the hot liquid. If you want a syrup to serve with the pears, remove the fruit from the pan after they're cooled and boil the remaining poaching liquid until reduced to about 1½ cups slightly thickened sauce, about 25 minutes.

The pears can be poached a day ahead and kept covered in the refrigerator. Bring them to room temperature before serving for the best flavor.

When ready to serve, use a serving spoon or small ice cream scoop to place a round of the "foam" alongside a poached pear. The foam will have the consistency of slightly softened butter and the flavor of Parmesan cheese.

> **TIP:** For a standing-up whole poached pear, just take a slice from its bottom to create a flat surface before poaching.

> **TIP:** If you want to serve poached pear halves, slice them from top to bottom before cooking and use a melon baller to neatly and easily remove the core and seeds.

Parmesan Foam

One 12-ounce piece Parmesan; do not use any cheese other than Parmigiano-Reggiano regardless of how good you think it is

1 cup half-and-half; do not substitute milk

Cut the cheese into pieces, each about ½ inch square. You should have enough to fill a 1-cup liquid measure. Try to cut the pieces equal in size so that they melt evenly.

Position the top of a double boiler or heatproof bowl over a pot of simmering water. Add the Parmesan and half-and-half to the pan. While maintaining a low heat, enough to keep the water simmering, slowly melt the cheese, stirring frequently.

After about 15 minutes, the cheese will have melted completely. *Don't let it boil.* Your goal here is simply to melt the cheese in the half-and-half. As soon as you've done so, remove the pan from the heat and pour the liquid into a heatproof bowl. It will look like a cheese sauce, and it won't be completely smooth.

Cool to room temperature, then cover with plastic wrap and refrigerate. After a couple of hours, it will solidify to resemble a firm ricotta cheese.

You can make the foam up to 2 days in advance. Any leftovers can be spread on bread and make a tasty addition to sandwiches.

Eleven Easy No-Cook Hors d'Oeuvres

When hosting a dinner party, I think it's better to serve just a few light hors d'oeuvres—your guests stay hungry, and you stay focused on the main cooking event. The alternative is to serve many hors d'oeuvres, skip the dinner, and call the event a cocktail party. That's fine, but that's, well, something else.

Luckily there are many simple homemade and store-bought hors d'oeuvres. Choose two or three that can be ready when your guests walk in the door and let you remain attentive to the rest of the meal. I like cocktail foods that can be eaten in a single bite, so there's no double dipping or juggling of plates, napkins, and drinks.

- Olives. I always serve the unpitted variety. Pitted olives are mushy, and the inevitable renegade pit in the bowl leaves your guests at risk for a broken tooth. Place a small plate next to the bowl for pits.
- Salted almonds or cashews. If you have the time, buy unsalted nuts, and just before serving, warm them in a large skillet over medium heat or on a sheet pan in a 350°F oven for 5 to 8 minutes, watching them closely and shaking the pan once or twice. Add a healthy pinch of sea salt and serve while still warm.
- Pistachios. I like to fill a large wooden bowl with a bounty of these nuts (please, not the red ones). Rest a smaller bowl on top for discarded shells.
- Cheese crackers. There are some very good store-bought crackers, like the boxed John Wm. Macy cheese sticks, but it's easy to make your own, so I've also included a recipe for cheese wafers (page 72). You can make the dough in advance and just slice and bake what you need.
- Small salty things such as sesame sticks, little pretzels, or potato sticks.
- Thin slices of English (seedless) cucumber with a square of smoked salmon on top.
- Endive leaves (not too big—a two-bite leaf) with a teaspoon of salmon caviar mounded at the end so that you get a bite of endive/caviar and then a second bite of just endive. Less costly fillings include a little olive oil-packed tuna fish, a dollop of chive cream cheese, a spoonful of store-bought black olive tapenade, or a single sundried tomato.
- Crab salad on a cracker or cucumber round or in an endive leaf. Buy a small container of fresh backfin crabmeat and mix with a little mayonnaise and a

few drops of fresh lemon juice and hot sauce. Put a mounded teaspoon on the cracker or cucumber or at the wide end of the endive leaf.

- Raw vegetables and hummus. Use finger food, one- or two-bite vegetables like baby carrots and celery pieces. Either buy or make your own hummus.
- Dried Turkish apricots with a teaspoon of softened goat cheese (thin with a little milk if it's too stiff) placed in the dent of each piece of fruit.
- Slices of dried salami or soppressata (the small ones that are about 1 inch in diameter) served with the little French pickles called cornichons.

How to Work with a Wine Merchant

Going into a wine store can be intimidating. Even for the practiced buyer, there's just so much to choose from! But a good wine merchant is an invaluable resource, and if you give him some clues, you'll make a better purchase.

- Try to choose a store that specializes in wine (versus a general liquor store) because the people who work there generally will have more knowledge about the inventory.
- Ask for help. There's no triumph in pretending you're a wine expert and then making a disappointing purchase.
- Know how the wine will be served. With a meal? As an apéritif? Mixed in a cocktail? Served soon or stored for the future?
- For wine with a meal, tell the merchant the details: type of cuisine, the whole menu and not just the main course, how the foods will be seasoned.
- Describe the kinds of wines you usually like—fruity or dry, heavy or light. The more detailed the snapshot of your wine tastes, the better the merchant can guide you.
- Ask if the wine you've chosen needs to be decanted, opened in advance, or chilled.
- Don't be put off by a large bottle or a screw top instead of a cork. What is in the bottle counts most, and wine producers are increasingly exploring new storage and production methods, including screw tops for very fine wines.
- Ask if a taste is available. Wine merchants frequently will have bottles open for tastings. This is one of the best ways to learn about wine and educate your palate.
- Give the merchant your budget. There are excellent wines at all price points, and wine merchants stock and sell for every budget.
- Enjoy the experience. Wine is one of life's greatest pleasures, so enjoy the learning and the shopping as much as the drinking.

Warm Bacon-Wrapped Dates Stuffed with Blue Cheese

With a flavor that is a perfect combination of sweet, salty, and smoky, this classic hors d'oeuvre can challenge a martini for the spotlight.

If you're serving these to guests, you can prep them hours in advance and then pop them into the oven just as the intercom rings. But don't bake them in advance because part of the pleasure is their combination of textures, including the warm melted cheese.

You'll need a hot oven, a shallow baking dish or sheet pan, and toothpicks. Have a pretty serving plate ready so that you can take them right out of the oven and out to your guests. Save one for yourself.

Makes 20 bite-size pieces

⅓ pound firm blue cheese, such as Danish blue, Maytag, or Great Hill Blue, cut into 20 pieces, each about 1 by ¼ inch

20 large or jumbo pitted dates

10 thin slices bacon, cut crosswise in half, at room temperature

Preheat the oven to 450°F.

Stuff one piece of cheese into each date and press it closed. Don't let too much spill out as it will melt faster than the entire date will cook and could burn. Wrap a piece of bacon around each date, securing it in place with a toothpick. Arrange on a sheet pan or in a shallow baking dish.

Bake for 5 minutes. Using tongs or carefully taking hold of the toothpicks, turn each date over. Bake until the bacon is crisp, the cheese has softened and melted a bit, and the edges of the dates have begun to caramelize, another 4 to 5 minutes. If you've used smaller dates, be careful to not overcook them.

Serve immediately.

> **TIP:** You can also use dates still on the vine or plump Medjool dates, but you will need to pit them yourself. It's easy to do with a paring knife by cutting an opening at one end and slipping the pit out, but take care to keep each date intact so it can be filled.

Roasted Red Peppers with Feta

Sometimes the most appealing way to start a meal is the simplest—as with glistening, slightly charred sweet red peppers topped with a crumble of salty feta cheese. But when a dish is so boldly plain, it's essential that each element be perfect. In this case, jarred peppers will not come close to achieving the potential poetry of this dish, so take the time to roast your own.

A few tips for roasting peppers:

- Use red or orange peppers because they are the sweetest.
- While kitchen lore says it's fine to roast a pepper over an open gas burner as if it were a marshmallow, you'll risk a terrible mess (and maybe damage your stove) because peppers fill with moisture as they cook and the roasting will tempt a leak.
- I prefer to roast peppers on a rimmed sheet pan (it captures any leaks) in a very hot oven, so the flesh cooks and softens and the skin blisters. Broiling is an alternative, but watch your pan carefully so that they don't go from blistered to burned.
- Don't rinse off the charred skin because you'll also rinse off the flavor. Take the time to remove the skins by hand.
- Roasted peppers can stand on their own as a starter, or they can be combined with other roasted vegetables or antipasti such as marinated artichokes. Cook a few extras and add to salads or sandwiches.

Serves 4

4 large red or orange bell peppers

1 tablespoon red wine vinegar

1 tablespoon extra virgin olive oil

Salt (this is a good time to use that artisanal salt you've been saving)

Freshly ground black pepper

½ cup crumbled feta cheese

Preheat the oven to 400°F.

Rinse and completely dry the peppers, leaving them whole. Place on a rimmed sheet pan. Roast for about 30 minutes until the skins blacken and blister, turning them several times to blacken every surface.

Remove the pan from the oven, put the peppers in a large bowl, and cover it with plastic wrap to create a seal. Let the peppers cool; the steam captured by the plastic wrap will help remove their skins.

After about 20 minutes, peel each pepper and remove the cores and seeds. Most of the skins will come off with your fingers, but you may need to help a bit with a paring knife. Don't be too meticulous; it's good if a few bits of blackened skin are left behind.

Cut the peeled peppers into thick slices and drizzle with the vinegar, olive oil, a pinch of good salt, and a few grinds of black pepper.

When you're ready to serve, toss with the feta cheese and serve with chunks of fresh bread.

Bloody Mary Sorbet with Crab Salad Brioche

Years ago on a trip to France—my first time there with my husband—I had a series of palate-changing meals. We rented a small car and braved unfamiliar country roads to explore Burgundy and Rhône-Alpes, including the city of Lyon, which many consider to be the food capital of France. For two weeks we drove across central France, eating in small cafés, simple bistros, and a few Michelin-starred restaurants. Whether it was a sandwich made of sweet rustic ham and soft Brie on a baguette or an elegant dinner, these meals forever raised my expectations for how good food can be.

One lunch was in a restaurant called Les Terrasses de Lyon, famed for its hillside view over the Saône River. I ordered a slice of fois gras served with a small spoonful of savory tomato sorbet. I had expected the fois gras to be the treat, but the sorbet's acidic and heated tomato taste confused my mouth with its icy surface and made a profound flavor memory.

Finding no recipe that duplicated what I had tasted, I began to experiment with my little ice cream maker. I came up with my own combination of cooked and raw

Making Sorbet

I apply the same principles for this savory sorbet as for one that is sweet:

- Make sure the mixture that you are going to freeze has a strong, rich flavor because freezing will diminish the taste.
- Chill the mixture for at least an hour before adding to the ice cream maker. It must be completely cold; otherwise as soon as you pour it into the drum, it will raise the drum's temperature, which may interfere with its ultimate freezing.
- Add 1 to 2 tablespoons alcohol—in this case, vodka—to the mixture just before freezing to lower the freezing temperature. This prevents the sorbet from turning into a block of flavored ice. (You don't need alcohol in ice cream because the addition of dairy creates the same effect.)

tomatoes, plus some seasonings often associated with a bloody Mary, to produce the right combination of bright tomato taste and spice.

Instead of serving fois gras (choose your reason: cost or politics), I serve a scoop of the sorbet alongside crab salad on a piece of brioche bread.

Bloody Mary Sorbet

Makes a little less than 1 quart

2 tablespoons extra virgin olive oil

¼ cup finely minced onion

2 sprigs fresh thyme

2 cloves garlic, finely minced

One 12-ounce can good-quality cherry tomatoes (LaValle is a good brand)

1 teaspoon salt

½ teaspoon sugar

⅛ teaspoon cayenne pepper (scant, meaning slightly less; you can always add more heat later)

12 ounces vine-ripened fresh cherry tomatoes

1 teaspoon good balsamic vinegar

1 to 2 tablespoons plain vodka

Optional: Tabasco sauce

Heat the olive oil in a sauté pan or a saucepan over low heat. Add the onion, thyme, and garlic and sauté until the onion and garlic are soft, 6 to 8 minutes.

Add the canned cherry tomatoes with their juice, the salt, sugar, and cayenne and cook over medium heat until the mixture becomes a thick paste, about 10 minutes. Remove from the heat and add the fresh cherry tomatoes along with the balsamic vinegar. Discard the thyme.

Transfer the entire mixture to a blender or food processor and purée until the tomatoes are entirely liquefied.

Pass the mixture through a sieve or food mill that's been placed over a large bowl.

This will remove the seeds and skin and anything else that will keep the sorbet from being totally smooth. Discard everything that's in the sieve.

Cover the strained tomato mixture and chill in the refrigerator for at least 1 hour—longer if you can—until the mixture is very cold.

Remove the mixture from the refrigerator, stir to make sure it is combined, and add the vodka. Taste and adjust for salt. Add a couple drops of Tabasco if you want a bit more heat but don't overwhelm the tomato flavor.

Pour the mixture into an ice cream maker and freeze according to the manufacturer's instructions. When the liquid has been turned into sorbet—which can take about 20 minutes—transfer to an airtight plastic container and freeze until it's ready to serve.

> **TIP:** If you can't find good-quality canned cherry tomatoes, you can use 12 ounces (about 2½ cups) San Marzano tomatoes that you've cut into small pieces or the flesh of best-quality summer tomatoes with the core and any thick skin removed. The goal is to begin with tomatoes that have a rich, bright flavor so that when they cook down, the mixture produces an intense, concentrated tomato flavor for the base of the sorbet.

Other Ways to Serve Tomato Sorbet

- Add a spoonful to a bloody Mary to add chill and flavor.
- Place a scoop alongside cold, cooked shrimp for a variation on shrimp cocktail.
- Gild the lily and serve a small spoonful alongside slices of fresh-from-the-garden beefsteak tomatoes topped with crumbled blue cheese or goat cheese.
- Use as a garnish in a bowl of gazpacho.

Crab Salad

Makes about 1½ cups

12 ounces fresh backfin or lump crabmeat

2 tablespoons finely minced chives

2 to 4 drops hot sauce

¼ cup good mayonnaise (I like Hellmann's Real or Light)

Pick through the crabmeat carefully for cartilage and shell.

Stir the chives and hot sauce into the mayonnaise, then combine with the crabmeat, taking care not to break up the crabmeat.

Open-Face Sandwiches

Makes 4 sandwiches

4 slices brioche or challah bread, about 1 inch thick

4 teaspoons unsalted butter, at room temperature

12 fresh cherry tomatoes, halved

Fresh chives

Very lightly toast the pieces of bread—just enough to toast the surface light golden brown, which keeps it from becoming soggy. Butter each piece of toast. Spread a generous spoonful of Crab Salad onto each slice.

Arrange each piece on a serving plate. Add a scoop of tomato sorbet next to the sandwich. Garnish with 3 halved tomatoes and a snip of fresh chives.

Serve immediately.

Cheddar Wafers

There are many versions of this classic savory. Here is mine.

Making hors d'oeuvres can be a challenge since many need to be finished just before serving, making it hard to be both with your guests and in the kitchen. Savory cheese crackers are a satisfying and easy choice because you can make them in advance. Even if you don't bake, these are simple to make if you have a food processor and a sheet pan. You can also make the dough in advance and slice off what you need, when you need it.

Makes about 48 wafers

8 ounces sharp cheddar cheese (about 2 cups when coarsely grated)

4 tablespoons (½ stick) unsalted butter, at room temperature

½ teaspoon Worcestershire sauce

¼ teaspoon dry mustard

⅛ teaspoon cayenne pepper

1 cup all-purpose flour

Coarse salt such as *fleur de sel* or Maldon for finishing

Using the grating disc of a food processor or the large holes on a box grater, grate the cheese.

In a food processor, combine the grated cheese, butter, Worcestershire sauce, mustard, and cayenne and process until smooth. Add the flour and process until combined. You may need to scrape down the sides of the processor once or twice to make sure all the ingredients come together.

Gather the dough into a ball and place it on a large sheet of plastic wrap. Use your hands to shape the dough into a long log, 12 to 14 inches long and about 1 inch in diameter. Wrap the plastic around the log to seal it and refrigerate until firm, about 2 hours.

Preheat the oven to 350°F.

Cut the log into ¼-inch slices and arrange the slices about 1 inch apart on a sheet pan (they will spread a little when cooked). Place a few grains of coarse salt in the center of each slice, gently pressing the grains into the dough.

Bake until lightly browned on the bottom and around the edges, 18 to 20 minutes. Be careful not to overbake them. Rotate the pan halfway through to help get even baking.

Transfer the wafers to a wire rack to cool before serving.

TIP: Use good-quality cheddar that has a sharp, full flavor. The color of the cheese, from pale yellow to rich orange, will be the color of the final wafers.

TIP: Because there is so much fat in the dough from the butter and the cheese, there's no need to grease the sheet pan, but placing a sheet of parchment paper or a silicone liner on the baking sheet will guarantee the finished slices won't stick.

TIP: The dough freezes very nicely so you can make a complete recipe, cut and bake what you need, and freeze the remaining dough, rolled into a log and wrapped in plastic, for another time.

Entertaining in a Small City Apartment

Apartment living shouldn't be an obstacle to hospitality.

Despite a lack of indoor acreage, many of us still prefer to entertain at home. It's a way to return an invitation, it's personal and welcoming, and it's usually more affordable than eating out. You don't need a formal dining room or eat-in kitchen to be a host. If you don't want to hold a formal dinner party, there are casual and easy ways to invite friends for a meal, even if you're an inexperienced host. For example:

Wine and Cheese Cocktail Party. Your local wine merchant and favorite cheese store can help you make all the choices. Add companions like nut bread, dried fruit, grapes, and *membrillo*, a Spanish quince paste. This is a perfect gathering for a late Sunday afternoon.

Soup and Dessert. If you don't have room for a sit-down dinner, it's easy to eat soup from a mug with a large napkin on your lap. Make three or four soups and give everyone a choice, keeping the soup pots hot on the stove where people can serve themselves. Pass a basket of great bread, a bowl of grated cheese, and toasted croutons. Finish with a plate of cookies and mini cupcakes, a dessert wine, and coffee.

Pizza and Beer. Make your own pizza—you can make your own dough or buy it already made. Let your guests choose their toppings, from traditional tomato and mozzarella to bacon, butternut squash, or raw arugula. Serve locally made beers and let everyone do some tasting to find a new favorite.

Weekend Brunch. Daytime entertaining lets both the cook and the guests have the remainder of the day to themselves. For a weekend brunch, make one thing that is warm (breakfast burritos or French toast) and then add help-yourself foods like bagels, smoked fish, and cream cheese; muffins or scones and fruit butter; baked apples or fruit cobbler; and generous servings of fruit juice and coffee and tea.

Salads

Making a salad is often the most time-consuming part of preparing a meal. There's all that trimming and washing, chopping and peeling, plus creating just the right slick of dressing that makes the raw ingredients sparkle with taste. But salads are so worth the effort because they are a satisfying year-round way to begin, conclude, or make a meal. For the best flavor, make your salad with what's in season, especially when it comes to tomatoes.

Raw Zucchini and Parmesan Salad

Red Cabbage Salad with Red Wine Vinaigrette

Winter Greens with Butternut Squash Croutons

Composed Salads

Plum Tomato and Chive Salad with Balsamic Vinaigrette

Green Pear, Romaine, and Blue Cheese Salad

Carrot and Chickpea Salad with Lemon Vinaigrette

Early Summer Green Vegetable Salad

Fennel Slaw with Citrus Dressing

Naples Tomato Salad with Crunchy Vegetables

Escarole and Red Onion Salad with Puntarelle Dressing

New Jersey Tomatoes and Red Onions

Blood Orange and Arugula Salad

Raw Zucchini and Parmesan Salad

Most of us think of zucchini as a vegetable to cook, whether pan-grilled, in a rata-touille, or steamed and tossed with a little sea salt. But small, tender, locally grown zucchini are perfect to eat raw. Combined with a few peels of salty Parmesan cheese and a toss of your best olive oil and lemon juice, this familiar vegetable will inspire new respect. Plus this salad is a perfect way to use the abundant zucchini in summer when the vegetable is bountiful and cheap.

Start by cutting small zucchini into paper-thin slices. The best way is with a mandoline, a ceramic kitchen slicer, or a very sharp paring knife.

Avoid making this salad with large, fat zucchini because these usually have developed little seeds and can be squishy in the middle. Instead always choose those that are firm, small, and tender.

Serves 4

4 small zucchini or 1½ pounds baby zucchini (the size of a finger)

1 block good Parmesan or Pecorino Romano (don't make this salad with any cheese of lesser quality)

1 lemon

Extra virgin olive oil (your best)

Salt

Freshly ground black pepper

Using a mandoline, ceramic kitchen slicer, or sharp paring knife, cut the zucchini into paper-thin slices. Place in a serving bowl.

Using a vegetable peeler, cut curls of Parmesan so that you have about ½ cup peels for 4 cups zucchini slices.

Gently toss to combine, taking care not to break up the cheese pieces too much.

Cut the lemon in half and squeeze it over the zucchini and cheese combination. Drizzle with about 3 tablespoons olive oil. Gently toss and taste. Add more lemon juice or olive oil to taste.

Add salt and pepper to taste. Remember that the cheese is salty so you may not need much added salt.

Serve immediately.

TIP: If you're uncertain about getting the lemon-to-olive oil ratio right, combine about 1 tablespoon fresh lemon juice and 3 tablespoons olive oil together in a small bowl and drizzle this combination over the zucchini and cheese mixture.

Salt and Pepper

We take salt and pepper for granted but add them to almost everything we cook. As ordinary as these ingredients may seem, choosing the right ones can make the difference between a bland or outstanding finish.

Salt

Unless you're trying to add iodine to your diet, buy one that is processed with no chemical additives. There are increasingly exotic and costly salts alongside the big boxes of plain kosher salt, but with a little label reading, you can find ones that suit your cooking.

- *Kosher salt.* Large-grained salt with a clean, bright taste and no additives, although some brands include an anticaking agent. It gets its name by being the type of salt used in making meats kosher by helping extract the blood from the meat. It's the choice of most professional chefs for its flavor as well as its large grain, making it easier to pinch and control how much is being added to food. I can't recall being in a professional kitchen that didn't have boxes of Diamond Crystal kosher salt on their shelves.
- *Sea salt.* Made by evaporating seawater. Some is done by hand, including the precious *fleur de sel,* which is mostly used as a final seasoning. Other sea salt is machine processed in large to fine crystals, the latter preferred by bakers because they dissolve more easily.
- *Flavored salts.* A recent innovation, these are sea salts to which flavors are added, for example, truffle, smoke, and other novelty tastes.
- *Gray salt.* Hand harvested in Brittany. The pans used to harvest the salt cause its pale silver color; it is naturally higher in some trace minerals such as magnesium, iron, and calcium.
- *Hawaiian salt.* Red or black sea salt harvested in the waters off Hawaii's red and black lava coastlines.

- *Maldon salt.* An English sea salt that has been processed into delicate flakes, it is a great choice for roasts and other foods that benefit from larger pieces of salt.

Salty Tips

- Be attentive to the size of the crystals and the amount of salt in a recipe. One teaspoon coarser kosher salt may have the same flavor as one-half teaspoon fine salt.
- Instead of using a saltshaker, keep your salt in a small bowl. You'll have far more control over the amount of salt you're adding to your recipes. And salt is stable, which means it won't spoil or attract bugs so it's safe to leave on the counter.
- Salt draws out moisture. This is a good thing when you add salt to a bowl of cut tomatoes. But if you're sautéing mushrooms, don't add salt until the end of cooking or the mushrooms will excrete lots of water, making it hard to get a brown, crispy surface.
- Likewise, only salt meat immediately before cooking or else the salt will draw out the juices and make it difficult to sear.
- When cooking pasta, add lots of salt to the water so that it tastes like the sea. This will flavor the pasta as it cooks; salting pasta *after* it cooks means the salt stays on the surface, making it taste salty.
- If you are making a sauce or gravy by reducing a liquid in which you've cooked meat, such as a pot roast, be very light-handed with the salt until you taste at the end. The process of reduction will intensify everything, including the saltiness.
- You can always add salt, but you can't take it away. (I've heard about that trick of putting a potato in something that's oversalted; I'd rather avoid the problem to begin with.) Add salt gradually and taste before adding more.

Pepper

- Invest in a good pepper mill and keep it filled with black peppercorns bought from a spice merchant or a market that has a busy spice department so the spices will be fresh. Then grind pepper as you need it to be sure that the flavor will be at its best. Grinding pepper in advance defeats the purpose of having a grinder because once the peppercorn is crushed it immediately begins to lose its flavor and aroma.

- Get into the habit of adding freshly ground pepper to your food. Add a little. Taste. Add more if your palate would like more of its liveliness. Because of the way it boosts flavor, very often adding pepper to your cooking means you can add less salt, which can be a good healthy choice. You can also add pepper during the cooking and then at the finish. But always taste first.

- Today pepper is grown and imported from Indonesia, Brazil, Ecuador, Malaysia, Vietnam, and various parts of India. Tellicherry, imported from India, has an extra bite, making it my favorite.

- What's the difference between black and white pepper? Both come from the fully ripe berries of the same tropical plant, but white pepper has had its outer surface removed. This means you won't get the little black flecks that come from grinding the black peppercorn, but you also won't get the full, pungent taste, much of which is in the black outer layer.

- Why pepper instead of chiles? The capsaicin in chiles is about one hundred times more powerful than the flavor compound in pepper. Plus the flavors are really different. Pepper is more woody and warm, some say more floral and less acidic, than chiles. In many dishes both will be used—pepper for complexity and chiles for heat and brightness.

Red Cabbage Salad with Red Wine Vinaigrette

This is my favorite salad and the simplest to make. It's good year-round because red cabbage is both a summer and winter vegetable.

Try to make this salad several hours before you're going to serve it because the salt in the dressing will soften the cabbage a little, making it easier to eat.

To cut by hand, take each cabbage leaf and cut out any thick rib so that you have large pieces of tender cabbage. Make a stack of the leaves and using a chef's knife, cut the leaves into very thin, shredded pieces.

A knife technique called chiffonade works perfectly here. You take a leaf (or two or three stacked on one another), roll them up like a cigar, and then cut the roll into ¼-inch slices.

While you can buy bags of already shredded red cabbage, please resist using it here because the pieces are very fine and your salad may wilt. Plus there's a big difference between the taste of precut vegetables and the ones you cut on your own. While you can use the slicing or shredding disc of a food processor to turn your fresh cabbage head into slaw, try to do this by hand because you'll get slightly larger and less uniform pieces, which in turn will make this more like salad than coleslaw.

Serves 4 to 6

1 head red cabbage	Freshly ground black pepper
2 tablespoons red wine vinegar	2 tablespoons extra virgin olive oil
Salt	3 tablespoons canola oil

Using a chef's knife, remove the bottom and the outer leaves of the cabbage head. Disassemble the cabbage head in order to have loose leaves. Stop at the point where the leaves become small and thick. Cut out any core or ribs, keeping the leaves whole.

Working in steps, cut using the chiffonade method: stack the individual leaves and roll them up like a cigar, then slice crosswise ¼ inch thick. Your goal is to produce about 6 cups thinly sliced cabbage.

In a smaller bowl, combine the red wine vinegar with a large pinch of salt and several grinds of black pepper. Using a fork, stir the vinegar until the salt dissolves. Continue to whisk with the fork as you add the olive and canola oils. Don't stop until they're fully combined.

Pour the vinaigrette over the red cabbage and toss.

This salad is best made 2 to 4 hours before serving so that the cabbage has some time to soften a little. Don't worry—it won't wilt! Refrigerate it but give it a few periodic stirs to make sure the dressing hasn't pooled on the bottom of the bowl.

Serve at room temperature.

Winter Greens with Butternut Squash Croutons

In midwinter we want big flavors in our salads. In this recipe cubes of butternut squash are roasted until caramelized and tender, and after they've cooled to room temperature, they're tossed with salad greens and pieces of crispy pancetta.

Any salad greens will work, but the sweet cubes of squash go particularly well with dark greens such as raw spinach, escarole, watercress, or arugula, each of which has a stronger flavor than most lettuces. The pancetta slices can be roasted alongside the squash. If you don't have pancetta, you can substitute bacon.

Finish with mustard vinaigrette, and if you like, a handful of toasted pumpkin or sunflower seeds.

Serves 4

1 medium to large butternut squash

2 tablespoons olive oil

½ teaspoon salt

Freshly ground black pepper

Optional: ground chipotle

4 slices pancetta or bacon

4 cups salad greens (baby spinach, escarole, watercress, arugula, romaine, or a mix of greens), rinsed and spun dry

¼ cup Mustard Vinaigrette (recipe follows)

Optional: ¼ cup toasted sunflower or pumpkin seeds

Preheat the oven to 400°F.

Peel the squash, remove and discard the seeds, and cut the squash into 1-inch cubes. Place on a sheet pan and drizzle with the olive oil. Sprinkle with the salt, about 6 grinds black pepper, and if you want a little contrast to the squash's sweetness, a pinch of ground chipotle. Using your hands, spread the cubes of squash in a single layer on the pan, making sure the olive oil, salt, and pepper coat the squash pieces.

Roast until the cubes are tender and beginning to brown, 25 to 30 minutes. Using a spatula, turn the pieces 2 or 3 times while roasting so that they cook evenly and don't stick.

While the squash is roasting, place the pancetta on a rack in another small pan and cook in the oven until golden brown and crispy, about 25 minutes depending on the thickness of the slices. (You can also cook the pancetta in a skillet on top of the stove.) When done, transfer to a paper towel and let cool.

Remove the squash pieces from the oven and let cool to room temperature, about 20 minutes.

Place the salad greens in a large salad bowl. Scatter the squash pieces on top of the greens and toss carefully (the squash will be soft). Crumble the pancetta on top of the salad and drizzle with the mustard vinaigrette. Toss one more time and serve immediately.

Add the optional seeds at the very end, after you've dressed the salad.

Mustard Vinaigrette

1½ tablespoons red wine vinegar

½ teaspoon salt

Freshly ground black pepper

1 teaspoon Dijon mustard

4 tablespoons extra virgin olive oil

In a small bowl, combine the vinegar, salt, 6 grinds of pepper, and the mustard. Using a fork or small whisk, stir until combined and the salt dissolves.

Add the olive oil and stir until emulsified.

If you don't use the vinaigrette immediately, be sure to stir it again before adding it to the salad because the oil and vinegar will separate once it sits for any amount of time.

Composed Salads

This is really a concept instead of a recipe.

In my years of cooking for company I've learned that everyone loves salad, and I've never served a more popular first course than a colorful variety of them. The idea is to make four or five different salads and arrange them either on one big platter from which people can serve themselves or in small portions on individual plates.

Although salads can be the most time-consuming portion of making any meal (my friend Pat always said that taking salad off the menu would cut dinner-making time in half), most salads can be made or prepped several hours in advance. Some flavors and textures will even improve if given a chance to marinate.

- Choose your salads by what's in season, giving thought to color and texture.
- Dress each salad separately and lightly. You can always pass extra vinaigrette at the table.
- Arrange the salads to show the colors and textures to best advantage.
- Add small accents, like half a hard-cooked egg or a scattering of oil-cured black olives.
- If you make any salads in advance, bring them to room temperature before serving.
- Served with good bread and some cheese, a platter of salads becomes a satisfying lunch.

Salad Ideas

- Chunks of in-season tomatoes with minced raw shallot and a drizzle of olive oil.
- White mushrooms with fresh tarragon vinaigrette.
- Diced crisp celery with Roquefort dressing.
- Roasted baby beets marinated in red wine vinegar.
- Little fresh mozzarella *bocconcini* with a tiny dice of tomato, a slick of olive oil, and shredded fresh basil.
- Drained and rinsed canned chickpeas with a light drizzle of chile oil.
- Mâche, a delicate, dark green lettuce, very lightly dressed.
- Roasted baby potatoes, cooked until tender and shriveled, served at room temperature.
- French green beans, cooked until tender and served at room temperature with a little lemon juice.

- Cooked long-grained rice or small pasta such as ditali with a tiny dice of red and green peppers.
- Little cubes of avocado (cut just before serving to prevent darkening).
- Paper-thin slices of English cucumber tossed with rice vinegar and a drop of sesame oil.

The Perfect Everyday Vinaigrette

Over many years of cooking for friends, this is the recipe I've been asked for more than any other. While I know I can make larger quantities in advance, I prefer to make it fresh, just for that day's salad. And I use no fancy tools—just a small bowl, a tablespoon for measuring, and a fork to whisk.

Most important in this recipe is the ratio of oil to acid, which determines how rich (oily) or bright (acidic) the dressing will be. I like mine to be a balance of both, so I use a ratio of 1 part vinegar to 2½ parts oil.

I also use two different oils. Olive oil has flavor and complexity, but the addition of tasteless canola oil lightens the dressing, avoiding any possible tannic taste that sometimes comes with olive oil.

You don't need lots of dressing for a big bowl of salad. Just toss a lot and you'll be surprised how far this goes. This amount generously dresses eight to ten cups of salad. Dress and toss just before serving so that the salad doesn't wilt.

2 tablespoons red wine vinegar

1 forkful (about ¾ teaspoon) good Dijon mustard (the smooth kind; my favorite brand is Maille)

½ teaspoon kosher salt (slightly less if you're using fine sea salt)

5 to 6 grinds of fresh black pepper

2 tablespoons extra virgin olive oil

3 tablespoons canola oil

In a small bowl, add the vinegar, mustard, salt, and pepper. Using the fork you just used to add the mustard, gently stir to dissolve the salt and break up the mustard. It will look slightly opaque and clumpy.

Add the olive and canola oils and gently whisk with the fork to emulsify the dressing. You also could mix everything in a glass jar, cover, and shake until combined.

Add to your completely prepared salad that's already in a salad bowl, and using salad servers, gently but thoroughly toss your salad to let the dressing coat everything.

Plum Tomato and Chive Salad with Balsamic Vinaigrette

When we think of tomato salads, most of us think of beefsteaks or gnarly heirlooms cut into chunks and scattered with fresh mozzarella and basil. But all year long, the firm plum, or Roma, tomato can deliver an intense tomato flavor; this salad combines peeled plum tomatoes with a rich, chive-studded balsamic dressing.

Select plum tomatoes that are firm and that have a bright, even red color. Also choose ones that are all about the same size so that when you peel them and remove the seeds, you have uniform "fillets." Because this salad only has two ingredients—tomatoes and chives—please don't even think about using dried chives, which do not get close to the peppery bite of their fresh counterparts.

Serves 4

6 to 8 medium-to-large plum tomatoes

1 tablespoon balsamic vinegar

Salt

Freshly ground black pepper

2 to 3 tablespoons canola oil

1 bunch fresh chives

Have ready a 3- to 4-quart pot of boiling water and a large workbowl filled with iced water. Drop the tomatoes into the boiling water 2 or 3 at a time. Count to 5 slowly—as in one Mississippi, two Mississippi—and using a spider or slotted spoon, transfer the tomatoes from the boiling water to the bowl of iced water to stop the cooking. Your goal is to loosen the skins, not cook the tomatoes. Take each post-boiled tomato and run your fingernail along the skin. If it loosens, it's ready to be peeled. If the skin is still taut, put it back into the boiling water for another 5 to 10 seconds. Shock in the iced water to stop any cooking. Take each tomato and, using a paring knife, remove and discard the skins. They should slip off easily.

Cut each tomato lengthwise in half. Remove the seeds and the rest of the insides so that you're left with just the skinned tomato flesh. Your goal is to have a bowl of halved or quartered tomatoes without skins or seeds.

In a small bowl, stir together the balsamic vinegar, a pinch of salt, and several grinds of pepper until the salt dissolves. Add the canola oil and stir until it combines. Taste for salt and the balance of oil and acid.

Pour the dressing over the tomatoes.

Hold the bunch of chives in one hand and use scissors to snip small bits, about ⅛ inch, over the tomatoes. Add about 2 tablespoons or to taste. Toss to combine.

This salad can be made several hours in advance and kept in the refrigerator until you're ready to serve. Bring to room temperature before serving.

TIP: The easiest way to snip chives into small bits is using a pair of scissors.

Green Pear, Romaine, and Blue Cheese Salad

What makes this salad special is the combination of sweet pear with salty cheese. The nuts and cranberries add both texture and color that stand up to the robust vinaigrette.

Serves 4

1 head romaine lettuce

1 ripe Bartlett or Anjou pear

⅓ cup dried cranberries

⅓ cup crumbled blue cheese, such as Danish blue, Maytag, Great Hill Blue, or other crumbly domestic or imported blue cheese

⅓ cup pine nuts

Balsamic Vinaigrette (recipe follows)

Rinse and dry the lettuce leaves, tear into bite-size pieces, and place them in a salad bowl.

Cut the pear in half and remove the core and stem. Leaving the peel on, cut the pear lengthwise into ¼-inch slices.

Add the pear, dried cranberries, and blue cheese to the lettuce.

Lightly toast the pine nuts in a skillet until fragrant and beginning to turn golden brown. Watch closely while you do this because the nuts can quickly turn from brown to burnt. Make the vinaigrette and toss the salad ingredients with the dressing and toasted pine nuts just before serving.

Balsamic Vinaigrette

2 tablespoons balsamic vinegar

3 tablespoons extra virgin olive oil

2 teaspoons finely minced garlic (or crushed through a garlic press)

1 teaspoon very hot mustard (Coleman's English, Löwensenf Extra, and Maille's Fine are all good choices)

½ teaspoon fresh lemon juice

Pinch each sugar, salt, and freshly ground black pepper

Put all the ingredients in a jar, cover, and shake well.

Carrot and Chickpea Salad with Lemon Vinaigrette

This simple salad gets its complex flavor from the sweetness of the carrots combining with nutty chickpeas and lemony vinaigrette.

This salad is perfect for a busy city cook. Because the chickpeas are canned and the carrots are bagged, you'll be able to make an easy salad for a weekday dinner after you've used up your more perishable fresh vegetables. Its beautiful orange color also makes it a good choice for a dinner party salad platter. If you can't find matchstick carrots at your market, buy whole carrots and shred them using the large holes on a box grater or your food processor.

Resist putting more lemon juice into the dressing; if it becomes too citrusy, it will be too sour against the carrots.

Makes 2 large or 4 smaller portions

One 10-ounce bag "French-cut" or matchstick carrots, or 2 cups shredded carrots

One 16-ounce can chickpeas, drained and rinsed

2 teaspoons red wine vinegar

2 teaspoons fresh lemon juice

Salt

Freshly ground black pepper

4 teaspoons extra virgin olive oil

4 teaspoons canola oil

Place the carrots and chickpeas in a serving bowl.

In a smaller bowl, combine the vinegar and lemon juice with a pinch of salt and several grinds of pepper. Stir with a fork until the salt dissolves.

Add the olive and canola oils to the vinegar mixture and whisk to emulsify. Taste for salt and the balance of acid and oil.

Pour the dressing over the carrots and chickpeas and toss to combine.

> **TIP:** Letting the carrots and chickpeas sit in the dressing for 2 to 3 hours helps develop flavor and softens the carrots. Refrigerate it if you're not going to serve right away, but it's best to bring it to room temperature before serving.

Early Summer Green Vegetable Salad

On a recent trip to France my husband and I had lunch in a brasserie under the direction of the great chef Paul Bocuse. Making the most of an early harvest of summer vegetables, the day's specials included a salad of green vegetables, mâche, which is a tender salad green, and lemon vinaigrette.

In this recipe, each vegetable is cooked separately just to tenderness, before they become too soft or their color fades. Once cooled, the vegetables are individually dressed and then arranged on plates in a green-on-green composed salad. While it may be possible to make this salad year-round, for the best flavor, it should only be made in the late spring or early summer when every ingredient is at its best.

Serves 4

4 medium to large artichokes

Fresh lemon juice

2 handfuls haricots verts (about 40 beans, 10 per serving)

8 to 12 spears asparagus

4 cups mâche (also called lamb's lettuce)

½ cup Lemon Vinaigrette (recipe follows)

Trim the artichokes to reveal the whole heart. Hold in a bowl of cool water (add a squeeze of lemon to prevent discoloration) until ready to cook.

Cook the whole artichoke hearts until tender by either steaming them over boiling water or cooking them in the microwave in a covered dish for about 4 minutes. Set aside and let cool to room temperature. When completely cool, cut each heart into quarters.

Trim and rinse the haricots verts. Have a bowl of iced water ready. Cook in a steamer, the microwave, or a pot of salted boiling water until fully tender but still bright green. Transfer to the bowl of iced water to stop their cooking and drain. Set aside.

Trim the asparagus and peel any stalks that have coarse or thick skins. Have a bowl of iced water ready. Cook in a steamer, the microwave, or a pot of salted boiling water until fully tender. Transfer to the bowl of iced water to stop their cooking and drain. Cut the asparagus stalks into discs about ½ inch each, leaving the tips fully intact.

Rinse and completely dry the mâche.

Make the vinaigrette.

On either a large single platter or 4 individual salad plates, arrange the mâche. On top of these leaves pile clusters of the other vegetables so that there are *haricots verts* alongside discs of asparagus and the quartered artichoke hearts. Place the reserved asparagus tips on top of the arrangement. Drizzle with the vinaigrette and serve immediately.

> **TIP:** Mâche, also called lamb's lettuce, has small, dark, velvety leaves that often come in small clusters. It is a delicate lettuce with a sweeter flavor than many other lettuces. If you can't find mâche, substitute a milder lettuce such as Boston or red-leaf lettuce.

Lemon Vinaigrette

1 tablespoon fresh lemon juice

1 tablespoon red wine vinegar

½ teaspoon salt

8 grinds of black pepper

3 tablespoons extra virgin olive oil

2 tablespoons canola oil

In a shallow bowl, combine the lemon juice, vinegar, salt, and pepper and use a fork to stir until the salt dissolves.

Add the olive and canola oils and stir with a fork or whisk until emulsified.

Vinegar

Its name comes from the French, *vin aigre*, which means sour wine. And today there are scores of different kinds. The more popular are red wine vinegar, white wine, Champagne, sherry, cider, rice, balsamic, white, plus lesser-known vinegars such as malt, honey, raisin, cane, or date, each with a taste and character derived from its original source.

Choose your vinegar depending upon how it will be used. For example:

- *Malt.* Popular with fish and chips and also used in pickling.
- *Balsamic.* Made from the *must* (concentrated juice) of white, sugary Trebbiano grapes. The best is aged in wood for up to one hundred years. Use a precious and aged balsamic to accent fresh figs or sprinkle a few drops on fresh strawberries. A less-expensive option is to boil a younger balsamic in a small saucepan until it reduces to a syrupy glaze to use in the same way.
- *Red wine.* Perfect in barbeque sauces or in mustard vinaigrette on mixed winter greens.
- *Champagne.* For a vinaigrette that will include crumbled cheese or for making your own mayonnaise.
- *White wine.* Good for salsas, marinades, and sauces that need an added tang.
- *Cider.* To deglaze a pan after sautéing pork chops that will be served with a side of cooked sliced apples or in a complex dish such as sauerbraten.
- *Rice.* Sprinkle a few drops over thinly sliced scallions and toss with brown rice, or add to a teriyaki glaze.
- *White.* Made by fermenting pure alcohol, this one is best for pickling and household cleaning.

Vinegar's acidity means it needs no refrigeration and has an almost unlimited shelf life. Still, sometimes you will find a growth inside a bottle. This is called a "mother," and it is cellulose that naturally occurs in vinegar, produced by the harmless bacteria that were used in fermentation. It doesn't mean the vinegar is spoiled or in any way harmed. Vinegar producers usually pasteurize the product to prevent a mother from forming, but should one develop in one of your bottles, simply pour the vinegar through a filter (a fine-mesh sieve or coffee filter would work), discard the mother, and enjoy the vinegar.

The difference between red and white wine vinegar? It depends on the color of the wine used to make the vinegar in the first place.

Fennel Slaw with Citrus Dressing

Many think a traditional slaw is dressed with a mayonnaise-based, tangy dressing, but in some parts of the country, the favorite dressing is light, vinegar based, and slightly sweet.

In this slaw I've combined raw fennel with red onion to make a fresh, crisp salad that is a perfect companion to fish or chicken. Fennel is a versatile vegetable, eaten both raw and cooked. Its faint licorice flavor deepens when it's cooked, but raw in this salad, it remains light and refreshing. Fennel and orange is a classic combination, so I've added a little orange juice to an otherwise simple vinaigrette.

To ensure that you end up with a slaw rather than just raw fennel, make sure your slices really are paper thin. Fennel bulbs can be coarse and a challenge to cut, so I recommend using a mandoline or a ceramic slicer.

Serves 4

2 fennel bulbs, trimmed and sliced paper thin (about 4 cups)

1 large or 2 small red onions, very thinly sliced (about 1½ cups)

1 tablespoon orange juice

1 teaspoon fresh lemon juice

1 teaspoon Dijon mustard

½ teaspoon salt

Freshly ground black pepper

3 tablespoons extra virgin olive oil

Combine the fennel and red onion in a serving bowl.

In a small bowl, combine the orange juice, lemon juice, mustard, salt, and 4 to 6 grinds of pepper, and whisk until the salt dissolves. Add the olive oil and whisk to combine. Immediately pour over the fennel and onion and toss to coat.

Refrigerate for about 30 minutes to let the dressing soften the fennel slices. Toss again and serve.

You can garnish the slaw with pieces of sliced orange and fennel fronds snipped from the fennel bulbs.

Olive Oil

Olive oil is a healthy fat, meaning that while it is high in calories, it's also high in monounsaturated fat. Purportedly a diet high in these fats reduces the risk of heart disease. Plus olive oil is full of antioxidants.

It's versatile for cooking and it has flavor, which means it adds dimension to salad dressings, can be drizzled on a bowl of soup or a platter of fresh mozzarella, or used to finish cooked or raw vegetables.

Most olive oil comes from the Mediterranean region, especially Italy, Greece, and Spain, but some is also produced in France and California. As with wine, getting acquainted with great olive oil requires some experimenting and tasting to find what you like.

Read the label to confirm the origin and character of the oil and get to know your favorite producers. As with most foods, you get the best quality when the folks who grow it and produce it also bottle and ship it.

Taste (and smell) different kinds of oils to find your favorites, choosing between the mellow gold oils of Sicily, the green and peppery ones of Tuscany, the bold oils of Catalonia in northern Spain, and the subtle oils of Provence.

Extra virgin olive oil is made from the first pressing of the olives and has less than 0.8% acidity, one test of superior flavor. It also means no chemicals were used to extract the oil, only physical pressure on the just-harvested olives. The first cold pressing is generally considered the best for flavor, and if an olive oil was produced that way, you can be sure it will say so on the bottle.

Virgin olive oil is the second pressing and usually cannot have more than 2% acidity, although standards for this vary.

Sometimes using virgin (not extra virgin) oil is a better choice for cooking because it has a higher smoking point, the temperature at which fats begin to decompose (and ruin whatever you're cooking). Extra virgin's is 375°F, while virgin olive oil's is 410°F, making it better for cooking at higher temperatures. So if you want to use olive oil for frying, keep a bottle of virgin on hand and save the extra virgin—which is also more expensive—for salads and other cooking.

Look for any declarations of quality. An important one is when a bottle says the oil was "cold pressed." This means no heat was used to extract the oil from the olives. I advise against buying oils labeled simply "olive oil," meaning a grade below virgin. By the time the olives get to their third or fourth pressing, there's a good chance heat or chemicals are being used to extract the oil and manipulate the flavor, and who wants to eat that?

Some better producers will also show proof of origin on a label, such as DOP or DOC in some parts of Italy (*Denominazione di Origine Protetta* or *Denominazione di Origine Controllata*) or DO (*Denominación de Origen*) in Spain. But an olive oil without such labeling can be excellent, so don't use these as your only criteria.

Olive oil doesn't need to be refrigerated, but once the bottle is opened the air can affect its flavor. Experts say to store olive oil in a cool place—not in the refrigerator but neither on a shelf over the stove where heat can affect its taste. Even better, only buy as much olive oil as you'll use in a few weeks, so that way it will always have great flavor.

Naples Tomato Salad with Crunchy Vegetables

I don't know why this salad is named for Naples, but that's the name it had when I first tasted it over twenty years ago. This is salad for the best of summer's vegetables, combining ripe tomatoes with large pieces of crunchy vegetables in a dressing made mostly from the tomatoes' own acidic juice.

Don't even think about making this salad unless the tomatoes are ripe, locally grown, and full of bright, juicy flavor.

This salad is versatile. You can add anything you like, but it's best to add big pieces of ingredients that can stand up to the acidic, juicy dressing. This salad is perfect on a summer night when it's too hot to cook, as a side to a store-bought rotisserie chicken, or simply served with great bread and a plate of assorted cheeses.

Serves 4

2 to 4 large, locally grown, ripe tomatoes

Salt, preferably good sea salt or kosher salt

2 stalks celery, cut into 1-inch pieces (inner, more tender stalks are best)

½ medium to large red onion, cut into ½-inch dice

1 cup thickly sliced radishes

1 cup 1-inch pieces peeled Kirby cucumbers

½ cup oil-cured black olives

1 teaspoon finely minced fresh basil

1 teaspoon finely minced fresh mint

Freshly ground black pepper

Extra virgin olive oil

Core the tomatoes and cut into large chunks, 1 to 1½ inches each (about 4 cups). Do not peel them unless the skins are very thick. Cut the pieces over your salad bowl to capture any juice that may run out of the tomatoes as you cut them. Remove any thick, white core so that your bowl is filled with beautiful pieces of juicy red tomato.

Salt the tomato pieces generously—about ¼ teaspoon salt for each cup—and toss to combine. Let the tomatoes sit for about 10 minutes while the salt draws out the juices.

Add the celery, onion, radishes, cucumbers, and olives to the tomatoes. Sprinkle with the basil and mint and about 4 grinds of black pepper.

Drizzle with about 2 tablespoons extra virgin olive oil. Toss to combine. Taste and adjust the seasoning, adding more olive oil if necessary.

Escarole and Red Onion Salad with Puntarelle Dressing

Because of its somewhat bitter taste, escarole is more commonly braised or added to a soup. But when dressed with a complex vinaigrette and contrasted with the big personality of red onion, escarole's satisfying flavor, similar to that of endive, its close cousin, becomes the centerpiece of a salad that can stand up to any other tastes at the table.

I've matched the escarole with a minced anchovy dressing, similar to one popular in Italy that's always served with a Roman chicory called *puntarelle*. Begin by marinating the onion in the dressing to soften and flavor it while you prepare the rest of the salad.

Serves 4

1 medium red onion

2 tablespoons red wine vinegar

2 anchovy fillets, finely minced

1 tablespoon Dijon mustard

½ teaspoon salt

Freshly ground black pepper

¼ cup extra virgin olive oil

1 large head escarole

3 to 4 tablespoons grated Parmesan cheese

Cut the onion crosswise into very thin (⅛- to ¼-inch) slices and separate the slices into individual rings.

In a bowl big enough to also hold all the onion rings, combine the vinegar, anchovies, mustard, salt, and 4 to 6 grinds of pepper and stir with a fork until the salt dissolves. Add the olive oil and mix until the dressing is emulsified. Add the onion rings to the dressing and mix to coat them completely. Let sit for up to 1 hour while you prepare the rest of the salad, giving the onion time to soften and almost pickle.

Trim the base and remove any damaged outer leaves from the escarole. Using a large chef's knife, cut the escarole into 2-inch pieces. Use your fingers to separate the inner pieces. Rinse and spin all the pieces dry and add everything to a salad bowl.

When ready to serve, spread the onion rings over the top of the escarole and pour any remaining dressing over the salad. Sprinkle with the Parmesan and toss to combine.

Serve immediately.

New Jersey Tomatoes and Red Onions

This is less a recipe than a tribute to the best of summer's tomatoes. Serve it for supper on a hot August night with slices of thick country bread and your favorite roasted chicken, served cold.

Serves 4

3 to 4 medium to large beefsteak or heirloom tomatoes

1 medium red onion

Sea salt

Freshly ground black pepper

Extra virgin olive oil

Core the tomatoes and cut into ½-inch slices. If the tomatoes have very thick skins, use a serrated knife or vegetable peeler to remove them.

Very thinly slice the onion crosswise and separate into rings.

On a serving plate, arrange the tomato slices in a single layer and scatter the onion rings on top.

Add a pinch of salt, several grinds of black pepper, and a drizzle of olive oil.

Serve immediately.

Blood Orange and Arugula Salad

Midwinter can be a dull time for salads, but the cold months bring us wonderful citrus fruits. Combined with peppery arugula, oranges produce a colorful plate and a fresh flavor.

Blood oranges are small, seedless fruits that have a slightly sweet taste and a deep red hue. Resist adding any dressing. The fruit's juice will combine with your best olive oil to help bring out the flavors.

If you can't find blood oranges—they seem to come and go all winter—substitute tangerines, ruby grapefruits, or any kind of orange.

Serves 4

4 or 5 blood oranges

1 medium red onion

1 pound arugula or baby arugula

3 to 4 tablespoons extra virgin olive oil

Salt

Freshly ground black pepper

Cut the peel and pith from each orange, leaving the orange flesh entirely exposed. Cut the oranges into thin slices.

Very thinly slice the onion crosswise and separate into rings.

Rinse and completely dry the arugula, then tear into large bite-size pieces.

Place the arugula on a large platter or on individual serving plates. Arrange the orange slices on top of the arugula and top with the onion rings.

Drizzle with about 3 tablespoons olive oil and season with salt and pepper.

Serve immediately.

Pasta, Rice, and Grains

Cooking pasta, rice, and grains is very city-kitchen friendly because these dishes can be made mostly right from the pantry. Add some vegetables and a little cheese, and many of these recipes can serve double duty as either the main course or a satisfying side dish.

Couscous Salad with Chickpeas and Vegetables

Farro Salad with Chopped Vegetables and Feta Cheese

Rigatoni alla Grecia

Spaghetti with Tomato Paste and Garlic

Penne with Canned Tuna and Cannellini Beans

Pasta Shells with Swordfish, Capers, and Black Olives

Paella Casserole

Red Rice Pilaf

Cacio e Pepe

Tomato Risotto

Whole-Wheat Pasta with Zucchini and Roasted Carrots

Greenmarket Fried Rice

Couscous Salad with Chickpeas and Vegetables

Couscous is fine-grained pasta made from semolina flour that is best known for its use in a spicy dish popular in Morocco and other parts of northern Africa. It's either steamed or quick-cooked in boiling water, and it takes on the flavor of the other ingredients in your recipe, making it a perfect partner to stewed vegetables or tomato sauce. In this recipe I use it as the base for a satisfying and versatile salad.

You can purchase instant couscous by the box, but for a better value look for it at bulk grocers, especially organic- and natural-food markets. When using it in a salad, it's preferable to cook couscous only with boiling water, not chicken or vegetable stock; adding a teaspoon of olive oil will help keep the grains from clumping together.

This salad can be made with any favorite vegetables you have on hand, but I like it best with ones that have texture and crunch, because they contrast with the tender grains of couscous. Others additions could include red or green bell pepper, red onion, fennel, and blanched haricots verts.

Serves 6

1¼ cups instant couscous (one 10-ounce box)

2 cups boiling water

1 teaspoon olive oil

2 cups halved cherry tomatoes

1 cup diced seedless or Kirby cucumber, peeled if the skin is thick

Red Wine Vinegar Vinaigrette (recipe follows)

¼ cup sliced scallions

½ cup canned chickpeas, drained and rinsed

¼ cup pine nuts, toasted

½ cup crumbled feta cheese

In a large mixing bowl, combine the couscous, boiling water, and olive oil and quickly stir with a fork. Cover the bowl with a pot lid or large plate so that the steam stays in the bowl. Let sit for 5 minutes, then fluff with a fork to break up the grains. Let cool to room temperature or place in the refrigerator to quickly chill.

While the couscous is cooling, prepare the vegetables and make the vinaigrette.

Just before you're ready to serve, combine the couscous with the vegetables, chickpeas, pine nuts, and feta and toss gently to combine. Add the vinaigrette and toss again.

Serve immediately.

Red Wine Vinegar Vinaigrette

2 tablespoons red wine vinegar

1 heaping teaspoon Dijon mustard

1 teaspoon kosher or sea salt

½ teaspoon freshly ground black pepper

5 tablespoons extra virgin olive oil

In a small bowl, combine the vinegar, mustard, salt, and pepper. Using a fork, stir until the salt is dissolved and the mustard is completely mixed.

Add the olive oil and whisk with the fork until it is combined with the vinegar. Remix it before adding it to the salad.

Toasting Pine Nuts

Pine nuts develop a richer flavor when toasted. Spread them in a pan and toast in a 350°F oven or on top of the stove over low heat. They should be ready in about 5 minutes. But watch them carefully; because they're high in fat, pine nuts burn easily. They are also quite costly, so it would be a shame to waste a whole batch.

Farro Salad with Chopped Vegetables and Feta Cheese

Farro is a hearty grain that's popular in some regions of Italy, especially Tuscany and Umbria. The first time I tasted farro was at a ristorante in Arezzo, the small Tuscan city famed for its exquisite frescoes by Piero della Francesca. It was a family restaurant, as so many are in Italy, and as my husband and I sat at an outdoor table waiting for our meal, the owner brought us small dishes of this nutty and satisfying salad. Tender grains of wheat had been mixed with small pieces of raw vegetables and a splash of oil and vinegar.

While farro is also used in soups and risottos, my memory of that art-filled day and wonderful lunch in Arezzo makes this recipe one of my favorites.

Here I've suggested diced peppers and cherry tomatoes, but you can choose any vegetables that have texture and bright flavors that will add color and crunch and contrast to the tender and nutty flavor of the grains. Chunks of avocado, fava beans, cubes of cooked beets, and a fine dice of seedless cucumber would all work as well.

If the salad is going to be a main course, serve with steamed asparagus spears or another green vegetable. If it's going to be a side dish, it is a perfect match to fish or steak.

If you can't find farro, substitute another whole grain such as wheat berries or barley, although be aware that these can take twice as long to cook.

Serves 4 to 6 as a side dish or 2 to 3 as a main dish

1½ cups farro

2 quarts water

Salt

½ cup diced red or green bell pepper (about 1 medium pepper) or other colorful and crunchy vegetable

1 cup cherry tomatoes, cut in half or in quarters, depending on their size (round cherry tomatoes that come on a vine have more juice and a brighter flavor than grape tomatoes but either is fine)

⅓ cup finely diced red onion or thinly sliced scallions, both white and tender green parts

⅓ cup diced feta or ricotta salata

1½ tablespoons red wine vinegar

¼ cup extra virgin olive oil

Freshly ground black pepper

In a large saucepan, combine the farro, water, and ½ teaspoon salt. Bring to a boil, then reduce the heat to medium-low. Cover and simmer until the farro is tender, about 20 minutes. Drain well. Place the drained farro in a large serving bowl and let cool to room temperature.

When the farro is completely cooled, add the vegetables and cheese and gently toss to combine.

In a separate bowl, combine the vinegar, olive oil, a large pinch of salt (about ¼ teaspoon), and 4 to 6 grinds of pepper, using a fork or whisk. Pour over the farro and vegetable mixture and toss to coat.

Serve either chilled or at room temperature on a bed of salad greens or radicchio leaves.

Rigatoni alla Grecia

This classic Roman pasta dish is made with only three ingredients: pasta, pork fat, and cheese. Similar to spaghetti carbonara but with no eggs, it is traditionally made with bucatini, a very thick spaghetti; guanciale (pronounced "goo-on-chi-ally"), cured pork jowls which is very similar to bacon but with a stronger flavor; and Pecorino Romano cheese. Because bucatini can be difficult to find, even in our most foodcentric cities, I've substituted rigatoni.

But try not to make substitutions for the other two ingredients. It's worth the effort to find guanciale because it is the pivotal flavor in this dish; it adds the perfect degree of unctuousness and gloss. If you give up on your search for guanciale, pancetta is a reasonably good alternative.

Pecorino Romano is a sheep's cheese from southern Italy that's used by Romans much as northern Italians use Parmesan. But Pecorino Romano has a sharper flavor and less subtle personality and thus works better in this recipe than the more complex—and costly—Parmesan.

Locatelli is an excellent imported Pecorino that is easy to find in city markets. Grate it by placing small chunks in a food processor and pulsing until the cheese has become a grainy powder. Don't use a Microplane zester because it will produce soft flakes that will melt too easily and not mix correctly with the hot pasta and pork fat.

Do not make this dish with fresh pasta as its tender texture will be overwhelmed by the guanciale and cheese. Instead, use a good-quality dried pasta such as DeCecco.

Finally, making this dish is all about technique. It's essential to have all your ingredients ready and your serving bowl warm so that the pasta, grated cheese, and pieces of pork all meld together into a creamy combo.

Serves 4 as a main course or 6 to 8 as a side dish

2 tablespoons salt

4 ounces guanciale, sliced ¼ inch thick (substitute pancetta only if you must)

⅔ cup grated Pecorino Romano cheese

1 pound rigatoni (a dry pasta such as DeCecco)

Bring a large pot of water to a boil. Add the salt.

Cut the guanciale into 1-inch pieces. In a large skillet or sauté pan, cook the guanciale over medium heat until golden brown and crisp. If you've never cooked with guanciale, you may be surprised by its strong aroma. Remove from the pan and drain on a piece of paper towel.

Pour off all but 2 tablespoons fat from the skillet. If the guanciale did not produce this much fat, add extra virgin olive oil to make up the difference. Keep the skillet on the stove over your lowest heat so that it stays warm but isn't cooking.

Fill your serving bowl with hot water from the tap to warm it.

Have your grated cheese ready.

When you have all the ingredients fully prepared, cook the rigatoni in the boiling salted water according to the package instructions. Be sure not to overcook it. Start checking for doneness at least a minute before the time on the box's instructions. When the pasta is cooked *al dente*, drain it, reserving a cup or so of the water.

Add the drained rigatoni to the skillet containing the warm pork fat and increase the heat to medium. Sprinkle with half of the grated cheese. Using tongs or a pasta fork, toss the pasta with the pork fat and grated cheese, adding 2 tablespoons of the hot pasta water to help everything combine. Stir until the water is absorbed and the cheese has melted to coat the rigatoni. Add a little more pasta water if the cheese and pork fat aren't combining to create a saucelike surface on the pasta.

Add the guanciale and gently toss to combine.

Turn off the heat under the pan and empty the hot water from the serving bowl (don't worry about making sure it's completely dry). Transfer the pasta to the warm serving bowl and sprinkle with the remaining cheese. Toss to combine.

Serve immediately.

Spaghetti with Tomato Paste and Garlic

Everyone has nights when you get home late and find there's nothing in the refrigerator. Or you just don't have the energy to stop at the market on your way. Or you get surprised with a dinner guest. Here's a solution—a pasta dish that's made with only four pantry ingredients: spaghetti, tomato paste, olive oil, and garlic.

Using tomato paste instead of a sauce or whole tomatoes produces an intense and tangy pestolike flavor. You may find you'll want to make this satisfying dish even when you have time to spare and a full refrigerator!

Serves 4

1 tablespoon salt

1 pound spaghetti, spaghettini, or linguine or other long pasta (ziti or another short pasta is fine as well, but the "sauce" slicks best on a long strand)

2 to 4 tablespoons extra virgin olive oil

2 to 3 cloves garlic, very thinly sliced

One 6-ounce can tomato paste (or the equivalent squeezed from a tube—about ¾ cup)

Bring a large pot of water to a boil. Add the salt.

Add the pasta to the boiling water and cook until *al dente*. Start checking for doneness at least a minute before the time given on the package to make sure you don't overcook the pasta.

While the spaghetti is cooking, add 2 tablespoons olive oil to a large skillet and place over medium heat. Add the garlic to the oil and cook until tender with just a little color. Don't brown it or it will become bitter.

Add the tomato paste to the garlic and, using a wooden spoon, spread the paste into the oil so that it can cook a bit. Add the remaining 2 tablespoons olive oil if you think the tomato paste is still too thick. Your goal is to remove the raw taste from the tomato paste and create a creamy mixture of tomato, oil, and garlic.

When the spaghetti is done, drain it and add it to the skillet. Toss with tongs so that the spaghetti gets completely coated.

Serve immediately.

Penne with Canned Tuna and Cannellini Beans

You can make this dish in the time it takes to cook the pasta. And every ingredient is something you can have on hand in your pantry.

   This dish is even nicer if made with high-quality imported tuna (such as Ortiz, Flott, or Callipo) that has larger pieces of tuna fillet. But make sure it is light, not white, tuna and that it is packed in oil and not water. Canned tuna is usually quite salty so you probably won't need to add any salt to this dish.

Serves 4

1 tablespoon salt

1 pound dried penne or another short pasta such as fusilli, medium shells, or ziti

2 tablespoons extra virgin olive oil

1 or 2 cloves garlic, finely minced

One 6-ounce can oil-packed tuna (do not drain)

One 16-ounce can cannellini beans, drained and rinsed

Freshly ground black pepper

Bring a large pot of water to a boil. Add the salt.

Add the pasta to the boiling water and cook until *al dente*. Start checking for doneness at least a minute before the time given on the box to make sure you don't overcook the pasta.

While the pasta is cooking, add the olive oil to a large skillet or sauté pan and place over medium heat. Add the garlic and cook until slightly softened and fragrant. Do not brown it or the garlic will become bitter.

Add the tuna—both the fish and the oil—to the skillet. Use a wooden spoon to combine with the garlic but don't overstir. You want to retain some reasonably sized pieces of tuna.

Add the cannellini beans and using the back of the wooden spoon, mash about two-thirds of the beans so that they soften and meld with the smaller pieces of tuna and garlic. Leave a few beans whole. Keep warm over low heat.

When the pasta is done, drain it and add it to the skillet. Add 4 to 6 grinds of black pepper. Toss to combine.

Serve with a crisp white wine and a simple green salad.

Pasta Shells with Swordfish, Capers, and Black Olives

This hearty pasta dish uses flavors from southern Italy, especially Sicily where seafood is king. Equal amounts of pasta and fish make it substantial enough to be a main course, but you could, of course, change the ratio to emphasize either the fish or the pasta. While you could use any pasta, I like to match the chunks of meaty swordfish with equally chunky dried pasta shells, which is also reminiscent of the sea.

This dish cooks in the time it takes to boil the pasta, making it an easy weeknight supper.

Serves 4

1 tablespoon salt

1 pound swordfish steak (it doesn't need to be in a single piece)

¼ cup pitted oil-cured black olives

1 tablespoon tiny capers

3 tablespoons extra virgin olive oil

1 teaspoon dried oregano

2 tablespoons finely chopped fresh flat-leaf parsley

Freshly ground black pepper

1 pound conchiglie or other medium-size pasta shells

Optional: 1 teaspoon fresh lemon juice

Bring a large pot of water to a boil. Add the salt.

Cut the swordfish into ¾-inch cubes. It will make about 2 heaping cups. If you've bought pitted olives, go through them carefully to make sure there are no errant pits (I almost always find one); if you've bought ones with pits, use the tip of a paring knife to cut out the pit. Coarsely chop the olives. Rinse the capers of any brine or salt and drain completely.

In a skillet, heat the olive oil over medium-high heat until shimmering. Add the fish cubes and sauté until just cooked through and slightly browned, 3 to 4 minutes; it may become slightly wet in the pan because of the liquid from the fish. Add the olives, capers, oregano, parsley, and several grinds of black pepper. Taste before adding any salt since the capers and olives are already salty. Cook until all the ingredients are hot, about 2 minutes. Remove from the heat while the pasta cooks.

Add the pasta to the boiling water and cook until *al dente*. Start checking for doneness at least a minute before the time given on the package to make sure you don't overcook the pasta. Drain and add to the swordfish mixture in the skillet. Taste and adjust the seasoning, adding lemon juice if you like.

Serve immediately.

Pasta—Dried, Fresh, and Artisanal

Dried pasta. Made in factories almost always from just semolina flour, water, and salt (most noodles and some fettuccine also contain egg), dried pasta comes in dozens of shapes and sizes, and which you choose depends on the sauce. My favorite brand is DeCecco, but Barilla is also good.

Fresh pasta. Almost always made with egg and sometimes with olive oil, fresh pastas are made from a softer flour. They cook very quickly and can have far more mouth and taste presence in a dish. Fresh pasta includes specialty items like gnocchi and cavatelli and filled pastas like ravioli.

Artisanal pasta. Artisanal pasta is made in small factories in small batches, dried at lower temperatures, and often made from durum wheat, which gives it a more complex flavor. The best-known brands sold in the United States include Latini, Benedetto Cavalieri, and Martelli.

Whole-wheat and farro pasta. Made with whole-wheat or farro (spelt) flour, this dried pasta has a nuttier taste, higher fiber content, and more texture and body. Because whole-wheat pasta can have more flavor than white pasta, I like it with hearty sauces and roasted vegetables.

No matter which kind you use, always check for doneness at least a minute sooner than the time suggested on the package.

Paella Casserole

City cooks often avoid certain recipes because we don't have room for what we think is essential equipment. Paella is a good example. Unless paella is a signature dish, it's hard to justify that big, hard-to-store pan.

For those who love this classic Spanish rice dish, this recipe produces the flavors—chorizo, saffron, chicken, and seafood—without the paella pan. By starting things in a skillet and finishing in the oven, it mimics the authentic paella textures. If you bake the casserole for a bit longer, the top will start to crisp and resemble a *soccarat,* the brown layer of crusty rice that develops on the bottom of perfectly cooked authentic paella.

For the sausage, I prefer to use dry-cured chorizo (Palacios is a good brand), but fresh is also fine. If you can't find chorizo, you can use tasso or andouille, but for authentic paella flavor, make sure it's made from pork.

It's worth a search for the short-grain rice that's used in classic paella, such as Spanish Valencia, which has a great texture. Goya also makes a very good medium-grain rice.

Serves 6 to 8 as a main course, more as a side

3 tablespoons extra virgin olive oil, or more if needed

8 ounces dry-cured chorizo, cut into ¼-inch slices (see headnote)

1 pound boneless, skinless chicken thighs, each cut into thirds

1 medium onion, minced (about 1 cup)

6 cloves garlic, very finely minced or crushed through a garlic press

1¼ cups raw short- or medium-grain rice

One 14-ounce can diced tomatoes, with their juices

2½ cups chicken stock (good-quality canned or boxed is fine)

½ teaspoon saffron threads

Salt

Freshly ground black pepper

12 ounces large or jumbo shrimp, peeled and deveined

3 jarred roasted red peppers or pimientos, drained and cut into ½-inch slices

½ cup frozen peas

Preheat the oven to 350°F. Have a large (9-by-13-inch) baking dish standing by.

In a very large skillet, heat 1 tablespoon of the oil over medium-high heat. Add the chorizo and brown, rendering some of its fat, about 2 minutes (a minute or so longer if you're using raw sausage). Remove from the pan and set aside. Pour off and discard the fat in the pan.

Put the pan back over medium-high heat, add the remaining 2 tablespoons oil, and heat until shimmering. Add the chicken and sauté for about 3 minutes a side until browned and almost completely cooked through. Remove the chicken pieces and set aside with the chorizo, leaving any fat in the pan.

Add the onion to the skillet, plus a tablespoon or so of oil if needed, and cook until softened, scraping up any chicken or chorizo bits from the bottom of the pan. Add the garlic and cook until fragrant, about 30 seconds.

Add the rice and cook, stirring, until the rice starts to look opaque, 1 to 2 minutes. Moderate the heat so that the onion and garlic don't burn.

Add the tomatoes with their juice and cook, stirring, until the liquid thickens a bit, about 2 minutes.

Warm the chicken stock in a saucepan or microwave so that it's not cold when added to the rice. Add the saffron to the chicken stock to "bloom," then add the stock and saffron to the rice mixture. Stir to combine—it will be soupy and the pan will be full. Add a generous pinch of salt and several grinds of black pepper. Bring to a boil, then turn off the heat.

Either by using a big spoon or by carefully pouring, transfer the rice mixture to the baking dish. Add the chorizo, chicken, raw shrimp, red peppers, and peas and carefully combine. Pushing the shrimp into the rice so that they are mostly covered will help to cook the shrimp better.

Bake for 15 to 18 minutes, a few minutes longer if you want the top rice to get crispy. The rice should be tender, all the liquids absorbed, and the shrimp completely cooked.

Serve immediately or hold to be reheated later.

Red Rice Pilaf

Pilaf with Bhutanese red rice is a nutty and beautiful alternative to traditional white rice pilaf. You can usually find Bhutanese red rice in city markets, gourmet shops, and specialty markets. The most common brand is Lotus Foods, a company that sells other imported and heirloom rices, including the exotic black Forbidden Rice.

This nutty pilaf is a perfect companion to any dish with which you might normally serve pilaf or a flavored rice, including fish, duck, and chicken. It's also great as part of a vegetarian menu that features vegetable gratin, curried vegetables, or ratatouille.

Serves 6

1 cup Bhutanese red rice

2 tablespoons unsalted butter

¼ cup finely minced yellow onion or shallots

1½ cups chicken stock (homemade or boxed, not from a bouillon cube), at room temperature or warmed

2 small or 1 large sprig fresh thyme

1 bay leaf

Salt

Freshly ground black pepper

Rinse the rice with cold water. Drain completely, shaking off any excess water.

In a large (about 3-quart) saucepan or a sauté pan with a cover, melt the butter over medium heat until the foam subsides. Add the onion and cook until soft and transparent, 1 to 2 minutes, keeping the heat low so that it won't brown.

Add the rice and stir to coat with the melted butter. Cook, stirring with a wooden spoon, over medium heat. Your goal is to cook the rice for 1 to 2 minutes, not to toast it, but to have the hot butter adhere to the surface of the grains. It's at this point when the rice begins to sound dry and scratchy as you stir it.

Add the warm stock, thyme sprigs, and bay leaf. If you've not used a salted stock, add ½ teaspoon salt.

Cover and gently simmer over low heat for about 20 minutes. It's done when all the stock is absorbed and the grains of rice are tender but still chewy. If you want the grains to be softer, add ⅓ cup more stock and cook for a few minutes longer.

Fluff the rice with a fork and remove the bay leaf and thyme sprigs. Taste for seasoning, adding salt and pepper as needed.

TIP: This pilaf can be made ahead of time and reheated just before serving. Depending on how long in advance it was cooked, you may want to add a tablespoon of butter as it's reheated to bring a gloss back to the grains of rice.

Rice

Rice feeds more people on earth than any other food and is essential for global nutrition. While there are thousands of varieties, these are the most popular.

Arborio. Its short grains and thick, starchy surface make this slow-cooking Italian rice essential for creating risotto's creamy texture. Carnaroli and Vialone Nano are similar to Arborio and also are good choices for risotto.

Long-grain white. With its long shape, this rice cooks as separate grains and is popular in all types of recipes, including jambalaya, rice pudding, gumbo, and pilaf. Carolina is a well-known brand.

Brown. Unmilled rice that still contains its bran, germ, and nutrient-rich layers, brown rice may be long-grain, short/medium-grain or one of the aromatics. It takes longer to cook and has a nuttier flavor. Store in the refrigerator for a longer shelf life.

Converted. This rice has been cooked before removing its hull to improve its nutritional quality, boost its flavor, and make it fluffy when it's cooked again at home. A versatile choice for rice salads, pilaf, and stuffing, Uncle Ben's is the best-known converted rice.

Quick-cooking. Partially cooked in a factory before it's packaged, this rice takes less time to cook in the home kitchen. What you gain in time, you lose in flavor and texture. Minute Rice is the best-known brand.

Basmati. This aromatic long-grain white or brown rice is popular in Indian cuisines.

Jasmine. This aromatic long-grain white rice is similar to basmati and is used in Thai cuisine. It is usually less expensive than basmati.

Medium-grain. This rice is popular in many Latin and Spanish dishes, including *arroz con pollo* and paella. Goya is a good brand.

Sticky. This short-grain rice becomes very clumpy when cooked. It is used in the foods of Laos and northern Thailand and in making sushi.

Bhutanese red. From the Himalayan kingdom of Bhutan, this red rice has a short grain, a nutty taste, and a beautiful deep red color. It is excellent when cooked as pilaf or as rice salad. Lotus Foods is an excellent importer.

Forbidden black. This medium-grain Chinese black rice cooks to a firm texture, nutty flavor, and deep purple, almost black, color. It makes a dramatic presentation alongside fish and vegetables.

Wild rice. Not really rice but a long-grain grass with a distinctive, nutty flavor, it is often combined with white or brown rice. Wild rice is more costly and takes much longer to cook than most rices.

Cacio e Pepe

For years this classic Roman pasta dish—its name means "cheese and pepper"—was a restaurant favorite, and I'd marvel at how something so simple—dry pasta, grated Pecorino cheese, and freshly ground black pepper—could taste so complex. After eating it many times in both New York and Italy, I figured, hey, how tough can it be to toss spaghetti with grated cheese and pepper? I was wrong. If you don't follow the cooking and mixing details carefully, you'll get a bowl of glop.

Like all great Italian recipes, the flavor comes from using great ingredients with a confident hand. Some recipes call for butter or oil, but this changes the finish and steals the chance for a perfect combination of tender strands of pasta, salty flecks of Pecorino, and the bite of freshly ground black pepper.

Follow this exactly and you, too, will have swooning guests asking for seconds.

Serves 4 to 6

1¼ cups grated Pecorino Romano (Locatelli is easy to find and an excellent cheese)

2 tablespoons freshly ground black pepper

1 pound dried spaghetti or spaghettini (DeCecco #11 spaghettini is perfect). Do NOT use fresh pasta for this recipe as it will deteriorate into a gluey mess, no matter how good the pasta or your skill in cooking it perfectly.

Have a large serving bowl ready to use.

Prepare the grated cheese and freshly ground pepper. Set aside.

Cook the spaghetti in boiling salted water according to the package instructions until *al dente* (do not overcook).

While the pasta is cooking, fill your serving bowl with very hot water from the faucet. This warms the bowl so that the hot pasta won't cool down when you place it in the bowl. Just before the spaghetti is finished cooking, drain the bowl but do not dry it. Just before draining the pasta, reserve ½ cup pasta cooking water.

When the pasta is *al dente*, drain it quickly in a colander (you don't have to shake off all the water as the extra moisture will help the cheese coat the pasta) and place it in the warmed serving bowl.

Immediately toss ½ cup of the cheese over the spaghetti, and using a pasta fork or large dinner fork, quickly toss to coat. Keep moving so that the cheese doesn't clump together. Continue to toss while adding more cheese a couple of tablespoons at a time, up to ¾ cup in total, as well as about ¼ cup of the hot, starchy pasta water. This will create a slightly creamy emulsion with bits of the cheese left whole. This is a good thing.

When you've incorporated about ¾ cup of the cheese, sprinkle with about 1 teaspoon of the ground pepper. Toss again. Taste for the combination of cheese and pepper and add more pepper, a teaspoon at a time. You want to be able to taste all three ingredients at once: pasta, cheese, and pepper. Add more of either or both the pepper and cheese if you think it's needed.

Serve immediately. You can pass a bowl with extra cheese, but if you've added the right amount, your guests won't ask for more.

> **TIP:** Use your pepper mill or a spice grinder to grind the pepper just before cooking so that the pepper has its fullest flavor. Coarsely ground pepper is best, but it should not be so coarse that it is in unpleasantly large pieces (smaller than you'd use in a steak *au poivre*). Your goal is to have lots of pepper flavor but not have pieces stuck in your teeth.

> **TIP:** Pecorino Romano is a hard sheep's cheese from the Lazio region of Italy where Rome is located. It resembles Parmesan but is less refined in its flavor, saltier, and more pungent. For this recipe it's essential that you use a coarser grated cheese so that when it's tossed with the warm pasta, it coats the strands while also staying a tiny bit unmelted, adding little bursts of salty cheese flavor. Do NOT use your Microplane zester to grate the cheese. Instead, put pieces of the Pecorino in your food processor and pulverize it into tiny bits, or use the small holes on a box grater. Cheese grated on the rasp will produce a melted gluey clump.

> **TIP:** If for some reason the cheese doesn't mix successfully and you need more "slip," try adding a small amount—only about ½ tablespoon—of good olive oil and toss thoroughly. Resist adding more oil because it will change the dish into pasta with oil and cheese and, frankly, that's another dish.

Tomato Risotto

This is a perfect way to use ripe summer tomatoes or to satisfy a midwinter craving when the best tomatoes around are from a can. But because the tomatoes are the star of this dish, use the best you can find. Use fresh only when they're local and in-season; otherwise choose canned San Marzanos or ones that a home canner put up last summer.

In this typical risotto recipe, you are instructed to cook half the tomatoes with the rice from the start to add depth and complexity. Adding the rest of the tomatoes toward the end preserves some of their bright flavor.

Using fresh tomatoes? Buy 2 pounds and peel by submerging them in a large pot of boiling water for 10 or so seconds. Transfer immediately to a bowl of iced water to stop the cooking. Use a paring knife, and the peels should slip right off. Cut the peeled tomatoes into 1-inch chunks over a bowl to retain the juices and seeds. You should have about 4 cups tomatoes with their juices.

Serves 6

4 cups canned San Marzano tomatoes with their juice, from a 28- or 34-ounce can (discard any basil leaves that may be in the can), or 2 pounds fresh tomatoes (see headnote)

4 cups chicken stock (homemade or good-quality boxed stock works best)

2 tablespoons extra virgin olive oil

1 tablespoon unsalted butter

¾ cup finely chopped onion

4 cloves garlic, thinly sliced

1 cup Arborio or Carnaroli rice

½ cup dry white wine

Salt

½ cup grated Parmesan cheese

Freshly ground black pepper

Divide the tomatoes and juice into 2 equal portions.

In a saucepan, bring the chicken stock to a low simmer and keep it at this temperature; you want the stock to be hot but not boiling as you add it to the rice.

In a large sauté pan or skillet, warm the olive oil and butter over medium heat until the butter melts. Add the onion and cook until soft and translucent, about 10 minutes. Be patient with this step because you don't want to brown the onion. Add the garlic and cook until soft and just golden, 2 to 3 minutes.

Add the rice and cook, stirring, until the rice is coated with the hot olive oil and butter and becomes opaque, about 3 minutes. You'll know it's ready when the rice sounds "dry" when you stir it.

Raise the heat to medium-high, add the wine, and cook, stirring, until the wine is absorbed.

Add one soup ladle of hot chicken stock (about 1 cup) and stir until completely absorbed.

Add half of the tomatoes—3 to 4 whole tomatoes—crushing them with your hands as you add them to the pan. Also add half the juice and stir until the juice is absorbed and the tomatoes begin to break up. Return to adding the hot stock, a cup at a time, stirring until absorbed, until nearly all the stock has been added and the rice is almost tooth-tender. This will take about 15 minutes. Keep the heat at medium-high and stir continuously.

If the rice is too firm, add any remaining tomato juice and chicken stock, ½ cup at a time, stirring after every addition. If you have used all the tomato juice and chicken stock, use hot water. Cook until the rice is tender but still firm.

When the rice is tender to the bite, crush the remaining tomatoes with your hands, add to the rice, and stir to combine. Taste for salt and also for doneness.

Remove from the heat and stir in the grated Parmesan. Season to taste with salt and pepper.

Serve immediately.

Whole-Wheat Pasta with Zucchini and Roasted Carrots

Some of us are trying to cut back on white pasta. Whole-wheat or farro pasta is a healthful way to satisfy a craving.

In this recipe, oven-roasted carrots combine with pan-sautéed zucchini and whole-wheat pasta to make a hearty and satisfying combination. If you can find pasta made with farro, a grain that is similar to spelt, that, too, will be a hearty partner to the roasted vegetables.

The easiest way to make this dish is to roast the carrots the night before, so that the pasta dish can be made the next day in the time it takes to boil the water and cook the pasta.

Serves 6 to 8

1 pound carrots, peeled and cut into 2-inch pieces

4 tablespoons extra virgin olive oil

Salt

Freshly ground black pepper

1 pound cut whole-wheat or farro pasta, such as fusilli or ziti

3 cloves garlic, finely minced

1 shallot, finely minced

Pinch of red pepper flakes

1 pound zucchini (about 3 medium), cut into ¼-inch slices

Optional: grated Parmesan or Pecorino cheese

Preheat the oven to 450°F.

On a rimmed sheet pan, spread the carrots in a single layer. Drizzle with 2 tablespoons of the olive oil and sprinkle with 1 teaspoon salt and several grinds of black pepper. Toss to coat the carrots with the oil and seasonings. Roast in the hot oven until completely cooked and tender, about 40 minutes. Remove from the oven and set aside.

Bring a large pot of water to a boil, add 1 tablespoon salt, and the pasta. Cook the pasta until *al dente*. Whole-wheat or farro pasta usually takes longer to cook than dried white pasta.

Meanwhile, heat the remaining 2 tablespoons oil in a large sauté pan or skillet over medium heat. Add the garlic, shallot, and red pepper flakes and cook until soft and fragrant but not brown.

Add the zucchini, raise the temperature to medium-high, and cook until the zucchini is completely tender and golden brown. Add the roasted carrots, toss to combine, and turn off the heat, leaving the pan on the stove.

When the pasta is cooked *al dente*, drain it. Add the pasta to the sauté pan and combine with the cooked vegetables. Taste and adjust the seasoning with salt and pepper.

Serve immediately, passing grated cheese at the table.

> **TIP:** This recipe can be made using any favorite vegetables. Choose ones that will combine well with the hearty pasta, such as roasted tomatoes, asparagus, red onion wedges, or cubes of butternut squash.

Greenmarket Fried Rice

I was given this recipe by my friend David Neibart, who is a writer, home cook, and father to Daisy and Archie. His splendid wife, Emma Murphy, and he often head to the popular Saturday greenmarket at Brooklyn's Grand Army Plaza and make this rice with whatever looks best that day or else leftovers from the previous week's visit.

You can make this recipe with either white or brown rice. It's particularly good when made with leftover rice, which is drier and will absorb less of the liquid and cook to a crispier finish. You can make your own leftover rice by cooking it in advance and keeping it refrigerated until ready to use in this recipe.

Serves 4

1 cup raw white or brown rice

Salt

8 strips bacon

1½ cups fresh or frozen vegetables cut into small pieces (fresh or frozen corn, diced fresh zucchini, small pieces of fresh cauliflower, frozen peas, green or yellow beans, diced red peppers, diced bok choy or Napa cabbage)

1 medium yellow onion, cut into ¼-inch dice

2 large eggs

¼ cup chopped fresh cilantro

1 to 2 teaspoons soy sauce

In a saucepan, cook the rice with 1 teaspoon salt according to the package directions. Try to cook in advance so that the rice has a chance to dry out.

Cook the bacon in a large skillet until brown and fully cooked but not to the crumbling point. Drain on paper towels and cut into ½-inch pieces. Pour off some of the bacon fat, leaving 1 to 2 tablespoons in the pan.

Prepare your vegetables. Cut any fresh vegetables into pieces and rinse any frozen vegetables with warm water to remove the freeze. Set aside.

Reheat the bacon fat in the skillet over medium heat. Add the onion and cook, stirring, until softened and very slightly golden brown, about 2 minutes. Add the cooked rice and stir for about 30 seconds. Add the vegetables and bacon and toss to combine. Cook for 1 to 2 minutes, making sure the vegetables are softened just slightly.

Push the rice mixture to the edges of the pan. Crack one egg into the exposed circle at the center and scramble until the egg has a consistent yellow texture but does not yet show signs of hardening. Mix the rice into the egg and push the egg-coated rice back to the edges of the pan. Repeat with the second egg.

Add the cilantro and soy sauce to taste (begin with about 1½ teaspoons and add more gradually because it can be very salty). Adjust the flavor with a pinch of salt and/or a little more soy.

Bringing Your Lunch to Work

When I first arrived in New York, I worked for a very large corporation with a subsidized cafeteria. When I began to work for smaller firms, I got sticker shock from what it cost to buy lunch every day in Manhattan. My solution was simple: I'd bring my own.

Trying to get out of the house every morning can be complicated enough, but with a little planning, you can make and carry a meal to look forward to. Invest in a thermal bag and some easy-to-clean carry boxes and what you pack will still be appealing midday.

- *Leftovers*. Most workplaces have microwaves so you can enjoy that bowl of last night's beef stew or quinoa pilaf. It's easy to create lunch from leftovers by just steaming some extra broccoli, sautéing one more chicken breast, or adding another sweet potato to the oven while dinner is on the stove.
- *A sturdy salad*. Assemble ingredients that can sit for a few hours and travel unrefrigerated such as cherry tomatoes and little balls of fresh mozzarella; cubes of cheese and salami or turkey; sliced raw peppers, mushrooms, and tuna fish (olive oil–packed but drained); tabbouleh salad bulked up with chopped raw vegetables; sliced raw fennel, sardines, and curls of Parmesan cheese. The idea is to combine protein and raw vegetables that won't easily get limp.
- *Sandwiches*. It costs less to buy the insides of a sandwich and then make your own. Buy your favorite deli meat and cheese at the grocer's, bring some pieces of lettuce and tomato, and pick up a fresh roll from a bakery on your way to work.
- *Desserts and snacks*. Fresh fruit, dried fruit, nuts, granola, containers of yogurt, baby carrots, a couple of cookies, leaving the whole bag at home.
- *Lunch-friendly foods*. Other foods that travel well and are easy to eat in a lunchroom or on a park bench on a nice day include hard-boiled eggs, pasta salad, peanut butter, cheese and fruit, and one of my all-time favorites, hummus with raw vegetables.

Vegetables

If I could take only one food group to that proverbial desert island, it would be vegetables. I will as easily make a snack detour to my neighborhood grocer for an avocado or tomato as someone else might choose a peach or a muffin.

It's essential to buy vegetables carefully, and when possible, buy in season. They should be treated gently and cooked simply, but given their versatility, this doesn't mean without flavor or personality.

Broccoli Rabe with Garlic and Red Pepper

Oven-Roasted Root Vegetables

French Beans with Lemon Shallots

Roasted Radicchio with Balsamic Glaze

Perfect Mashed Potatoes

Long-Cooked Green Beans with Oregano

Roasted Cherry Tomatoes

Potato Latkes

Smashed Potatoes with Thyme

Roasted Asparagus Wrapped in Pancetta

Tuscan Kale with Crispy Garlic

Puréed Vegetables for Grownups: Roasted Carrots, Cauliflower and Garlic Chips, Peas with Parmesan, Roasted Beets, Butternut Squash and Apple

Green Beans with Tomatoes and Prosciutto

Luscious Potato and Mushroom Gratin

Broccoli Rabe with Garlic and Red Pepper

Broccoli rabe is a vegetable that many only eat at Italian restaurants, never thinking that it could be simple and quick to make at home. In fact, it is. Plus it's a vegetable that can be cooked in advance and then easily reheated, making it a great side dish for a more elaborate meal or for company.

Sometimes called rabe, rape, or rapini, broccoli rabe is a leafy green vegetable that is popular in Italy and is increasingly garnering fans here. It's extremely good for us (full of beta carotene and vitamin C) and has a slightly bitter taste that makes it perfect on its own or mixed with other ingredients, such as Italian sausage or pasta.

I particularly like broccoli rabe when the rest of the meal has other robust flavors, such as ossobuco or a pot roast. Some think of it as a winter vegetable, but it's available year-round. It's not fragile and both the leaves and stalks cook easily and quickly. It reduces when it cooks (not as much as spinach), so keep this in mind when gauging portions. It can be served warm or at room temperature.

This is a two-step process: first steam the broccoli rabe, then finish it with a little olive oil and garlic.

Serves 4

1 large or 2 smaller bunches broccoli rabe

Salt

2 tablespoons extra virgin olive oil

2 cloves garlic, very thinly sliced

Pinch of red pepper flakes (more or less to taste)

Untie the bunch of broccoli rabe, and holding the bunch together with one hand, cut off the thick, coarser ends of the stalks. Pick through the leaves, discarding any that look unappetizing or yellow. Rinse the rest in a generous amount of cool water, just as you would spinach. Rinse several times until the water is totally clear.

Lift the broccoli rabe out of the water and either shaking by hand or using a salad spinner, remove the excess water, leaving a few droplets on the leaves. Use a vegetable peeler to trim off any coarseness on the remaining stalks.

Put the broccoli rabe in a large pan that has a cover—a 12-inch skillet or shallow roaster with a cover would be good—with a pinch of salt. Cover and set over medium heat. The remaining water on the leaves, plus the moisture in the leaves themselves, will cause the broccoli rabe to steam to tenderness in 3 to 5 minutes. You don't have to watch the pan constantly but do rotate the vegetables in the pan once so that it all cooks evenly and nothing sticks to the pan. If you're concerned it's too dry, add no more than a teaspoon or so of water.

When the leaves and stalks have softened, drain the broccoli rabe and wipe the skillet dry with a paper towel.

Heat the olive oil in the skillet over medium-high heat. Add the garlic and red pepper flakes. Stirring with a wooden spoon, cook the garlic just until it begins to turn golden brown (don't overcook the garlic or else it will turn bitter). Return the cooked broccoli rabe to the pan and turn to coat in the oil and garlic mixture. Cook, stirring, until warmed through.

Serve immediately.

> **TIP:** If you want to cook this ahead of time, you can steam the broccoli rabe up to 2 hours in advance. Just before serving, finish cooking it with the oil, garlic, and red pepper flakes.

Oven-Roasted Root Vegetables

Oven-roasting is an easy and tasty way to cook vegetables. Asparagus roasts quickly and easily, its tips caramelizing. Tomatoes get a richer taste, especially when roasted for a long time at a low temperature. Roasting can even turn the often-scorned Brussels sprout into something that tastes more like popcorn than cabbage.

But root vegetables—especially carrots, parsnips, turnips, and potatoes—may be best of all to roast. The high temperature causes their natural sugars to become more pronounced. Their tips and edges get brown and crispy, while their insides become soft and tender. Parents take note: this simple roasting turns ordinary vegetables into something that even an anti-vegetable kid will eat.

This cooking method is so simple it may be an overstatement to call it a recipe.

Serves 4

1 pound parsnips

1 pound carrots

1 pound small potatoes (baby Yukon Golds or fingerlings are best, but you can also use Red Bliss or another non-baking potato)

Extra virgin olive oil

Sea salt

Freshly ground black pepper

Preheat the oven to 400°F.

Peel the parsnips and carrots and trim the tops and tips so that you have clean, trimmed vegetables. If they are thick or large, just slice them the long way to have long spears of approximately equal size.

You can scrub the potatoes well and leave the peels on or else peel them completely. Cut any larger potatoes into 1- to 2-inch pieces.

Make sure all the vegetables are dry. Spread all the prepared vegetables on a rimmed sheet pan, doing the best you can to have them in a single layer. As they cook they will shrink, so any overlap will disappear within 10 minutes or so.

Drizzle about ¼ cup olive oil over the vegetables. Sprinkle with a pinch of sea salt and several grinds of fresh pepper. Using your clean hands, toss everything together to get a light coating of oil on everything (just a slick; we're not frying here).

Roast for 30 minutes, shaking the pan every 10 to 15 minutes. You may need to use a pair of tongs or a spatula to turn the pieces over so that different surfaces get brown. The vegetables should be tender and the edges brown and crispy and a bit caramelized.

Remove from the oven and taste and adjust the seasoning. Toss and serve.

TIP: Roasted root vegetables are wonderful when eaten hot right out of the oven, but you can also let them cool to room temperature and add them to a salad of winter greens dressed with a simple vinaigrette.

Buying in Season

Global food production lets us eat any food at any time of the year, but you can't deny the truth of the growing season: if you eat a summer fruit in the winter, it's had to travel a long distance to reach your table. This not only adds to its carbon footprint but also takes away from its taste. If you're not sure what's in season, here are two shopping tips: one, in-season choices will usually be the cheapest; and two, these in-season foods are featured front-and-center at most markets.

It's the opposite of buying an air conditioner in August: you'll get the best value if you buy foods when they're in season.

Buy in season and you'll also get the best flavor. Think citrus in the winter, squash in the fall, and tomatoes in the summer. Consider canning fruits and vegetables when they're at their top taste and lowest cost, or make favorites like soup or tomato sauce and freeze them for later in the year when they will be even more of a treat.

The flavors from your kitchen will benefit from cooking in harmony with the calendar.

French Beans with Lemon Shallots

This deceptively simple recipe makes a special addition to a meal cooked for company. The beans can be cooked in advance and warmed just before serving.

You can use either regular green beans or the very thin and more tender French beans known as haricots verts. While melted butter is a luxurious addition, you can easily substitute olive oil. And finally, if you prefer to cook your vegetables in the microwave, go right ahead: it will make no difference except that you may need to add salt to the finished beans.

Serves 4

1½ pounds green beans or haricots verts

Salt

2 medium or 1 large shallot

2 tablespoons unsalted butter or extra virgin olive oil

2 teaspoons fresh lemon juice

Trim the beans by snipping off the ends. Rinse completely to make sure there's no debris or dirt on the beans.

Bring a 3- to 4-quart pot of water to a boil and add about 1 tablespoon salt. Add the beans and cook until tender, about 5 minutes. Drain.

Very finely mince the shallots, ⅛- to ¼-inch pieces.

Melt the butter either in the microwave or in a small pan on the stove, taking care to make sure it doesn't burn or darken. In a small bowl, combine the melted butter with the shallots and lemon juice.

Transfer the drained green beans to a serving bowl and drizzle with the shallot mixture. Toss to combine.

Serve immediately.

Roasted Radicchio with Balsamic Glaze

Most of us were first introduced to radicchio in a popular salad called *tre colore*, after the tricolored red, white, and green flag of Italy. Its leafy appearance might lead one to assume it was a kind of lettuce, but this somewhat bitter vegetable is actually a part of the chicory family.

As with many vegetables, its flavor changes when it's cooked. As much as I love raw radicchio in a salad, I also love to cut it into wedges, give it a little drizzle of olive oil, and roast it until the leaves soften and the flavor becomes milder and almost sweet. For an easy glaze, simply boil inexpensive balsamic vinegar until it reduces to a syrup.

Radicchio leaves are thin and so can go from perfectly cooked to burnt in an instant. Just keep an eye on it. Choose firm heads of radicchio with tightly compressed leaves.

Serves 4

2 large heads radicchio

2 tablespoons extra virgin olive oil

Salt

Freshly ground black pepper

1 cup balsamic vinegar (use medium-priced vinegar for this, not a precious aged one)

Preheat the oven to 375°F.

Remove any blemished outer leaves from the radicchio and trim the bottoms, leaving the cores intact. Quarter each head, leaving the core in place.

Place on a rimmed sheet pan, drizzle with olive oil, and season with a pinch or two of salt and several grinds of black pepper. Roast until the radicchio softens and the leaves slightly separate, about 15 minutes.

While the radicchio is roasting, put the balsamic vinegar in a small saucepan and place over high heat. Bring to a boil and continue to cook at a medium boil so that the liquid is reduced by half and becomes syrupy. Remove from the heat and hold at room temperature until ready to serve.

Remove the radicchio from the oven, drizzle about a tablespoon of the balsamic glaze over each wedge, and serve 2 to each person.

Perfect Mashed Potatoes

When it comes to making perfect mashed potatoes, the details make all the difference in getting a smooth, rich result. Here are some tips that can help.

- Use potatoes that will have a smooth, creamy finish. Yukon Golds are best. Some people prefer russets—also known as baking potatoes—because they mash to a fluffy texture. But I prefer the smooth texture and richer flavor of Yukon Golds.
- If you make mashed potatoes more than once or twice a year, buy a potato ricer, which can cost less than $10. Buy one that has removable discs because this will make the ricer easier to clean (mashed potatoes become like hardened glue when dried) and allow you to use the ricer for other purposes.
- The ricer will produce a bowl of perfectly and uniformly mashed potatoes. An old-fashioned wire masher will also do the job, but you'll get an uneven texture—those famous lumps—which means that the butter and milk won't combine evenly.
- Placing the potatoes in a pan of salted cold water and then bringing to a boil (instead of adding them to already boiling water) helps the potatoes cook evenly.
- If you make mashed potatoes in advance of the rest of the meal, don't reheat them in the microwave. Instead, keep them warm in a double boiler or a heatproof bowl set over a pot of simmering water. Cover them so that the potatoes don't dry out on the surface. Mashed potatoes kept warm this way for an hour or so will be as nice as when you first cooked them.
- Given all the effort to make mashed potatoes, make extra. They will be less smooth the next day, but you can use the leftovers to make potato patties (kids love them). Just combine the leftover potato with a beaten egg and grated cheese, then sauté in a little butter or olive oil.

Serves 4

2 pounds Yukon Gold potatoes

Salt

4 tablespoons (½ stick) unsalted butter, at room temperature

¾ cup lowfat or whole milk, or half-and-half (avoid the extremes of skim milk or heavy cream)

Peel the potatoes and cut into uniform pieces—about 2-inch squares are ideal. Place in a large saucepan filled with cold water. Add about 1 tablespoon salt. Bring to a boil.

Cook the potatoes at a gentle boil for 15 to 20 minutes total and check for doneness with a sharp knife. The potatoes should be easily pierced with the knife but not be falling apart. While the potatoes are cooking, fill a heatproof bowl with hot water to get it ready to hold the mashed potatoes.

Drain the potatoes completely. Dump the hot water out of the heatproof bowl.

Using a potato ricer, mash the potatoes into the warmed bowl. Add the butter and stir until the butter is completely melted and dispersed.

Warm the milk in a small saucepan or in a heatproof measuring cup in the microwave. Add it to the potatoes a little at a time, using a large spoon to combine. Keep adding more, about ¼ cup at a time, until you get a soft, mashed consistency.

Taste and add more salt if necessary.

Either serve immediately or keep the finished potatoes covered and warm until ready to serve by placing them in a double boiler or over a pan of simmering water.

> **TIP:** If you peel the potatoes in advance, keep them in a bowl of cool water so that they don't discolor.

Long-Cooked Green Beans with Oregano

Despite the popularity of crispy just-cooked vegetables, in traditional Italian cuisine green beans and other vegetables are cooked until they are soft.

When green beans are well cooked, their bright color fades and they look like canned beans. But with a taste and texture nothing like their canned counterparts, these green beans are deeply flavorful and tender without being gummy.

Green beans cooked this way are especially nice when served with pot roast, other braised meat or poultry, or with a dish that has deep flavors such as a tagine or stew.

Serves 6

¼ cup extra virgin olive oil

6 cloves garlic, thinly sliced

1 tablespoon coarsely chopped fresh
   oregano leaves (from 6 to 8 sprigs), or
   1 teaspoon dried oregano

Small pinch of red pepper flakes

2 pounds green beans, rinsed and ends
   trimmed

2 teaspoons kosher salt

Freshly ground black pepper

Juice from 1 medium lemon (about 3
   tablespoons)

½ cup water

Heat the olive oil in a heavy 3- or 4-quart saucepan over medium heat. Add the garlic, oregano, and red pepper flakes and cook until the garlic softens and just begins to take on color, about 2 minutes.

Add the beans to the pan along with the salt, about 6 grinds of black pepper, the lemon juice, and water.

Bring to a boil and immediately reduce the heat for a low simmer. Cover the pot and cook until nearly all the liquid in the pan has evaporated, about 30 minutes. While cooking, occasionally turn the beans with tongs so that all the beans are combined with the garlic and oregano and coated in the oily, salty water. Each time you do this you'll see the bright green color continue to fade.

Allow to cool briefly and serve.

TIP: If you're thinking of using dried herbs in this or any other recipe, but they're so old they've lost their scent and flavor, just leave them out entirely.

Roasted Cherry Tomatoes

Local summer tomatoes are lovely, but let's face it, their season is short and the rest of the year we're lucky if we can find tomatoes with any taste or spark at all. Lately what we can find are cherry tomatoes. I particularly like the little round tomatoes still on the vine because they are firm and juicy with bright acidic flavor.

One of the best ways to enjoy cherry tomatoes is simply to roast them until the skins wrinkle and the juice seeps out. Their acidity delivers a great contrast to any fish or strong-flavored meat like lamb or beef. They can also be tossed with couscous or a grain such as farro.

Don't substitute little sweet grape tomatoes because those won't give you the juice or the acid that makes this dish so winning. If you want to make a larger quantity, just multiply the ingredients but make sure the tomatoes are able to sit in a single layer in your roasting pan.

Serves 4

3 tablespoons extra virgin olive oil

3 large cloves garlic, finely chopped (about 1 tablespoon)

2 or 3 shallots, finely minced (about 2 tablespoons)

2 pints cherry tomatoes

¼ teaspoon crushed red pepper flakes

Pinch of salt

Preheat the oven to 350°F.

Add the olive oil, garlic, and shallots to a large ovenproof skillet or sauté pan and cook over medium heat until they slightly sweat and soften, 2 to 3 minutes.

Add the tomatoes and toss to coat. Add the red pepper flakes and salt. Roast in the oven until the tomatoes are wrinkled and beginning to throw off juice, 18 to 20 minutes. Halfway through cooking, shake the pan a bit so that the tomatoes cook evenly.

Serve immediately.

Potato Latkes

My husband loves latkes with meatloaf. I'll eat them with anything.

What's not to love about shredded potatoes held together with a little egg and flour and then pan-fried to a golden, crispy finish? These simple potato pancakes are particularly popular during the eight days of Hanukkah, but they are also a great year-round side dish to anything that goes well with *frites* or home fries. You can also turn them into hors d'oeuvres by topping each with a little sour cream or Greek yogurt and a piece of smoked salmon.

There are three keys to success: One, use starchy, rather than waxy, potatoes. Two, drain the shredded potatoes of their excess liquid before cooking. Three, use very hot oil. When choosing oil, it's better to fry in peanut, vegetable, or virgin olive oil because of their higher burn temperatures; avoid frying in extra virgin olive oil. (Yes, it gets hot enough to sauté, just not hot enough to fry!)

Some prefer their latkes to have a more pancake than potato texture. If that's you, use matzo meal instead of flour.

Serves 4 as a side dish

3 or 4 large russet baking potatoes (Yukon Golds are a good alternative.)

¼ cup all-purpose flour

2 large eggs, slightly beaten

Vegetable, peanut, or canola oil

Peel the potatoes and grate them either by hand, on the large holes of a box grater or with the grating blade of a food processor. Your goal is to have about 6 cups shredded potatoes.

Once all the potatoes are shredded, transfer them either all at once or in batches onto an immaculately clean kitchen towel and fold the towel around the potatoes so that you can wring the moisture out of them. Working over the sink, wring the excess water out of the potatoes. Place the dried potato shreds in a large, dry mixing bowl.

Add the flour and eggs to the potatoes and combine.

Pour enough oil in the bottom of a large skillet or sauté pan to cover it by ¼ inch and heat it on high heat until very hot (the surface should be shimmering but not smoking). Place heaping soup spoonfuls of the potato mixture in the oil, each spoonful being one serving size (if you're making mini pancakes, use a teaspoon). Using the bottom of the spoon, flatten the mixture into pancake shapes so that they have an even thickness. Cook for 2 to 4 minutes a side, until golden brown and crispy. If you give them a chance to brown before trying to turn them over, the patties will be less likely to fall apart—so be patient!

Serve immediately with sour cream or applesauce.

> **TIP:** Fry in small batches so that the oil stays hot. If you're making a large batch of latkes, keep them warm in a 200°F oven while you cook the rest.

> **TIP:** Fry in a cast-iron or other heavy skillet instead of a nonstick because getting a nonstick pan blazing hot can damage the surface. Plus browning latkes is a challenge with Teflon. And if you're using all this fat, what is the point of a nonstick anyway?

Smashed Potatoes with Thyme

This is an easy twice-cooked way to get a crisp finish to potatoes without frying.

I like to make this recipe with Yukon Gold potatoes because of their buttery flavor and creamy texture that survives both the boiling and the baking. You can use either small potatoes that are individually smashed, or larger ones that are cooked whole and then cut in half before they're smashed.

You can boil the potatoes up to two hours in advance and finish them in the oven just before serving. If you do boil the potatoes in advance, leave them at room temperature until you finish them because refrigerating the boiled potatoes will change the texture, making them grainy.

The potatoes can be finished with a simple sprinkle of sea salt or a mixture of salt and fresh herbs, especially thyme or rosemary.

Serves 4

Extra virgin olive oil

8 small or 4 large Yukon Gold potatoes (about 2 pounds), scrubbed clean

Sea salt or kosher salt

1 tablespoon fresh thyme leaves or finely chopped fresh rosemary

Preheat the oven to 400°F.

Brush a rimmed sheet pan with a thin coating of olive oil. This is most easily done with a pastry brush, but you could also use a paper towel dipped in oil.

Add the potatoes to a pan of salted cold water and bring to a boil. Continue to cook the potatoes at a soft boil until the potatoes are just tender when tested with a fork or paring knife, about 15 minutes. Be attentive, so they don't overcook.

Drain the potatoes and let cool until you can handle them. If the potatoes are small, place them on the oiled sheet pan and using a large fork or potato masher, crush each potato, splitting the skin but leaving the potato in a single piece. If the potatoes are large, cut each in half at its width and place them skin side down on the sheet pan. Use a fork to crush the cut side of each potato. Whether the potato is whole or halved, the skin and shape should still be intact.

Drizzle each smashed potato with a little olive oil, enough to glaze the surface. Sprinkle with salt and herbs.

Bake until the edges of the potatoes get brown and crispy, 10 to 15 minutes.

Serve immediately.

Santa Fe Farmers' Market
Santa Fe, New Mexico

Roasted Asparagus Wrapped in Pancetta

Spears of asparagus are peeled and wrapped in slices of pancetta, an unsmoked Italian bacon. As the asparagus becomes tender, the bacon becomes crisp, forming a little package around the green spears.

Pancetta is easy to find at most delis, butcher shops, and Italian grocers, either presliced and packaged or sold by the pound, sliced or in a single chunk. It's not as salty as regular bacon and thus adds a subtler flavor. Plus since pancetta is almost always produced in a round shape instead of a flat slab, its round slices are easy to wrap around other ingredients, in this case asparagus.

This recipe can be made ahead of dinner and served at room temperature either as a starter—you can add sliced tomatoes alongside—or as a side to a main course of meat, fish, or poultry.

Serves 4 either as a starter or side dish

16 asparagus spears, about ½ inch thick (if the asparagus is very thin, buy more so that there are at least 4 spears per bundle)

4 ounces sliced pancetta (you'll need 8 slices, about ⅛ inch—thin enough to wrap around the asparagus without breaking)

Salt

Freshly ground black pepper

Extra virgin olive oil

Preheat the oven to 375°F.

Trim the asparagus of any tough, woody ends so that all the asparagus stalks are about the same length.

Rinse carefully to remove any sand in the tips and dry completely with paper towels.

Using a vegetable peeler, peel the thicker stalks. If using very thin asparagus, do not peel.

Take 2 thick or 4 thin asparagus stalks and hold them together in a bundle and wrap a slice of pancetta around them. Place the packages, seam side down, on a rimmed sheet pan.

Sprinkle with a little salt and pepper and drizzle olive oil on the exposed tips and stalks.

Cook until the pancetta is crispy and the stalks are tender, 18 to 20 minutes. Serve either immediately or at room temperature.

Penn Quarter Freshfarm Market
Washington, DC

Tuscan Kale with Crispy Garlic

Tuscan kale, also called *cavolo nero*, is new to many home cooks, but it's increasingly easy to find in our farmers' markets and organic food stores. Since its deep green, wrinkly leaves are unfamiliar, you may reach past it to instead buy regular kale, spinach, Swiss chard, or another leafy green, but if you do, you'll be missing out on a richly flavored, versatile, and hugely healthy vegetable. Its leaves are less bitter than those of regular kale, and it cooks a little more quickly.

Your eye doctor will praise you—kale is one of the best vegetables for eye health.

If you can't find Tuscan kale at your local market, you can cook regular kale in the same manner.

Serves 4

2 pounds Tuscan or other kale

Garlic Chips (recipe follows)

2 tablespoons extra virgin olive oil

Pinch of salt

Pinch of red pepper flakes

One 8-ounce piece Parmesan, large enough to produce curls

Using a kitchen scissors or knife, trim and discard the stalks from the kale. Remove any discolored leaves. Wash the kale by submerging it in cool water as many times as needed to get it clean.

Place the kale in a large pot of salted boiling water and cook until tender, 8 to 10 minutes. Drain it, and when it's cool enough to handle, squeeze out any excess water. With a large knife, coarsely chop the kale, just enough to break the large leaves into medium pieces.

While the kale is cooking, make the garlic chips.

Heat the oil in a large skillet over medium-high heat. Add the salt and red pepper flakes. When the oil is hot, add the kale and toss to coat and reheat. Remove from the heat, sprinkle with the garlic chips, and toss again. Use a vegetable peeler to put curls of Parmesan on top.

Serve immediately.

Garlic Chips

1 head garlic

Extra virgin olive oil

Preheat the oven to 400°F.

While the kale is cooking, peel all the cloves of garlic and slice very thin. You should end up with about ½ cup sliced garlic.

Transfer the garlic to a shallow baking dish or rimmed sheet pan and use your fingers to separate the slices into a single layer. Drizzle with a little olive oil, enough to lightly coat but not make the chips wet; you are roasting, not frying, the chips.

Place the garlic in the oven and bake until golden brown, 4 to 5 minutes. Give the pan a shake or stir a couple of times so that the pieces cook evenly. Watch them carefully because you don't want the garlic to burn or get too dark.

> **TIP:** Don't cook the garlic too far in advance, or the chips will become soft and you'll lose the pleasure of crispy garlic combined with the kale.

Puréed Vegetables for Grownups: Roasted Carrots, Cauliflower and Garlic Chips, Peas with Parmesan, Roasted Beets, Butternut Squash and Apple

Purées have long been used to get kids to eat vegetables, but most adults I know also love them. The soft texture can nicely complement other foods on our plate that have more texture. Unlike roasted vegetables, which really taste best right out of the oven, a purée can be made in advance and reheated at mealtime. They are also versatile. Combine purée with good chicken stock and you'll have soup! You can boost flavors with crispy garlic chips or shots of hot sauce. Plus purées travel well, which means any leftovers make a good addition to your lunch box if you've got a microwave at the office.

Some of the best-flavored purées are made with winter root vegetables, and they come in beautiful colors that add to their "we eat with our eyes" appeal.

Whenever you're going to purée a vegetable, cook it completely so that little bits of uncooked vegetable don't take away from the smooth texture.

Once you get the technique down, you can boil, roast, and purée almost any vegetable, adjusting the seasoning to your liking. And a final tip: always make extra because for the effort and extra cleanup of your food processor, you'll be glad to have leftovers.

Roasted Carrot Purée

Makes about 4 cups

2 pounds carrots, whole or baby, peeled and trimmed

2 cloves garlic, smashed with the side of a chef's knife and peeled

2 to 4 tablespoons extra virgin olive oil

Salt

Freshly ground black pepper

1 teaspoon fresh lemon juice

1 teaspoon freshly grated ginger (use a Microplane zester to finely grate the ginger so that it almost melts into the carrots)

½ cup half-and-half

Preheat the oven to 400°F.

Cut the carrots into 2-inch pieces and spread on a rimmed sheet pan (you may need 2 pans) in a single layer. Add the garlic cloves. Drizzle everything with olive oil, 2 tablespoons per pan. Sprinkle with a pinch of salt and several grinds of black pepper.

Roast until the carrots are completely tender and have begun to char and caramelize on their edges, about 30 minutes.

Purée the carrots, garlic, any oil remaining in the pan, lemon juice, ginger, and half-and-half in a food processor until completely smooth.

Cauliflower Purée with Garlic Chips

While the cauliflower in our markets is usually white, sometimes we can find purple or green ones, either of which results in a beautifully colored purée.

Makes about 3 cups

1 medium head cauliflower

3 cloves garlic

3 cups chicken stock

2 tablespoons extra virgin olive oil

2 tablespoons sour cream or crème fraîche

1 tablespoon unsalted butter

Salt

Hot sauce

Cut up the cauliflower by first removing its core and outer leaves and then chopping the florets into pieces. You should have about 4 cups florets.

Peel the garlic cloves. Cut 2 cloves into paper-thin slices and cut the remaining clove in half.

Combine the chicken stock, cauliflower pieces, and halved garlic clove in a pot and bring to a boil. Reduce the heat and simmer until the cauliflower and garlic are tender, about 10 minutes. Drain but reserve about ¼ cup of the cooking liquid.

While the cauliflower is cooking, sauté the sliced garlic in the olive oil, cooking carefully so that the slices become golden brown and crispy. Be careful: if it gets too dark, it will become bitter. Drain on a paper towel.

Transfer the simmered cauliflower and garlic to a food processor and process, adding a little of the cooking liquid to help create a smooth purée.

Add the sour cream and butter and process until blended. Season to taste with salt and several drops of your favorite hot sauce.

Serve with a sprinkle of crispy garlic slices.

Pea Purée with Parmesan

Makes about 3 cups

4 cups freshly shelled peas, or one 16-ounce bag frozen peas (if frozen, be sure to use the kind without butter)

3 cups chicken stock or water

1 tablespoon unsalted butter or extra virgin olive oil

¼ cup grated Parmesan cheese

Salt

Freshly ground black pepper

Cook the peas in boiling chicken stock or water until very tender. If you're using frozen peas, this will take only about 5 minutes because the peas are already cooked. If using fresh peas, it will take about 10 minutes. Drain the peas but save the chicken stock or cooking water.

Place the peas in a food processor and pulse until completely smooth. Thin the purée to the consistency that you like by adding a little of the chicken stock or water. Add the butter and Parmesan and pulse to combine. Season with salt and pepper to taste.

Serve immediately.

Roasted Beet Purée

Makes about 4 cups

2½ pounds trimmed medium red beets (about 4½ pounds with greens)

2 sprigs fresh thyme

1 tablespoon extra virgin olive oil

2 tablespoons water

1 teaspoon salt

1 tablespoon tomato paste

4 teaspoons fresh orange juice

Freshly ground black pepper

Preheat the oven to 375°F.

Scrub the beets and place on a 2-foot-long piece of aluminum foil. Add the thyme, olive oil, water, and salt, distributing evenly. Seal the foil into a package and place it on a rimmed sheet pan or in a shallow roasting pan (to catch any leaks).

Roast the beets until very tender, 50 to 60 minutes. If you're not certain if the beets are done, carefully (the packet will be hot) give the beets a squeeze.

Remove from the oven and let sit until cool enough to handle. Peel the beets and purée them in a food processor until completely smooth. Transfer to a large bowl and add the tomato paste. Add the orange juice 1 teaspoon at a time, tasting before adding more. Season to taste with salt and pepper.

Butternut Squash and Apple Purée

In this combination, the apple and brown sugar add sweetness to the squash. You can use any type of apple but I like Rome apples.

Makes about 4 cups

1 large or 2 medium butternut squash

1 Rome apple

1 to 2 teaspoons light brown sugar (taste before adding more because the apple adds sweetness)

1 teaspoon fresh lemon juice

Optional: 2 tablespoons unsalted butter, at room temperature

Salt

Freshly ground black pepper

Peel the squash and trim the top and bottom. Cut the squash into 1-inch pieces.

Peel and core the apple and cut into large chunks.

Cook the squash and apple either in a steamer over boiling water or in the microwave until completely tender and soft. Using either a food processor or immersion blender, process the squash and apple together until completely smooth. Add the brown sugar, lemon juice, and butter and stir to completely combine. Season with salt and black pepper to taste.

> **TIP:** You can either discard the seeds or save them to toast. To toast squash seeds, first rinse and dry the seeds with a paper towel. Toss with 1 tablespoon olive oil, a large pinch of salt, and a small pinch of cayenne pepper, then spread on a sheet pan that's been lined with parchment paper. Toast in a 275°F oven until fragrant and crisp, 30 to 40 minutes.

How to Buy an Onion

Like the woman I met in a produce aisle whose confusion over buying onions inspired me to create TheCityCook.com, many of us can get stumped by all the choices we have when buying fruits and vegetables. There are many different types of onions and which you buy will depend on what you're cooking.

Yellow. These full-flavored and versatile onions turn golden brown when sautéed and are a good choice for onion soup. High levels of sulfuric acid—the stuff that makes you cry—make them too sharp to eat raw.

Spanish. Bigger and sweeter than yellow onions but not sweet enough to eat raw. Good in a pilaf and ideal for onion rings.

White. Some as large as a softball, white onions become sweet when cooked, making them a great choice for Mexican dishes.

Red. Red onions range from small to huge. Raw, they add a fresh, spicy taste to a salad. They also grill well.

Scallions. Also called green onions, scallions are eaten both raw and cooked.

Shallots. A species of their own, shallots have a mild, onion-garlic flavor and are often substituted for onions. They can be eaten cooked or raw.

Pearl onions. Usually these are boiled whole and used in stews and stir-fries. Yellow pearls have more flavor than the white, and the red are mild enough to eat raw in a salad when peeled and marinated in a vinaigrette.

Leeks. With a white bulb and long green stalk, leeks are almost always eaten cooked. Leeks are grown in sand and must be cleaned very carefully so as not to add grit to your dish.

Sweet onions. Vidalia, Walla Walla, Texas Sweet, Maui. Sweet onions are regional prides with mild flavor that is best tasted raw on a burger or as the centerpiece of a recipe like onion pie.

Cipolline. With a distinctive oval shape, cipollines are an Italian onion now also grown in the U.S. They become sweet when cooked and hold their shape when grilled.

Ramps. Ramps are wild spring onions that look like bulbous scallions and have a pungent and savory onion-garlic taste. Eaten both raw and cooked, these in-demand delicacies have a very short season.

Green Beans with Tomatoes and Prosciutto

Green beans and haricots verts, their more tender cousins, are available year-round. Add slices of raw, bright little tomatoes and shreds of prosciutto to make a satisfying and easy bean salad that tastes best at room temperature.

Serves 4

1 pound haricots verts (also called French beans)

1 pint cherry tomatoes

3 paper-thin slices prosciutto

1 teaspoon sherry vinegar

1 teaspoon salt

¼ teaspoon freshly ground black pepper

1 tablespoon extra virgin olive oil

Clean and trim the beans but leave them whole.

Bring a large saucepan of salted water to a boil. Add the beans and simmer until tender, about 4 minutes.

Drain and rinse the beans with cool water to stop the cooking. Make sure the beans are completely drained. Pat dry with paper towels and place the beans in a serving bowl.

Cut the cherry tomatoes in half and add to the serving bowl with the beans.

Using a knife or your fingers, shred the prosciutto into about 1-inch pieces. Add to the beans and tomatoes.

In a small bowl, combine the sherry vinegar, salt, and pepper and whisk with a fork until the salt dissolves. Add the olive oil and continue to whisk until the dressing emulsifies. Pour over the beans and tomatoes and toss to combine.

Serve immediately at room temperature.

Luscious Potato and Mushroom Gratin

There are two big appeals to vegetable gratins: First, you can make them in advance, keeping them warm while finishing other cooking. A little sitting only makes the gratin even more melded and intensely flavored. But second, most gratins are made with milk and cream, creating a luxurious and rich side dish for any meal.

Gratins also reheat well the next day. Put the baking dish in a preheated oven, letting it warm through, and the top becomes crusty again. Or else just zap in the microwave, which means you can take leftover gratin to work for lunch.

This gratin is a classic, combining sliced potatoes with mushrooms and cream. Although its top gets golden brown, the finished dish is mostly white so plan your meal to include other dishes that have color. You can use olive oil instead of butter to prepare the baking dish and substitute half-and-half for the heavy cream.

Serves 6 to 8

1 large clove garlic, peeled and halved

1 tablespoon unsalted butter

4 to 6 large Yukon Gold potatoes (about 8 cups when sliced)

10 ounces fresh white mushrooms

Salt

Freshly ground black pepper

1½ cups heavy cream

Preheat the oven to 350°F.

Rub the inside of a gratin or shallow baking dish with the cut surface of the garlic and then butter the dish. Save the garlic pieces.

Peel and slice the potatoes ⅛ inch thick, using a sharp knife, food processor, or mandoline. Be sure all the slices are uniform so that the gratin will cook evenly. If it's taking you a while to slice the potatoes, keep them in a bowl of cool water so that the peeled slices won't darken. Dry them with a paper towel before putting them into the baking dish.

Brush the mushrooms clean with a dampened paper towel. Remove the stems and slice the mushrooms about ⅛ inch thick.

Place a layer of potatoes in the buttered gratin dish. Season lightly with salt and pepper and add about half the cream. Tuck the garlic pieces into the potatoes. Spread the mushrooms over the potato layer, arranging the slices evenly so they cover the potatoes.

Finish by adding a top layer of the remaining potatoes, covering all the mushrooms. Season again with a little salt and pepper and pour the remaining cream over the assembled dish.

Bake until the top is golden brown and the edges of the gratin are bubbling, about 1 hour.

Ferry Plaza Farmers Market
San Francisco, California

Frozen Vegetables and a Non Sequitur

Many vegetables are better frozen and all can turn your freezer into a pantry, letting you keep key ingredients on hand without concern about spoilage.

Peas. Once peas are harvested, they begin to toughen and lose flavor. But frozen peas have been flash-frozen right after being picked, keeping them sweet and tender. There's also the work factor: you have to shell about 1 pound of pea pods to produce 1 cup of peas. Buy frozen peas by the bag with no added butter or sauce.

Baby onions. If you have ever made *boeuf bourguignon*, you will know how tedious it is to prep the pearl onions. Plus I find that by the time I get a tiny onion peeled, I've reduced it in size by half. Frozen baby onions packaged without any added sauce or seasoning are an excellent alternative, especially if the onions are headed to a stew or soup.

Spinach. There is no substitute for fresh spinach when spinach is the main event. But when a recipe calls for spinach to add color, flavor, or nutrition (as in a pesto, ravioli stuffing, quiche, dip, or soup), frozen spinach can save you prep time and cost. A 10-ounce box of frozen spinach is the equivalent of 3 or so pounds fresh.

Artichoke hearts. The first person that figured out how to eat an artichoke was either very adventuresome or very hungry. Fresh artichokes are one of the greatest pleasures to cook and eat but, wow, are they a lot of work. They are also seasonal. Frozen artichoke hearts can be an excellent alternative. Buy them plain with no added sauce, then defrost and drain them of any water in a colander. If they still seem damp, just take a paper towel and give each a gentle squeeze before using in your favorite recipe.

Puff pastry. Okay, it's not a vegetable, but for me frozen puff pastry is a freezer pantry essential. Available in most grocery freezer cases, it's both hugely versatile and remarkably easy to work with. Even if you are a baking novice, you'll be able to put together desserts, cheese sticks, and savory tarts with ease. Making puff pastry from scratch is time consuming, requires both skill and patience, and in most recipes you can scarcely (if at all) tell the difference. Pepperidge Farm and Dufour are both good choices.

Meat, Poultry, and Game

Beef, lamb, pork, chicken, and other poultry and game are the centerpiece of many dinners, and the cost of these ingredients can range from modest to hugely expensive. But price isn't a guarantee of taste. That, of course, depends on how you cook them.

These recipes make extensive use of less expensive cuts of poultry and meat. Matching cooking technique with an ingredient is almost always the route to the best result.

Baked Peach and Bourbon Ham

Eggs in Purgatory

Weeknight Roast Chicken-in-Parts

Pan-Grilled Lamb Chops with Harissa

Seared Duck Breasts with Port-Shallot Pan Sauce

Spicy Broiled Chicken Drumsticks

Roasted Pork Tenderloin with Aleppo Pepper Rub

Slow Roast of Pork or Lamb for Company

London Broil

Slow-Cooker Lamb Shanks with Tomato Sauce

Pan-Seared Skirt and Hanger Steaks

Chicken Breasts Ten Ways

Tasty Pan-Grilled Turkey Burgers

Simple Oven-Roasted Whole Duck

Baked Peach and Bourbon Ham

There's an old expression about eternity being a ham and two people. Baked hams are mostly large to huge, and while many of us love ham, it can take a holiday or big buffet dinner to justify baking one. But many city butchers and markets now offer small and even mini hams that weigh in at about five pounds.

While this recipe is written for the ten-pound "half-ham," you can use this method for baking a ham of any size. At the end of the recipe I've added adjustments for the larger whole ham and the smaller three-to-five-pound version.

This recipe is for a fully cooked bone-in ham, either uncut or spiral cut. The only thing I love more than baked ham are its leftovers, so if you're a fan of ham salad, sandwiches, and omelets, go ahead and bake a ham that's bigger than you'll need for dinner.

A ten-pound bone-in ham will serve about twenty as a main course.

One 9- to 11-pound fully cooked bone-in ham (either sliced or not)

One 15- to 20-ounce can sliced peaches in syrup

1 shot bourbon (3 tablespoons)

1 cup light brown sugar

3 tablespoons dry mustard (Coleman's is always a good choice)

Unsalted butter

Remove the ham from the refrigerator 1 hour before you plan to bake it so that it comes to room temperature. Remove any plastic wrapping. Rinse the ham and pat it dry with paper towels.

If you've bought a ham that has skin on it, carefully cut off the skin as well as all but about ¼ inch of fat.

If you wish to add a traditional decorative diamond pattern, use a knife to score the surface of the ham in 1-inch diamonds. Take care not to cut much deeper than ¼ inch into the surface.

Preheat the oven to 300°F. Place a rack in the lower third of the oven to accommodate the roasting pan and ham.

Drain the can of peaches, saving the syrup. Depending on the size of the can, you should have about 1 cup syrup. Add the bourbon to the peach syrup and set aside.

Place the ham in a large roasting pan, cut side down, so that the mound of the ham rises out of the pan.

In a small bowl, combine the brown sugar and dry mustard; mix well.

Using your hands, rub the mustard mixture all over the ham. Expect some of it to fall into the bottom of the pan.

Bake the ham for 12 to 15 minutes per pound, about 2 hours altogether. The purpose here is to heat the ham completely. After 1¼ hours' baking, remove the ham from the oven, pour the bourbon mixture over the ham, and return it to the oven. Bake for the remaining 45 minutes, basting every 15 minutes with a long-handled spoon or bulb baster.

Remove the ham from the oven and let rest for 10 minutes before slicing.

In a sauté pan on top of the stove, sauté the sliced peaches in a little butter until warmed through and the surface and edges of the peaches become a light golden brown.

Slice the ham and serve, passing the sautéed peach slices.

Going Bigger: Baking a Whole Ham (about 22 pounds)

Thanks to Lorrie Stuart, an extraordinary home cook in New York City who provided the instructions for making the same recipe work for a 20-plus-pound whole ham:

Before applying the brown sugar and mustard coating, place the whole ham in a large roasting pan, add 1 cup water to the pan, cover it with aluminum foil, and bake for 1 hour at 300°F.

Remove the ham from the oven and raise the temperature to 325°F. Remove and discard the aluminum foil and pat on the mustard coating; you may want to double the amount of sugar and mustard if your ham is really big. Return the ham to the oven and bake, uncovered, at 325°F for 2½ hours.

Pour the peach syrup and bourbon mixture (syrup from one 29-ounce can and one 15-ounce can peaches plus ½ cup bourbon) over the ham. Bake, basting the ham every 15 minutes, for 45 minutes.

Let rest for 20 to 30 minutes before carving.

Going Smaller: Baking a Small Quarter-Ham (3½ to 5 pounds)

For a mini ham, with or without a bone, follow the same recipe as for the half-ham with the following changes: use half the amount of brown sugar and mustard and cook for a total time of 1½ hours at 300°F. Baste with the bourbon mixture for the last 45 minutes of the total time.

Let rest for 10 minutes before carving.

Alternative to Canned Peaches

If fresh peaches are in season or you prefer frozen peaches, substitute 1 cup peach nectar (canned or bottled) for the canned peach syrup. For a side dish with the finished ham, warm about 2 cups fresh or frozen peach slices in a skillet with a little butter and brown sugar.

Eggs in Purgatory

This simple egg and tomato sauce combo is often compared to the popular Latin American huevos rancheros. Its name is attributed to Naples, Italy, where *uova al purgatorio* is said to have originated.

You can make your own marinara sauce by simmering a can of crushed red tomatoes and sliced garlic in olive oil for about 10 minutes. But for this dish, a jar of good-quality store-bought marinara will work just as well and reduce your dinner-making time to about 20 minutes.

If your tomato sauce seems too thick, just thin it with a few tablespoons of water. Make sure the sauce is really hot before adding the eggs so that the eggs begin to cook immediately.

If you don't want to include the pancetta, guanciale, or other pork fat, you can simply skip the first step entirely and only use tomato sauce.

Serve this with a heap of broccoli rabe and thick pieces of grilled bread and you'll be in heaven.

Serves 2

2 to 4 ounces good-quality pancetta or guanciale, sliced medium-thick so that the pieces have some body, cut into 1-inch pieces

4 cups tomato or marinara sauce

Small pinch of red pepper flakes

Generous pinch of dried oregano

4 eggs, preferably free-range or organic

½ cup grated ricotta salata or Parmesan cheese

In a large sauté pan or skillet that has a cover, cook the pancetta over medium heat until the lean meat is cooked through and the fat is opaque but not brown.

Add the tomato sauce, red pepper flakes, and oregano (warm the oregano between your fingers before adding). Stir to combine and bring to a gentle simmer.

Add the eggs, one at a time, so that each egg settles into the sauce but isn't covered. You want the yolks to remain exposed. Cover the pan. Reduce the heat to medium-low so that the sauce gently simmers but doesn't boil. Cook until the egg whites are cooked completely but the yolks are still runny, about 5 minutes.

Serve immediately with a dusting of freshly grated cheese and spears of toasted bread for dipping.

Weeknight Roast Chicken-in-Parts

When I was growing up, my mother would bake pieces of chicken once a week, and we never tired of it. As I began to cook, I became a bit of a snob and instead insisted upon the iconic whole roast chicken. But after years of trying dozens of different recipes, my chickens never cooked evenly. I tried blasts of high temperature, stuffing the cavity with lemons, sticking compound butters under the skin, and even used one of those oven-challenged metal racks on which you poise the chicken in a humiliating upside-down position. The results were never completely satisfying.

Roasting a whole chicken means limited choices of white meat or dark. And unpredictable amounts of leftovers. My solution is to cook only those parts I want and need. If you're handy with a boning knife, you can buy a whole chicken and cut it up yourself (a whole chicken always costs less than the pieces). Some markets also sell a whole chicken already cut up, usually in eight pieces, including the back, which you can freeze for stock.

Cooking chicken parts lets you cook the pieces to their ideal doneness since white meat cooks faster than dark. Pieces always cook faster than a whole bird, so this is a perfect weeknight dinner done in less than an hour.

The other essential for flavorful chicken is to buy a good one: free-range or organic and, if possible, from a local poultry producer. The happier the chicken when it roamed in its yard, the happier you will be at dinner. Finally, use fresh seasonings instead of that dusty tin of paprika, and you'll experience how a recipe this simple can result in a most satisfying weekday supper.

Serves 4

4 pieces chicken on the bone (your preferences for breasts, drumsticks, or thighs)

Salt

Freshly ground black pepper

Paprika (sweet or hot)

Preheat the oven to 350°F.

Rinse the chicken with cool water and pat dry with paper towels. Leave the skin on. If you prefer to not eat it, remove the skin after cooking because otherwise the meat will dry out.

Sprinkle the salt, pepper, and paprika on both sides of each piece. Place in a shallow roasting pan or rimmed sheet pan.

Bake the breasts for 45 minutes and the leg and thigh pieces for 55 minutes.

Serve with a favorite vegetable and a grain such as rice pilaf. If you bake extra pieces, they make a wonderful lunch to take to work.

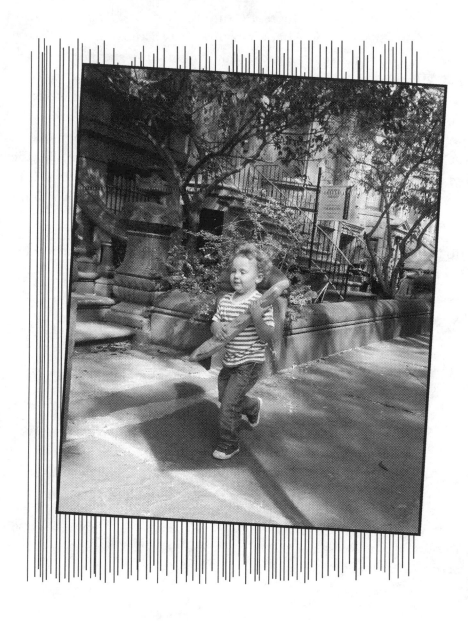

Pan-Grilled Lamb Chops with Harissa

Harissa is a spicy red pepper paste used in Moroccan and Tunisian cuisine. It's made with a combination of chiles, cumin, garlic, paprika, coriander, and olive oil. While you can certainly make your own, there are many excellent varieties sold by grocers and specialty markets in jars, cans, and tubes. All are spicy and pack some heat, but some are stronger than others. Be sure to check the label, and once you bring it home, taste a little so you'll know what you're working with.

In this recipe, harissa is used as a rub. I usually prefer the cheaper and more flavorful shoulder lamb chop, but for a treat you can use either loin or little rib chops, which are more expensive but have less gristle and bone.

The longer the harissa sits on the chops, the hotter the final flavor will be. This is not, however, like some chili-based rubs that can quickly go from subtle flavor to dangerous heat. The spices in harissa are more subtle and complex, and there's little risk of fire damage. Still, you may want to only let the coated chops sit for 15 to 30 minutes, about the time it takes for the meat to come to room temperature.

Serves 4

6 double-rib lamb chops, cut in half for 12 single-rib chops, or four ½-inch-thick
   shoulder chops
½ cup harissa

Remove the lamb chops from the refrigerator, rinse, and pat dry.

Place the chops in a single layer on a platter or in a large ceramic dish. Using your hands, spread the harissa on the lamb chops so that there's a thin coating of the red paste on both sides of all the chops. Let the chops sit long enough to come to room temperature, 15 to 30 minutes. The longer they sit with the harissa on them, the spicier the final flavor will be.

Heat a ribbed grill pan (cast-iron is best) or other robust skillet (NOT nonstick) over high heat for 2 to 5 minutes so that it is blazing hot. Add no fat to the pan.

While the pan is heating, use a spatula, your hands, or a paper towel to wipe the harissa off of the chops. The meat will be stained a little red from the red pepper paste. Discard the harissa.

Pan-grill the lamb chops in batches, letting each side cook for 3 to 4 minutes for medium-rare. The fat on the chops plus any residue from the harissa will bring up some smoke, so you might want to turn on your fan or open the kitchen window.

Serve with warm couscous to which you can add chickpeas, sliced cherry tomatoes, and toasted pine nuts, plus a green vegetable or salad.

City Potluck Cooking and Carrying

Potluck dinners are a popular way to share the cost and the cooking of a meal. It also lets both the host and guests show off some culinary skill because if you're only cooking one dish, you can be more ambitious.

But potluck isn't always easy to plan, cook, or carry. Without some coordination of every contribution, a meal can end up being all macaroni and cheese or all chocolate desserts. Plus not every recipe was meant to be mobile: some foods travel better than others, especially on the subway.

If you're the host and are asking a guest to bring something to your next dinner party, or you're a guest who volunteers to cook and carry, here are some tips for a more successful city potluck:

- Advance planning needs to be both specific and descriptive; the host should give assignments with details about the whole meal. For example, if your host asks you to bring a salad, it would help to know that the main course is honey-glazed Indonesian chicken before you decide to make your favorite honey mustard vinaigrette. Same thing for dishes that have lots of spice or dairy. Everyone will enjoy what you bring more if it really complements the rest of the meal.
- Some dishes can be assembled at their destination. If you're bringing a salad, wash, cut, and prep each element in your kitchen, including the dressing. Pack each in its own separate plastic bag or container, then toss and dress the salad just before serving. Same thing for dishes with sauces or that need last-minute seasoning.
- Ask your host in advance about serving utensils. Will there be a serving bowl big enough for your pasta, a tray and dish for your dip and crudités, a large serving spoon for your rice pilaf? What about soup bowls and spoons? Maybe every dish has been committed to the other courses, and you'll have to bring extra. So ask.
- If the rest of the menu isn't using every burner in your host's kitchen, consider dishes that can be mostly cooked in your own kitchen but finished at your destination. For example, pasta almost always tastes best when cooked and assembled just before serving. So make your sauce in advance, pack it in recycled plastic deli containers, and then cook and sauce the pasta in your host's kitchen.

- Don't forget to bring any necessary seasonings. If you assume your host has grainy mustard, hot sauce, red wine vinegar, grated Parmesan cheese, confectioners' sugar, or any other detail needed to finish your dish, you may be disappointed.

- Some foods travel well but, frankly, others don't. If you're a public transit user, this further complicates the carrying so consider the transport of what you're making before committing to your recipe. Foods such as couscous salad, soup, hummus, rice pudding, and sesame noodles are good choices because they can be decanted from their plastic containers at your destination. Frozen foods, like baked lasagna, are easy to carry and can go directly from your freezer to your host's oven (ask your host first if the oven will be available).

- Dishes such as casseroles that can't be removed from their baking dishes are the toughest to carry. You can wrap the baking dish with several layers of aluminum foil and then a kitchen towel and place it in the bottom of a sturdy shopping bag that's been lined with an additional towel or two. If your casserole is still fragrant from baking, expect to have fellow subway passengers follow you to dinner.

- Some foods require special carrying containers. Cupcakes and layer cakes really need one of those hard plastic carrying cases with a locking lid. I've never seen a jerry-rigged cake carrier actually work. If you love to bake and always volunteer to bring dessert, consider investing the $20 or so in a reusable carrying case to prevent the heartache of smashed icing.

- For carrying shallow baked goods like a fruit tart, I use a clean pizza box from my local pizza shop. Tuck a crush of aluminum foil in each corner to keep the pan stable, then place the box flat in a shopping bag, ideally one with a square, flat bottom. Leave the tart in its metal baking pan until it's safely at your final destination. This also works for a quiche or savory tart, which are perfect first courses for a potluck. Bake them a few hours in advance, let them cool enough to carry, and then warm in your host's oven before serving.

Seared Duck Breasts with Port-Shallot Pan Sauce

The great Jacques Pépin has a recipe that combines pork tenderloin with a rich port wine sauce. It inspired me to do the same with boneless duck breasts, which like Chef Pépin's pork are complemented by sweet prunes and port.

Browning the duck is essential for achieving a rich and complex flavor. Do not use a nonstick pan because you won't develop the flavorful brown *fond* that forms on the bottom and is deglazed into the sauce.

This dish is quick enough for a weekday dinner but it's special enough for company. Serve with rice pilaf or couscous.

Serves 4

6 ounces pitted prunes (15 to 20 small prunes; fewer if they're large)

½ cup port

2 boneless duck breasts, trimmed of all but ½ inch of fat (Pekin or Long Island breasts will be about 8 ounces each, but a Moulard breast can be as large as 1 pound)

Salt

Freshly ground black pepper

2 tablespoons finely minced shallots

3 tablespoons red wine vinegar

⅔ cup good-quality chicken stock

1 tablespoon seedless raspberry jam

2 teaspoons ketchup

About 1 hour before cooking, pour enough boiling water over the prunes to cover them and let them sit for 30 minutes. Drain. Pour the port over the drained prunes and let sit for another 30 minutes.

Preheat the oven to 200°F. Have ready an ovenproof platter or a sheet pan.

Make shallow cuts on the skin of each duck breast on the diagonal and about 1 inch apart. Cut into the fat only, not the meat. Season with salt and pepper.

Set a skillet or sauté pan over high heat. Add no fat. When the pan is hot, add the duck breasts, skin side down, and immediately reduce the heat to medium. Cook the duck breasts until the fat has largely rendered and the breasts are browned, 8 to 10 minutes. Do not cook them too fast because you'll cook off all the fat without cooking the meat. Turn the meat over and cook until browned, about 5 minutes. A total of 15 minutes cooked at medium should result in medium-rare meat. If you're cooking large Moulard breasts, you may need to finish them in a 400°F oven for 5 minutes.

Place the duck in a 200°F oven to keep warm while you make the sauce.

Pour off all but 1 tablespoon fat from the skillet and place the pan over medium heat. Add the shallots and sauté until they begin to soften and take on a little color, about 30 seconds. Add the vinegar, being careful not to get a noseful of the acidic fumes that will rise when the vinegar hits the hot pan. Stir with a wooden spoon to deglaze the pan. Add the chicken stock and continue stirring as you add the port and prunes.

Remove the duck breasts from the oven. Pour any accumulated juices into the sauce and stir to combine. Transfer the duck breasts to a cutting board and let rest. Bring the sauce to a gentle boil and cook until slightly reduced and thickened, about 5 minutes.

When the sauce has become slightly thickened, stir in the raspberry jam and ketchup.

Cut the duck breasts on the diagonal into 1-inch slices, cutting along the shallow marks made before cooking. Arrange the slices on a serving platter. You can pour the sauce over the breasts or pass it separately.

Serve immediately.

> **TIP:** Port is a fortified wine that is often served as a dessert wine because it is particularly sweet and spicy. Some vintage ports can be notably pricey. As with any wine used in cooking, you should choose a port you'd be willing to drink, but there's no need to use a precious vintage port in your cooking. Instead select a medium-quality ruby or tawny port. If you don't have or don't like port, you could use Madeira or a fruity Zinfandel instead.

> **TIP:** If you can't find seedless raspberry jam, use another dark seedless jam such as black cherry or blackcurrant.

Spicy Broiled Chicken Drumsticks

Since I don't have a grill, I use the broiler in my oven to give certain foods the finish that only a blast of high heat can produce. Indoor broiling may not produce charcoal-flavored finishes, but it does deliver high heat close to the surface of meats and fish. Plus broiler cooking doesn't overheat my small city kitchen as much as having the oven on for 45 minutes.

Chicken drumsticks are a perfect broiler food. Their dark meat cooks in only 20 minutes, about half the time they take to bake, and the broiler gives them an appealing crispy skin. While you can simply give the drumsticks a light rub of olive oil and a sprinkle of salt and pepper, I prefer a spicy rub that is inspired by jerk flavors that I first saw several years ago in a magazine. The paste is easy to make and flavors the meat in only ten minutes. Instead of the traditional Scotch bonnet chile, I use a jalapeño, which is milder but also more likely to be in your pantry. You could also use a serrano chile.

Serves 4

8 to 10 scallions, white and tender green parts only, cut into 1-inch chunks

2 tablespoons Champagne vinegar

1 tablespoon fresh thyme leaves, or 1 heaping teaspoon dried thyme

4 cloves garlic

1 teaspoon ground allspice

1 heaping teaspoon finely minced jalapeño or serrano pepper (include the seeds for more heat)

1 teaspoon salt

10 chicken drumsticks with skin (about 3 pounds)

Combine all the ingredients except the chicken drumsticks in a food processor. Pulse until the garlic is finely chopped and everything combines in a thick paste.

Place the chicken in a large bowl or ceramic baking dish and toss with the paste to coat. Leave at room temperature for about 10 minutes.

Position a rack under the broiler so that the chicken will be 5 to 6 inches from the flame. Preheat the broiler to high.

Use either the stove's broiling pan or a rack placed on a sheet pan. Because the paste coating the chicken and the fat that will cook out of the meat can combine to be a bit messy, it is a good idea to first line your pan with foil.

Arrange the chicken pieces, still covered with the paste, on the broiling pan. Broil for 10 minutes. Using tongs, turn the drumsticks over and cook until the drumsticks are fully cooked and brown, another 10 minutes or so.

Serve with a steamed green vegetable and rice pilaf.

TIP: The chicken can also be cooked in a 500°F oven for 20 minutes and then finished under the broiler, close to the flame.

Roasted Pork Tenderloin with Aleppo Pepper Rub

I was late in falling in love with pork tenderloin. For the longest time I somehow missed recognizing how this value-priced cut of meat was so tasty and versatile. Plus the tenderloins, which typically weigh about a pound, are a good size for smaller households.

The tenderloin is from the part of the animal below the ribs and when butchered with the adjacent bone, sold as a loin pork chop. The meat is tender, lean, mild in flavor, and has about the same amount of fat as a boneless, skinless chicken breast. The fillet can be cut into thick medallions to be sautéed or grilled, but cooked whole, it makes a perfect centerpiece for a weekday meal.

Because this cut is small and low in fat, roasting can leave it overcooked, dry, and flavorless. But with just a little care and the help of an instant-read thermometer, a pork tenderloin can be a frequent go-to dinner choice. It doesn't need fussing to add flavor, but a quick spice rub will enhance the meat's taste.

Aleppo pepper is a smoky pepper, mild but with a kick, that is often used in Middle Eastern cooking. Here I simply combine it with sea salt to add a little heat to the pork without overwhelming its delicate flavor.

This recipe serves two. For more servings, just increase the number of tenderloins and cook them all at the same time.

Serves 2

1 pork tenderloin (about 1 pound)

2 tablespoons Aleppo pepper

1 tablespoon sea salt

2 tablespoons olive oil or canola oil

Remove the pork from the refrigerator about 30 minutes before cooking to let it come to room temperature.

In a small bowl, combine the Aleppo pepper and salt and rub over all surfaces of the meat.

Preheat the oven to 400°F. Position a rack in the center of the oven.

Heat the oil in an ovenproof sauté pan or skillet (do not use nonstick) over medium-high heat until the oil shimmers but doesn't smoke. Place the seasoned tenderloin in the pan and brown on all sides. This will take about 6 minutes. Don't rush it.

Put the pan in the hot oven and cook for 8 to 10 minutes. Using an instant-read thermometer, check the tenderloin's internal temperature by inserting the thermometer in the thickest part of the meat. Your target is an internal temperature of 140°F. This will result in medium-rare, or slightly pink, meat. Remove from the oven and let rest for 10 minutes.

Cut into 1-inch-thick slices and serve. Thick slices of roasted pork tenderloin can be placed on top of a green salad or alongside your favorite vegetables. Thinly slice the meat for sandwiches.

TIP: To accompany a simple pork tenderloin, sauté sliced apples in a little butter until they soften and brown a bit on the edges. Prepare them while the tenderloin is in the oven and serve them as a side dish along with roasted sweet potatoes or sautéed bitter greens.

Slow Roast of Pork or Lamb for Company

Roasting is one of the easiest ways to cook, whether it's vegetables, a whole fish, or a piece of meat. Requiring essentially no effort once the item is in the oven, a large roasted piece of meat can be the main event in a dinner for company. If it's just for you, you'll have tasty leftovers for another meal or sandwiches. But a roast can also be very costly since the cuts of meat that are almost always recommended for roasting, whether beef, lamb, or pork, are the more expensive leg or loin.

One of the first lessons I learned in culinary school is that the cut of meat determines how it should be cooked. For instance, pieces of the loin are best if cooked rapidly at high heat, as when we grill a rib-eye steak. But other cuts from the animal's hardest-working parts, like the shoulder, should always be slow-cooked, giving the collagen and intramuscular fat time to become tender.

When we think of slow-cooked meat, we usually think of cooking in liquid, as a braise or stew, but you can achieve the same result with roasting, as long as you cook at a low temperature and for a long period of time.

In this recipe a boned shoulder of either pork or lamb is seasoned, tied into a compact roast, and cooked for five hours at low heat. The surface will become brown and the meat will be falling-apart tender. These cuts are forgiving, so you can take some latitude in the timing. What I also love about this cooking method is that it makes a lower-cost cut of meat special enough for company.

The selection of the roast is key to this recipe, so buy your meat at a good butcher shop where you can order precisely what you want. Ask for a boneless shoulder, trimmed of excess fat on one side. You want the other side to still have fat (and skin, if possible) because this is the surface that will be exposed to the oven's heat; it will cook to exquisite crispness. The lean surface will be rolled up with herbs and garlic. Request that the meat be left untied but ask the butcher for a long piece of butcher's twine if you need it.

If you don't have access to a good butcher, you can find this cut of meat at your grocer's. Ask someone from the meat department to remove the bone for you, since deboning a roast is tricky to do at home and you'll probably end up wasting much of the meat. You'll still be charged for the bone, but there should be no cost for its removal. If you're buying a pork roast with the skin intact, you can also ask the butcher to score the skin if you think your knives aren't sharp enough to do this at home.

Keep in mind that shoulder cuts have lots of cartilage, fat, and gristle, so you'll need to buy a bigger roast than you would if you were cooking a leg or loin. The shoulder will reduce as it cooks, so plan for this as well. If you're lucky enough to have leftovers, you can shred the meat and add it to a favorite barbecue sauce for a sandwich, make tacos, or add it to a ragù for pasta.

A final suggestion: While your roast is cooking, slip a sheet pan filled with halved plum tomatoes and peeled whole garlic cloves (topped with a little olive oil, salt, and pepper) into the oven. They'll slow-cook right along with your roast and make a perfect side dish. Remove the pan after about 3 hours when the edges of the tomatoes get brown and the flesh has reduced.

Serves 6

Leaves from 4 sprigs fresh thyme

Leaves from 2 sprigs fresh rosemary, chopped

6 fresh sage leaves for pork, or 2 teaspoons dried oregano for lamb

6 cloves garlic, peeled

¼ teaspoon ground cumin

2 teaspoons salt

1 teaspoon freshly ground black pepper

3 tablespoons extra virgin olive oil

One 4- to 5-pound boneless pork or lamb shoulder, with skin (see headnote)

½ cup dry red wine

Preheat the oven to 275°F.

Combine the herbs, garlic, cumin, salt, and pepper in a food processor and pulse to finely chop and mix everything together. Add 1 tablespoon of the olive oil and pulse to mix into a paste.

Open the roast skin/fat side up. Use a sharp knife to score the surface with cuts 1 inch apart in a diamond pattern. Cut into the skin and fat but try not to cut the meat underneath. Turn the meat over and, using the tip of a knife, make little ½-inch slits in the meat. Rub about two-thirds of the herb mixture over the meat and into the slits. Roll the meat into a roast and tie it securely at 2-inch intervals with butcher's twine.

Place the roast fat side up in a roasting pan. Rub the surface with the remaining 2 tablespoons olive oil and then the remaining herb mixture. It's okay if some falls into the pan.

Roast for 2 hours, uncovered. Remove the roast from the oven and pour the wine over it. Roast for an additional 3 hours, for a total cooking time of 5 hours. The roast is done when the surface is crispy and browned and the meat is very tender. Use your fingers (it's hot so be careful!) or a fork to press and probe the meat in between the strings to test for doneness. It should be so tender that the meat is falling apart.

Let rest for 15 minutes before carving.

How to Work with a Butcher

Nearly everything I know about buying and cooking meat I've learned from butchers.

Butchers have taught me how to choose a smoked ham, how to make a perfect crown roast of pork, and why a bargain-priced shoulder lamb chop is more flavorful than the pricey rib.

Here's what's important to know: The butcher isn't there just to wrap and weigh what you want. He's also there to finish the item to your exact needs. So if you're shopping at a butcher shop or at a store with a great meat department, here's what a butcher can do for you:

- Give cooking advice. Tell him what you're shopping for and what you're going to do with it.
- Match cuts of meats to recipes. If you're buying a roast and even if you already have your recipe, ask him how he'd cook it (most butchers are excellent home cooks).
- Guide serving size. Need to know how many strips of baby back ribs for four people? Your butcher will have the answer.
- French (I'm using the word here as a verb and not an adjective) lamb or pork chops or a bone-in roast. This means scraping the bones down so that the ribs are exposed, making them prettier and easier to fit in a pan.
- Pound chicken breasts thin enough for chicken piccata, or pieces of veal into cutlets for scaloppine.
- Debone almost anything. For example, he can remove the bone from a leg of lamb to butterfly it or cut out the bone from a budget-priced veal breast to make it easy to stuff. You'll still pay for the bones if that's how the item was originally priced, but you'll be able to take them in a separate package (I freeze mine for stock).
- Give you a length of butcher's twine so that you can tie up the legs of that whole chicken you plan to roast.
- Cut anything into a smaller size. This is particularly helpful if you need to cut through bones. For example, he can cut those 1-inch bone-in pork chops into chops ½ inch thick.

All this and for no extra cost.

London Broil

London broil is not so much a cut of meat as a way of cooking. In some butcher shops and meat departments, London broil is synonymous with flank steak, but any piece of beef that has been marinated, broiled, and then sliced thin on the bias qualifies. As flank steak becomes more expensive, other cuts, including top round, bottom round, and chuck, are increasingly being butchered to be sold as London broil.

Although it's sometimes called a "steak," it is not cooked, sliced, or eaten as you would a strip, rib-eye, porterhouse, or other tender cut of beef. London broil comes from the part of the cow's body where the meat is prone to toughness. As a result, it is significantly less expensive than other cuts of beef, making it a popular and affordable option for city cooks.

The key to London broil is in its slicing.

Serves 4 to 6

1 London broil (flank steak or top round, about 2 pounds and 2 inches thick)

Salt

Freshly ground black pepper

Remove the meat from the refrigerator and place it on a large plate. Generously salt both sides of the steak and let it come to room temperature, which will take about 1 hour. During this time, the salt will pull liquid from the meat. When you're ready to cook, discard any liquid, rinse the steak, and pat it dry using paper towels.

Salt (yes, again) and pepper both sides of the steak and place on a broiling pan or a rack set on a rimmed sheet pan.

Preheat the broiler. Adjust the upper rack so your steak will be about 4 inches below the heat source.

Broil the steak for 10 minutes per side. The steak is done medium-rare when it has an internal temperature of 130°F. Use an instant-read thermometer to check for doneness.

Remove from the heat and let rest for 10 minutes before slicing. All the juices will run out of the meat if you cut it too soon.

If you attempt to serve and eat London broil like another steak, you will find it tough, stringy, and almost inedible.

But all you have to do is simply slice the beef on the bias, meaning at an angle that is against the grain, and it will be fine. It is important to cut thin (about ½ inch) slices, since this too will counter its toughness.

Thin-sliced London broil is a great choice for steak sandwiches, fajitas, and salads. It can also be served on its own with horseradish or a horseradish-cream sauce (add white grated horseradish—fresh or from a jar—to sour cream or whipped cream).

Slow-Cooker Lamb Shanks with Tomato Sauce

When I first learned how to use a slow cooker, I consulted as many cookbooks as I could find to show me how to get the best flavor from what I used to think was an inferior way of cooking. Shame on me, because trial and error taught me that great flavor and convenience can, in fact, come together.

I adapted this recipe from a favorite cookbook by Lynn Alley who is gifted at using a slow cooker to make traditional ethnic dishes. I exchanged her method of grinding her own spices for the convenience of ones ready to use. And because the lamb's aromatic tomato sauce is so flavorful, I doubled it to make enough for a side of fluffy couscous or another day's plate of roasted vegetables.

This recipe can either be made in a slow cooker or braised slowly in the oven. Browning the lamb shanks in a skillet and then braising them with liquid and seasonings tenderizes this otherwise tough cut of meat. Puréed canned San Marzano tomatoes seasoned with garlic and aromatic spices such as cinnamon provide the braising liquid.

Lamb shanks come from the lower portion of the leg. Shanks from the animal's front legs are smaller in size, while shanks from the rear legs can be very large and take much longer to cook. But because here they're cooked for several hours in a slow cooker, size doesn't matter. Whether your shanks weigh more or less than a pound each, they will still cook perfectly as long as you adjust the amount of tomato purée so that there's enough liquid. And if you add more tomato purée, increase the seasonings accordingly.

You can buy canned tomato purée, but I prefer to buy a 28- or 34-ounce can of whole tomatoes and purée them with my immersion blender. I think whole tomatoes have more flavor.

This dish is wonderful with traditional Greek lemon potatoes or with couscous and a green vegetable.

No slow cooker? Use a heavy covered pot and bring to a simmer on the top of the stove, then cook in a 275°F oven for about 2½ hours. Check periodically to make sure the liquid has not cooked off and, if necessary, add a little water or chicken stock.

⅛ teaspoon ground cinnamon

Pinch of ground cloves

Pinch of ground allspice or nutmeg

2 tablespoons extra virgin olive oil

Salt

Freshly ground black pepper

4 lamb shanks (8 to 16 ounces per shank)

1 medium onion, finely minced

2 cloves garlic, minced (about 1 heaping teaspoon)

¼ cup brandy or Cognac

4 cups tomato purée (see headnote)

Combine the ground cinnamon, cloves, and allspice in a small dish and set aside.

Heat 1 tablespoon of the olive oil in a large sauté pan or skillet over medium-high heat until very hot but not smoking. Salt and pepper the lamb shanks and brown them in the oil on all sides. This will take 8 to 10 minutes. Because of the shape of a lamb shank, you won't get every surface browned but try to get a nice brown on the largest sides of the shanks. Transfer the shanks to your slow cooker.

Add the remaining 1 tablespoon olive oil to the same pan and heat over medium heat. Add the onion and cook until softened and slightly browned, 3 to 4 minutes. Add the garlic and cook until fragrant, about 1 minute. Sprinkle the spice mixture over the onion and garlic and stir to coat.

Add the brandy to deglaze the pan, scraping up any brown bits as the brandy cooks off. Add the tomato purée to the other ingredients and cook, stirring, until everything is hot. Remove from the heat and pour the tomato mixture over the lamb shanks.

Cover and cook on low for 6 to 8 hours. About halfway through, check the shanks to be sure they are not sticking to the bottom and that the sauce is well dispersed around the meat. Cook until the meat is completely tender and coming away from the bone.

Pan-Seared Skirt and Hanger Steaks

Skirt and hanger steaks are among the most overlooked and unappreciated cuts of beef. They are inexpensive, very flavorful, quick to cook, and adaptable to a variety of recipes. They have such a rich, beefy flavor that I actually eat less than when I have one of my favorite New York strip steaks. But a warning: if skirt or hanger steaks are cooked too long—to medium or well-done—they will be tough.

These cuts are particularly versatile. Slicing on the diagonal helps counter any toughness, making them perfect for fajitas and stir-fries. Skirt and hanger steaks are best cooked fast and simply. No need for a fancy marinade: you can choose either a simple spice rub or an easy pan sauce. Slices can be placed on top of a simple romaine and raw red pepper salad dressed with a balsamic vinaigrette, seasoned with a rub of cayenne and sea salt, and served with a side of steamed broccoli, or tossed with oven-roasted tomatoes and added to rotini pasta.

Skirt steak is a long, thin cut from the belly of a cow, adjacent to the larger hanger steak. Both are flavorful, slightly chewy, and have a coarse texture.

This recipe works for both skirt and hanger steaks with the adjustment that a thicker hanger steak will need to cook a bit longer in the oven.

Serves 4

1½ pounds skirt steak, cut into pieces that will fit into a sauté pan, or hanger steak, cut into 2 pieces along the center membrane

3 to 4 tablespoons spice rub (suggestions follow)

2 tablespoons canola or extra virgin olive oil

Put the steaks in a sheet pan or baking dish. Make a spice rub, if using, and apply the rub to each piece on both sides. Let the steaks come to room temperature for about 20 minutes.

Preheat the oven to 400°F.

Place an ovenproof skillet over high heat. Add the oil and heat until it's very hot, almost but not quite smoking. Place the steaks in the pan and cook until nicely browned, about 1½ minutes a side. Transfer to the oven. Cook skirt steaks for about 5 minutes for medium-rare. Cook hanger steaks for 12 to 15 minutes for medium-rare. Check with an instant-read thermometer to be sure: 130°F is medium-rare. You will also know that the steaks are medium-rare when they're still slightly soft but also firm to the touch. If they still feel very squishy, put them back in the oven for another minute or two before you check them again.

Let the steaks rest for about 10 minutes to let the juices settle back in place. Cut on the diagonal into ½-inch slices.

Spice Rubs

2 tablespoons ground cumin, 2 teaspoons salt, 1 tablespoon freshly ground black pepper, and ¼ teaspoon cayenne pepper

or

2 tablespoons sumac, 2 teaspoons salt, and 1 teaspoon freshly ground black pepper

or

1 teaspoon each finely minced garlic, ginger that's been scraped on a rasp, salt, and freshly ground black pepper

Simple Pan Sauce

Instead of a spice rub, you can just season the steaks with salt and pepper, cook them exactly the same way, and serve them with a simple pan sauce made with the tasty browned bits left behind in the sauté pan.

4 tablespoons (½ stick) unsalted butter	2 teaspoons Dijon mustard
¼ cup finely minced shallots	Salt
½ cup red wine	Freshly ground black pepper
½ cup chicken or beef stock (good boxed broth is fine)	

While the steaks are resting, add 2 tablespoons of the butter to the pan you used for the steaks (be careful—the handle will still be hot!). Melt the butter over medium heat. Add the shallots and cook until soft and translucent, about 2 minutes.

Add the wine, using a wooden spoon to scrape up the browned bits on the bottom of the pan. Turn up the heat a little so that the wine bubbles and boil the wine until it's syrupy, about 2 minutes. Add the stock and boil over medium-high heat until reduced by two thirds.

Reduce the heat and stir in the mustard. Stir in the remaining 2 tablespoons butter, ½ tablespoon at a time. Season to taste with salt and pepper.

Drizzle the sliced steak with the sauce. Serve with steamed potatoes and green beans.

Apartment Grilling—Oven Broilers

Feeling deprived because you don't have any way to grill? Cheer up! You can do indoor grilling with your oven broiler.

Your broiler is simply an upside-down grill. You control the pace and intensity of the cooking by adjusting the distance from the heat source—in this case it's above the food, not underneath it—as well as the cooking time. An oven broiler gets better flavor than a countertop grill because it blasts heat against the food's surface, resulting in rapid browning and more intense flavor. Since broiling is faster than roasting, the oven needs less time to heat up and cool down, making it a great choice for small kitchens, especially in hot weather.

- Get to know your broiler. Turn it on and get down on your hands and knees to take a look at how the flame works. Notice the size of the heat source, where the flame is most intense, and how large its expanse—all essential for knowing where to place a pan.
- Preheat the broiler just as you preheat an oven. Once a broiler is turned on, it's throwing off heat, but you want to be sure that it's at full force before you put food under it. Unlike an oven that may need 20 minutes to preheat, most broilers will be at full heat in about 3 minutes.
- Adjust the level of the rack. As with a grill, you control broiler cooking by adjusting the distance between the food and the flame. So if you place a steak too close to the heat, you can easily get a dark brown surface with a rare-to-raw interior. Many foods broil best about 4 inches from the heat.

- Can't adjust your rack? Sometimes ovens have broilers in separate drawers, and these are usually not adjustable, leaving the distance between the heat and your pan at about 3 inches. If that's the case with yours, you can first roast your dish in a very hot (500°F) oven and then finish it under the broiler just to give a crispy surface. See the recipe for Spicy Broiled Chicken Drumsticks (page 170).
- Broiler pans: Many ovens come with a 2-piece broiler pan with a shallow bottom part and a perforated insert that lets food cook on top while fat drips into the pan below. But you can just as easily use a sheet pan with a rack set in it. Always be sure that any pan you use under a broiler is totally heatproof because the temperature can exceed 500°F; this rules out using anything nonstick.
- Never use parchment paper under a broiler because it will burn.
- Clean ovens help. If there's any spilled or spattered food, you can get lots of smoke.

Which foods broil best? Anything that benefits from high heat and browning. Meat, poultry, and fish of course, but also stone fruits like peaches and plums, polenta squares, tomatoes, ham steaks, and fruits naturally high in sugar that will easily caramelize with the high heat, such as fresh figs.

Chicken Breasts Ten Ways

For many home cooks, chicken breasts are a go-to meal. They're not expensive, are often on sale (good for stocking the freezer), can be cooked in small portions, and are low in fat.

The down side? They can be so boring. But chicken breasts are very versatile—do a quick recipe search either online or on your cookbook shelf and you'll see what I mean. Sometimes we just need a prompt to treat a familiar ingredient in a new way. So if chicken breasts are a favorite, here are ten different ways to cook them:

1. Roasted, on the bone, skin on, with a spoonful of herbed goat cheese or Boursin tucked under the skin.
2. Chicken tacos. Pan-sauté the breasts until cooked through and golden brown. Cut into strips to fill a corn taco shell along with shredded lettuce, tomatoes, guacamole, Jack cheese, hot sauce, and finely diced red onion.
3. Chicken salad. Roast the breasts on the bone with the skin (they'll have more flavor), then let cool and remove the meat. Add mayonnaise, minced celery and scallions, tarragon, and sliced seedless grapes.
4. Chicken potpie. Make your own pastry dough or top it with a disc of frozen puff pastry.
5. Cobb salad. Pan-cook or roast the breasts, cut them into cubes, and add to other chopped ingredients—avocado, blue cheese, lettuce, tomatoes, bacon, and hard-cooked eggs.
6. Chicken Parmesan. Pound boneless breasts flat using a meat pounder or the bottom of a heavy skillet, coat in a mix of panko and grated Parmesan, and sauté as a cutlet. Surround with a favorite tomato sauce, top with thin slices of fresh mozzarella, and bake in the oven until the cheese melts.
7. Roast on the bone, let cool, and shred into pieces to top your own pizza.
8. Toss pieces of cooked chicken breast with a favorite pasta and steamed broccoli florets.
9. Bake breasts still on the bone with tandoori spices (garam masala, cumin, chili powder, garlic, ginger) and yogurt. Finish under the broiler until slightly charred and serve with seasoned basmati rice.
10. Chicken hash. Since its main ingredient is precooked meat or poultry, hash is a perfect use for leftover roasted or sautéed chicken breasts. Dice the breasts

and combine with diced potatoes, an egg to hold everything together, and favorite seasonings like minced jalapeño or chopped onions. Be careful not to overcook because with a second cooking, the chicken can dry out.

The Versatility of Rotisserie Chickens

A rotisserie chicken cooked by a favorite grocer or butcher can be a city cook's best friend. The rotisserie oven guarantees a juicy bird; many stores add spices and seasonings; and the cost is usually not much more than what you'd pay for a whole raw chicken.

One whole chicken serves four, two with leftovers, or more if added to a salad or pasta.

- *Serve it whole*. Heading home from work for dinner? Put the chicken in a 200°F oven as you walk in the door to keep it warm. Don't reheat in the microwave because it will toughen the meat. Add a green vegetable and sliced tomatoes for a meal that's faster than takeout.
- *Make a salad*. Shred the pieces of meat off the bone and combine with chopped raw vegetables, toasted pecans, dried cranberries, and pieces of goat cheese. Pass a mustard vinaigrette on the side and serve with chunks of bread.
- *Add to pasta*. Discard the skin and add pieces of chicken to a favorite homemade or jarred tomato sauce and pasta. Or instead of sauce, combine with roasted tomatoes and a drizzle of olive oil.
- *Chicken pizza*. Make your own or buy pizza dough and use the chicken as a topping. Add ricotta for a more substantial pizza bianca.
- *Tacos and burritos*. Make a favorite recipe for tacos or burritos and fill with the shredded chicken.
- *Chicken melt*. Instead of tuna salad, add the cooked chicken to a grilled cheese sandwich.
- *Chicken fried rice*. Combine cooked rice, frozen peas, pieces of cooked chicken, and a scrambled egg. Season with soy sauce.

Tasty Pan-Grilled Turkey Burgers

Turkey burgers often sound better than they taste. That's because low-fat ground turkey is frequently overcooked, becoming unappealingly dry and flavorless.

To counter this problem, I've added cooked aromatics—finely minced garlic and shallot—to add both flavor and moisture.

Served with rolls and a side of salad or coleslaw, these burgers make an appealing weeknight meal.

Serves 4

2 tablespoons extra virgin olive oil

2 shallots, finely minced (about 2 tablespoons)

2 to 4 cloves garlic, finely minced (about 2 teaspoons)

1 pound ground turkey

1 tablespoon finely minced fresh parsley

2 teaspoons Dijon mustard, plus more for serving

4 to 6 drops hot sauce or Tabasco

1 teaspoon salt

Freshly ground black pepper

Heat 1 tablespoon of the olive oil in a large sauté pan or skillet over medium heat. Add the shallots and garlic and cook until they are soft and the shallots are translucent but not browned, 2 to 3 minutes. The goal here is to get rid of the raw taste. Remove from the heat and set aside to cool slightly.

In a large bowl, mix together the ground turkey, parsley, mustard, hot sauce, salt, several grinds of black pepper, and the cooked shallots and garlic. The best way to mix everything is with your (clean) hands.

Divide the meat mixture into 4 parts and form patties, taking care not to press too hard. Because ground turkey is very soft and sticky, wet your hands to make it easier to handle.

Heat the remaining 1 tablespoon olive oil in the same sauté pan over medium heat. Add the turkey patties, lower the temperature to medium-low, and cook until the underside is brown, about 5 minutes. Turn and continue to cook the second side until brown and the center is no longer pink, about 10 minutes total. Remember that poultry should always be completely cooked and not eaten rare or medium-rare.

Transfer the patties to plates and serve immediately with rolls, pieces of romaine lettuce, your favorite condiments, and maybe a side of tossed salad or creamy coleslaw.

> **TIP:** Some butchers and meat departments sell ground turkey with different amounts of fat. If given a choice, buy ground turkey with 7% fat instead of all-white meat (usually 3% fat), for a less dry and more full-flavored result.

Simple Oven-Roasted Whole Duck

Many of us love the taste of duck but are intimidated by its reputation as tricky to cook. Plus there's all that fat. Cookbooks can intimidate us with recipes that advise steaming, poaching, piercing, fast cooking at high temperatures, slow cooking at low, and even drying with a hair dryer. No wonder we instead satisfy our duck appetites with an occasional pan-seared breast.

While there may be some benefits to marinating, air drying, steaming, and other tricks before roasting, the results are only subtly different and, in my view, not usually worth all the trouble. If you're a duck lover but have never roasted one before, try this simple method. Roasting at a moderate heat gives the layer of fat time to melt while also producing a crispy skin and tender meat below.

This recipe is for domesticated, not wild, duck. Wild duck is a true game bird, and most game has far less fat and thus needs to be cooked using a different method. Game birds also usually benefit from being roasted with a layer of bacon or other fat placed on the entire surface of the bird.

Most ducks sold in city markets and butcher shops are Long Island ducks, also called Pekin. These typically weigh four to five pounds and after cooked, will produce three or four servings. Less commonly found is the Moulard, a hybrid of a Pekin and a Muscovy duck, which is about twice the size of a Long Island duck. All ducks can be cooked in the same way, but you'll need to adjust the amount of time in the oven to account for the bird's larger size. Also note that Muscovy ducks have much thinner skins and a slightly stronger flavor.

Serves 3 to 4, depending on the size of the duck

1 whole Long Island or Pekin duck (4 to 5 pounds)

Salt

Freshly ground black pepper

½ lemon, cut into wedges

½ orange, cut into wedges

3 or 4 sprigs fresh thyme

Preheat the oven to 375°F. Place a rack in the center of the oven.

Remove the duck from the refrigerator and remove any giblets that may be in the duck's cavity. Rinse the duck with cool water and pat it completely dry inside and out with paper towels. Using the prongs of a fork or the sharp tip of a skewer, pierce the skin of the duck all over every ½ inch or so, pushing the prongs through the skin and into the fat below but not through to the underlying meat. This step will help the fat release as it melts and cooks.

Generously season the duck inside and out with salt and pepper, then place the pieces of lemon and orange plus the thyme sprigs inside the duck's cavity. Tie the duck's legs together with a piece of butcher's twine. Use a small skewer, the kind used on a turkey, to close and secure the neck opening.

Place the duck breast side up on a rack in a roasting pan. It is important to use a roasting pan that has some depth so that the fat rendered from the bird doesn't spill into the oven.

Place the bird in the preheated oven and roast for 1 to 1½ hours. Every 20 minutes or so, take the bird from the oven and pour off any rendered fat to a heatproof dish or bowl. Each time you return the bird to the oven, rotate the pan to help the duck cook and crisp evenly.

After about 50 minutes of cooking, use an instant-read thermometer to check the duck's progress. The duck will be done when the skin is golden brown and crispy and a thermometer pierced into a thick part of the bird's thigh registers 165°F.

Remove the duck from the oven and pour out and discard any liquid and the solids from the cavity. Let rest for about 10 minutes before carving.

Carve the duck as if it were a chicken, removing each breast in a single piece and detaching the wings and leg-thigh pieces.

Serve with roasted little potatoes and braised red cabbage. Red currant jelly and applesauce are nice accents to the duck's rich flavor.

> **TIP:** The rendered duck fat can be cooled and saved for other uses, such as frying sliced potatoes or making duck confit. Seal the duck fat in a clean plastic container and store it in the refrigerator or freezer.

Fish and Shellfish

I love seafood for its flavor, delicacy, nutrition, and variety, but for many home cooks it's a challenge. The answer is to cook it simply. Other lessons: Buy it the day you'll cook it. Don't overseason or oversauce it or you'll lose its flavor. And learn about buying fish in today's environment because there is much to know that affects not only your dinner table but also the future of the oceans.

Warm Bean and Broiled Shrimp Salad

Baked Red Snapper with Artichokes and Cherry Tomatoes

Baked Salmon with Leeks and Dill

Pan-Seared Arctic Char

Whole Fish Baked in a Salt Crust

Jumbo Shrimp with Teriyaki Glaze

Broiled Black Cod with Miso

Pan-Fried Tilapia with Crispy Panko

Salade Niçoise with Pan-Grilled Fresh Tuna

Salmon Cakes with Spicy Sriracha Mayonnaise

Warm Bean and Broiled Shrimp Salad

I love creamy cannellini beans and always keep cans of them in my pantry. They're versatile, very nutritious, and add wonderful flavor to other ingredients, as in this warm salad made with broiled shrimp and raw cherry tomatoes.

While you can soak and cook dried cannellini beans in advance, I find it easier and just as tasty to use the canned ones, making this the kind of dinner that can be made almost completely from the pantry. Just purchase a pound of jumbo shrimp and a package of cherry tomatoes on your way home from work, and you'll have dinner on the table within an hour.

Serves 4 as a side dish or starter, or 2 as a main course

1 pound jumbo shrimp (about 15)

4 cloves garlic

4 tablespoons extra virgin olive oil

1 tablespoon finely minced fresh rosemary

Small pinch of red pepper flakes

One 14-ounce can cannellini or Great Northern beans, rinsed and drained

2 cups cherry tomatoes, halved and set in a dish to collect the juice

1 tablespoon fresh lemon juice

Salt

Peel, clean, and devein the shrimp.

Finely mince the garlic. Place half the garlic in a bowl, add the shrimp and 2 tablespoons of the olive oil, and stir to combine. Cover with plastic wrap and refrigerate for 30 to 60 minutes.

Combine the remaining garlic, remaining 2 tablespoons olive oil, the rosemary, and red pepper flakes in a medium saucepan. Cook over medium heat until the garlic has cooked a bit but has not browned, about 1 minute.

Add the beans to the pan and stir to coat. Cover and cook over low heat until warmed through, about 5 minutes. Remove from the heat and stir in the cherry tomatoes with their juice, the lemon juice, and a pinch of salt. Taste for seasoning. Let sit at room temperature while you cook the shrimp.

Preheat the broiler.

Arrange the shrimp in a single layer on a rack on a rimmed sheet pan or on a broiler pan. Broil about 4 inches from the heat for 2 minutes per side until the shrimp are cooked through. Let cool for a few minutes.

Arrange individual servings of the bean and tomato mixture on plates and place the cooked shrimp on top. Serve slightly warm or at room temperature.

Baked Red Snapper with Artichokes and Cherry Tomatoes

Some city cooks don't cook fish because it smells up their apartments. For days! But baking keeps the stink at bay, and it's a gentle way to cook delicate white fish like snapper or sea bass.

Choose any firm white fish, such as red snapper or tilapia. Sole is too fragile and will be overwhelmed by the tomato and artichoke. Also avoid meaty fish such as salmon or tuna. If you're buying your fillets from a good fishmonger, ask to have a whole fish of your choice filleted. You may be surprised at its better flavor.

When choosing cherry tomatoes, look for the round kind, not the little grape tomatoes (too sweet and not juicy enough). The ones that come in a mesh bag and are still on the vine are ideal.

Fresh artichokes are seasonal (spring and fall) and not always available. They are also a huge amount of work to prepare for this recipe. If it's the time of year when the artichokes are gorgeous and you have the time to trim four large artichokes down to their hearts, then by all means use fresh instead of canned or frozen. But this is the kind of recipe for which there is no shame in using something that comes out of a can.

Serves 4

2 cups cherry tomatoes

1 tablespoon grated lemon zest (a Microplane zester is perfect)

8 cloves garlic, smashed with the heel of your chef's knife and peeled

1½ tablespoons small capers, rinsed

⅓ cup extra virgin olive oil

Four 4-ounce firm white fish fillets, such as tilapia, snapper, or flounder

One 13.5-ounce can artichoke hearts, rinsed, or one 9-ounce box frozen artichoke hearts, completely defrosted

1 to 2 tablespoons fresh lemon juice

Salt

Freshly ground black pepper

Preheat the oven to 350°F.

Place the tomatoes, lemon zest, garlic, and capers in a large baking dish or small roasting pan. Drizzle with half of the olive oil and gently toss so that everything is coated and combined. Bake for 20 minutes.

Remove the pan from the oven. Add the fish fillets, skin side down, inserting them into the tomatoes, which by now will have cooked and wrinkled a bit, throwing off some juice.

Squeeze the artichokes to remove any excess moisture and cut each one in half. Add the artichokes to the fish and drizzle with the remaining oil. Cook until the fish is fully opaque, a little golden, and cooked through, 15 to 20 minutes. At this point the tomatoes will be wrinkled and their juice will be mixed with the oil and liquid that cooked out of the fish.

Drizzle with lemon juice, sprinkle with salt and pepper, and serve.

Baked Salmon with Leeks and Dill

I was given this recipe by Dorian Mecir, owner of Dorian's Seafood Market on Manhattan's Upper East Side, who credited it to a long-ago customer. It's become my absolutely favorite way to cook salmon. In this easy dish a quick sauté of leeks and herbs is baked with salmon, producing tender fish and a flavorful sauce.

Serve with boiled rice and a green vegetable such as steamed green beans or broccolini, letting any extra sauce combine with the rice and vegetable.

Serves 4

1 large or 2 small leeks, white and tender green parts only, well rinsed

1 pound salmon fillet, center cut is preferable

1 tablespoon unsalted butter

2 tablespoons extra virgin olive oil

1 teaspoon finely minced fresh dill or thyme

Salt

Freshly ground black pepper

Preheat the oven to 375°F.

Thinly slice the leeks. You will need about ¾ cup.

Rinse the fish and pat dry with a paper towel. Cut the fillet into large 1½-inch chunks and place in a baking dish.

Heat the butter and olive oil in a sauté pan or skillet over medium-high heat. When the butter foams, add the leeks, fresh herbs, a pinch of salt, and several grinds of fresh pepper. Cook over medium heat until the leek pieces sweat and soften but do not brown.

Pour the leek mixture over the fish. Cover the baking dish with aluminum foil and seal the edges.

Place the fish in the oven and bake for 15 minutes, until the fish is cooked through and opaque.

Serve immediately.

> **TIP:** Leeks are grown in sandy soil, and even if the outside of the stalk is carefully washed, there still may be lots of sand inside. Trim them carefully, then run a knife down the center of the stalk from the top almost through the root. Fan them open and thoroughly rinse with cool water.

Pan-Seared Arctic Char

For the longest time I was reluctant to cook fish, and for good reason—I would often overcook it or fuss too much with it, which meant the result was always disappointing. I finally learned that the best way to cook fish is simply. When I see a fish I'm unfamiliar with, I ask my fishmonger what it's like and how he or she likes to cook it.

This is how I learned about arctic char, a cousin of the salmon that is either wild or raised sustainably. It looks like salmon, has a slightly milder flavor, is a thin, quick-cooking fillet, and is sturdy enough to be prepared in a variety of ways.

But I like arctic char best cooked in a hot skillet with just a little olive oil. I cook mine with the skin still attached because this helps hold it together. If you don't like to eat fish skin, you can always remove it after it's been cooked.

Serves 4

4 skin-on arctic char fillets (about 1½ pounds)

Salt

Freshly ground black pepper

2 tablespoons extra virgin olive oil

1 lemon, cut into wedges

Rinse the fillets and pat dry with a paper towel. Lightly season with salt and pepper.

Heat the olive oil in a large skillet over medium-high heat until the oil shimmers but doesn't smoke.

Add the fish, skin side down, in a single layer. (If your pan is too small to cook it all at once, cook the fish in batches and keep warm in a 200°F oven.) Leave the fish undisturbed—don't fuss with it—for 3 minutes. Turn the fillets over and cook an additional 2 to 3 minutes until cooked through.

Serve immediately with fresh lemon.

Whole Fish Baked in a Salt Crust

In this roasting method, a whole fish is covered in a crust of salt and baked. The crust gives you a tender, juicy fish with a clear, refined flavor, but surprisingly, it doesn't make it salty.

This is the time to buy a whole fish from an excellent fishmonger. Tell him or her how you're going to cook it so that they can prepare it correctly: it should be left whole, with the head and tail on, but it should be gutted and scaled.

It is essential that you use kosher salt, which is coarse. Do not use fine-grained salt because the crust will not hold together.

Serves 2

One 3-pound box kosher salt (Diamond Crystal is perfect but any brand is fine)

6 egg whites

One 2-pound whole fish (sea bass and branzino are both excellent choices), cleaned and scaled

Salt

Freshly ground black pepper

2 to 4 sprigs fresh thyme or rosemary

1 lemon, thinly sliced

1 to 2 teaspoons extra virgin olive oil

Preheat the oven to 375°F. Line a large rimmed sheet pan with a piece of parchment paper.

Combine the kosher salt and egg whites in a large mixing bowl. Using your clean hands, mix the salt and egg whites together until combined. The texture will seem like wet beach sand—and if you have any tiny cuts on your hands, you'll feel the sting of the salt!

Remove the fish from the refrigerator and rinse it with cool water. Pat it completely dry, inside and out, with paper towels. Place the fish in the center of the parchment-lined sheet pan.

Season the fish cavity with salt and pepper and insert the fresh herb sprigs and 3 or 4 lemon slices. Rub the fish with the oil. Using your hands, completely cover the fish with the salt-egg mixture. The crust should be about ½ inch thick. Pat the crust all over to make sure it's intact and sturdy. Make sure that every bit of fish is covered, so that when the crust bakes, the airtight surface keeps in the moisture.

Place the pan in the center of the oven and roast for 25 minutes. The crust will become light golden brown, especially around the edges, and it will completely harden.

Remove from the oven and let rest for about 20 minutes (it will stay warm for up to an hour). When ready to serve, use a small hammer, the back of a chef's knife, or another kitchen tool to crack the crust's hard exterior. Break the crust off in pieces until the fish is entirely revealed. Discard all the pieces of salt crust.

The cooked fish will now be exposed. Remove any skin and cut around the fillet— below the head and above the tail—and place on a serving platter. Remove and discard the center bone and skeleton to access the bottom fillet. Again, cut around the fillet and place it on the serving platter. The skin should remain behind, but if it doesn't, just remove it gently. Discard the head and tail.

The meat will be very tender, so handle it carefully. Serve with slices of fresh lemon.

Jumbo Shrimp with Teriyaki Glaze

Japanese teriyaki sauce is an easy and flavorful way to transform fish, chicken, shellfish, and steak. The slightly sweet sauce is made from a combination of soy sauce, sugar, ginger, and garlic. You can buy it ready-made in a bottle at most grocery stores. But why buy it when it's so easy and quick to make yourself with fresh ingredients?

Because it has sugar in it, teriyaki sauce caramelizes when it's cooked, which also means it can burn. Avoid this by keeping the shrimp 5 to 6 inches below the broiler element.

Serves 4

6 tablespoons regular or low-sodium soy sauce

3 tablespoons firmly packed light brown sugar

1 teaspoon finely grated fresh ginger

1 large clove garlic, finely minced

Small pinch of cayenne pepper

½ teaspoon sesame oil

1½ pounds jumbo shrimp (about 20), peeled and deveined

In a small saucepan, combine the soy sauce, sugar, ginger, garlic, and cayenne pepper and stir to dissolve the sugar. Bring the mixture to a boil over medium-high heat and simmer until it has thickened slightly and coats the back of a spoon, about 2 minutes. Stir in the sesame oil and remove from the heat.

Position your oven rack so that the shrimp will be 5 to 6 inches away from the broiler element. Preheat the broiler to high.

Line a small rimmed sheet pan or broiler pan with aluminum foil. Place a rack in the sheet pan or position the top of the broiler pan back in place. Arrange the shrimp on the rack in a single layer.

Broil the shrimp for 2 minutes, then generously brush the teriyaki glaze on each piece and broil for another 2 minutes.

Using tongs, turn the shrimp over. Brush with glaze, and broil for 2 minutes. Re-apply the glaze and broil for 2 minutes more, for 8 minutes total cooking time. The shrimp should be totally opaque and their surface caramelized with the glaze.

Serve with rice and steamed vegetables such as broccoli and carrots. This glaze works with almost any type of fish and is particularly nice with salmon, tuna, black cod, and halibut.

TIP: You can also serve this recipe as an hors d'oeuvre by using large shrimp instead of the jumbo; serve 2 or 3 on bamboo skewers.

L.A.'s Original Farmers Market
Los Angeles, California

Broiled Black Cod with Miso

Nobu Matsuhisa is a gifted chef whose New York restaurant, Nobu, is famous for its black cod cooked with white miso, a paste made from fermented soy beans. Miso is salty but also complex and meaty, a unique flavor best described by the Japanese term *umami*.

In Nobu's masterful recipe, black cod is marinated for twenty-four hours in a mixture of sake, mirin, and white miso and then grilled and finished in a very hot oven. The result is sweet fish, almost like fish candy. And it is irresistible.

While there is nothing quite like Nobu's version, if you crave the combination of miso's *umami* flavor and black cod's creamy texture on a weeknight, try this recipe.

A tip about black cod: this fish, also called sablefish, is a big fish and is usually sold in large slices that have a centerpiece of bone. You can either cook the piece whole or cut this bone out before cooking. Either way, take this into account when buying the fish—you'll simply need a little more than usual. Also, do not salt the fish because the miso is already very salty.

Miso is sold in most grocers and natural-food stores, usually in the dairy or other refrigerated section.

Serves 4

1½ pounds black cod (leave the skin on so that it holds together while cooking)

1 cup white or red miso

Cut the fish into 4 large serving portions, removing and discarding the center bone. Using your fingers, rub the miso on the fish, coating both sides entirely. Place on a plate, cover with plastic wrap, and refrigerate for 20 to 30 minutes.

When ready to cook, preheat the broiler and arrange the rack so that the fish will cook 4 to 6 inches below the element—if it's too close to the heat, it will cook unevenly.

Remove the fish from the refrigerator and scrape the excess miso off the fish. Place the fish on a broiling pan, skin side up. Broil for 2 to 3 minutes, then turn each piece over and cook until the fish is firm but not flaking apart, another 2 to 3 minutes.

Serve immediately.

How to Get Fish Smells Out of an Apartment

Your kitchen may look clean, but just a few tiny drops of fishy oil can make it smell like a fried clam shack in Essex, Massachusetts. For those of us who don't have a window in the kitchen or a stove that vents to the outdoors, here are some ways to get rid of the fish smells.

- After your fish dinner, clean everything near the stove—surfaces, walls, cabinets. Really clean it, using warm soapy water, and follow it with something like Windex.
- Instead of frying or sautéing fish, poach it (in seasoned water or fish stock) or bake it.
- Make sure any fish garbage is separately bagged and tossed down the trash chute as soon as possible. Just get it out of your apartment.
- If you have a garbage disposal, send half a lemon down the disposal after you've scraped and washed the fishy dishes.
- Got fishy smells on your hands? Wipe them with a cut lemon (open and close your hand so that the lemon juice gets into its tiny creases) and follow with soapy warm water.
- Some people like scented candles, but I think that they only create an olfactory combo of hibiscus and fried tilapia. Not nice.
- Finally, if all the quick cleaning and trash management doesn't work, boil a saucepan of water to which you add some white vinegar and a few cloves, or else a teaspoon of cinnamon and lemon peels. There's something about the acid in the vinegar and lemon peels that seems to counter the oiliness in the air. Whatever the reason, it seems to work, but expect a little lingering vinegar smell in place of the fish.

A final comment: despite the sometimes stink of cooked fish, fresh fish has no smell. I suppose if we only ate sashimi or ceviche or tuna tartare, we'd never have this housekeeping challenge. But who wants to give up perfect pan-seared salmon? Not me.

Pan-Fried Tilapia with Crispy Panko

Tilapia has become a very popular fish and for good reason. It's inexpensive, it's sustainable, much is farmed in U.S. environmentally friendly systems, and it has a mild taste that is flavorful on its own but can also stand up to other ingredients. The fillets are also almost always boneless, a plus for those who have a fear of fish bones.

I like tilapia best when cooked simply, as in this recipe where the fillets are simply coated in panko and pan-fried. This is a cooking method that's good for any home cook who is a bit intimidated by cooking fish because the panko will hold the fillet together and protect it from overcooking. The panko also gets crispy, giving the fish the taste and texture of a modern fish stick without any deep frying. I find it's inevitable that one side of the fish—the first side down—cooks to a more attractive golden brown than the second side. My suggestion is to serve the fish best side up (who checks the underside of a fillet?).

Serve with wedges of fresh lemon, a dab of spicy mayonnaise (page 212), or in the traditional fish-and-chips style with a sprinkle of malt vinegar.

Serves 4

1½ pounds tilapia (about 3 pieces, each of which has 2 fillets)

Salt

Freshly ground black pepper

2 eggs

2 tablespoons water

2 cups panko

2 tablespoons extra virgin olive oil

If the fillets are still in doubles, cut them in half. Rinse, pat dry with a paper towel, and lightly salt and pepper each fillet.

Set up an assembly line with 3 shallow dishes. Add the eggs to one dish, add the water, and lightly mix with a fork. Add the panko to the second dish. Working with one fillet at a time, dip each piece of fish first in the egg mixture and let any excess drip off. Coat both sides of the fillet in the panko. Use your fingers to press the crumbs onto the fish to help them adhere. Place in the third dish in one layer while you repeat with the remaining fillets.

Heat the olive oil in a large skillet over medium-high heat until hot but not smoking. Add the fillets and sauté on both sides until golden brown and completely cooked through, about 3 minutes per side. If the pan is not big enough to hold all the fillets at once, cook the fish in batches, adding more oil if necessary to the skillet. Keep any cooked pieces of fish warm in a 200°F oven.

Serve immediately.

Panko

Panko are light, crunchy Japanese bread crumbs. Unlike dry store-bought crumbs that come in a cardboard cylinder or the soft, fresh bread crumbs you make yourself, panko produces a crunchier, less greasy crust when used to coat fried, sautéed, or baked foods.

Made from rice or wheat flour, most panko crumbs are bland-to-tasteless (so you'll taste the dish and not the topping) and have less salt and fewer calories than regular bread crumbs. They're also coarser and larger than ordinary crumbs, stay crisper longer, and are an appealing alternative to cracker, matzo, or cereal crumbs that cooks sometimes use in an effort to get a crunchier finish.

Panko is usually sold by the bag. Look for it near the bread crumbs or in the Asian food or fish departments of most supermarkets. Once you open a package, store it in the refrigerator or freezer.

Use panko to coat foods that will be sautéed or fried, including turkey cutlets, chicken breasts, pork chops, fish fillets, whole shrimp, onion rings, whole mushrooms, and even tofu. Just dip whatever you're cooking in flour (shake off any excess), then egg, and finally the panko, and proceed with your recipe.

Panko is also great for the top of fish fillets or casseroles such as macaroni and cheese because the crumbs will add only texture, not flavor, to the dish (unless you season the crumbs).

Salade Niçoise with Pan-Grilled Fresh Tuna

This main-course salad is easiest to serve on a huge platter with each element arranged separately. Then everyone can take what he or she likes. This also makes it a perfect dish for entertaining in a small apartment, where buffets are sometimes easier than a sit-down meal.

There are three keys to the wonderful flavor of this salad. First, dress each element separately and lightly so that the flavors of the vegetables and fish stand on their own. You can pass a small dish of extra vinaigrette for anyone who wants more dressing. Second, buy top-quality tuna steaks and cook them only to medium rare, to keep the fish from drying out and becoming tasteless. Finally, the salad tastes best if everything is served at room temperature rather than chilled.

Serve with a loaf of great bread and a chilled white wine, and add a fruit crisp or cobbler for dessert to make a perfect and bountiful meal.

Serves 4

Anchovy Vinaigrette (recipe follows)

1 pound baby fingerling, Yukon Gold, Red Bliss, or other locally farmed potatoes, with the skins left on, scrubbed (about 2 cups potatoes)

Salt

1 pound haricots verts (also called French beans), trimmed

2 cups shredded red cabbage

2 ripe large tomatoes, or 1 heaping cup cherry tomatoes

4 eggs

1½ pounds top-quality tuna steaks, at least 1 inch thick

Olive oil

Freshly ground black pepper

2 cups baby arugula, mesclun, or other young salad greens

1 cup small mozzarella balls, often called bocconcini (not traditional but good)

1 to 2 cups roasted or marinated artichoke hearts, cut into large pieces (from a good Italian deli; not frozen or canned)

Make the Anchovy Vinaigrette.

Place the potatoes in a saucepan filled with salted cold water. Bring to a boil over high heat, then lower the heat for a strong simmer and cook for 12 to 15 minutes total. When the potatoes are just tender through—be careful not to overcook them—remove from the heat and drain. Transfer to a medium bowl. If the potatoes are not bite-size, cut them in half. Toss the warm potatoes with 2 to 3 tablespoons of the vinaigrette. Set aside.

Fill a saucepan (the one you just used to cook the potatoes is perfect) with water, add a generous pinch of salt, and bring to a boil. Add the haricots verts and cook until just tender, about 3 minutes. Using a slotted spoon, remove the beans and immediately plunge them into a large bowl of iced water. This stops the cooking and also helps retain the bright green color. Drain completely and pat dry with paper towels. Transfer to a bowl and toss with 1 to 2 tablespoons of the vinaigrette. Set aside.

Place the shredded cabbage in a large bowl and toss with about 2 tablespoons of the vinaigrette. Set aside.

Core and cut the large tomatoes into large chunks. If using cherry tomatoes, either leave them whole or cut in half. Set aside.

Bring the eggs to a boil in a small saucepan filled with cold water, then simmer for 10 minutes. Cool the eggs in cold water. Peel and cut into quarters. Set aside.

To cook the tuna steaks, place a cast-iron grill pan or sauté pan over high heat and let it become blazing hot. Cut the tuna steaks into large pieces, about 6 by 2 inches, and rub with a small amount of olive oil, enough to just slick the surface. Sprinkle with salt and pepper. Place the fish in the hot pan and cook for about 2 minutes per side. You want to sear and slightly crisp each surface but leave the interior red. Be careful not to overcook the fish.

Remove the fish from the pan and let it cool to room temperature on a plate. Cut each piece on a diagonal into thick 1-inch slices.

To assemble the salad, begin by placing a mound of arugula or mesclun in the center of a very large platter. Working around the center, arrange each ingredient in its own pile. Take color and texture into account and insert the quarters of the hard-cooked eggs between the other components. Gently place the pieces of pan-grilled tuna on top of the center mound of salad greens. Add the mozzarella balls and artichoke hearts.

Let each person serve her or himself from the platter. Pass a bowl of extra vinaigrette separately.

Anchovy Vinaigrette

2 anchovies (oil-packed are perfect), very finely minced

3 tablespoons red wine vinegar

1 generous teaspoon Dijon mustard

½ teaspoon salt

¼ teaspoon freshly ground black pepper

¼ cup extra virgin olive oil

¼ cup canola oil

Place the anchovies, vinegar, and mustard in a medium bowl. Using a fork or a whisk, combine them.

Add the salt and pepper and stir to dissolve the salt.

Gradually whisk in the olive and canola oils.

Taste and adjust the seasoning. Set aside until you're ready to serve, but remix before adding to the vegetables.

> **TIP:** If you want to leave out the anchovies, that's fine. But anchovies are a classic Niçoise ingredient that add a complex salty but not fishy flavor to the dressing. If you leave them out of the vinaigrette, you may want to add a couple of anchovies to the salad platter for anyone who loves these salty little fish.

Salmon Cakes with Spicy Sriracha Mayonnaise

Canned salmon is wild salmon, processed and canned right as the fish are caught wild in Alaska. A 14-ounce can will make six cakes, serving three as a main course or six as a starter. Because canned wild salmon is significantly less expensive than fresh, this becomes a real budget meal.

Canned salmon is already cooked, so making these cakes is similar to making crab cakes—you just combine the flaked fish with something to bind it together and then sauté until it's heated through. In this recipe I use cracker crumbs and an egg as a binder. Any saltine cracker will do, but choose ones without salted tops, otherwise your salmon cakes may be too salty. If you can't find no-salt saltines, you can substitute panko for the crushed crackers.

It's fine to discard any pieces of skin that you find in the can, and you should drain off any liquid. But don't throw away the tiny bones—instead just crush the larger ones in your fingers and mix in with the fish where they'll disappear during the cooking—you won't know they're there but the calcium will be a healthy boost to your diet.

I like to serve these cakes with the spicy mayonnaise.

Serves 3 as a main course or 6 as a starter

Spicy Sriracha Mayonnaise (recipe follows)

1 large egg

½ teaspoon dry mustard

¼ teaspoon Old Bay seasoning

1 teaspoon Worcestershire sauce

¼ teaspoon sriracha sauce (see Tip) or other hot sauce

Pinch of salt

¼ teaspoon freshly ground black pepper

One 14-ounce can wild salmon, drained and flaked into large pieces

½ cup no-salt saltine cracker crumbs or panko

3 tablespoons extra virgin olive oil

Make the Spicy Sriracha Mayonnaise. Refrigerate until ready to serve.

In a mixing bowl, combine the egg, mustard, Old Bay seasoning, Worcestershire sauce, sriracha sauce, salt, and black pepper.

Add the salmon and cracker crumbs and, using a fork, gently combine, taking care not to break up the pieces of fish too much.

Using your clean hands, form the fish into 6 cakes of equal size, about 3 inches in diameter and about ½ inch thick. If the patties fall apart a little, use your fingers to push them back together again.

Add the olive oil to a sauté pan and heat over medium high heat. Add the salmon cakes and sauté until the surface is golden brown and crusty, about 2 minutes a side.

Serve immediately and pass the spicy mayonnaise.

Spicy Sriracha Mayonnaise

½ cup regular or reduced-fat mayonnaise (homemade always makes a big difference but if you don't have the time, Hellmann's is excellent)

½ to 1 teaspoon sriracha or other hot sauce, or to taste

Combine the mayonnaise and hot sauce. Taste and add more hot sauce if you want more heat. Add more gradually and keep tasting until you get it right.

Refrigerate until ready to serve.

> **TIP:** Sriracha sauce is a spicy sauce made from chiles and garlic. It can be found in Asian markets and many supermarkets and grocers either in the Asian food section or alongside other hot sauces.

Fish Talk—A Guide to Buying Seafood

As more of us buy and cook seafood, we need to know where it comes from and how it was caught. Our best fishmongers are giving us help by labeling the fish and shellfish sold in their stores. Here are some of the terms you'll see.

Farmed. These are fish and shellfish—most commonly salmon, tilapia, catfish, shrimp, mussels, and trout—that are raised commercially in tanks, nets, or other enclosures. A third of our seafood comes from farms around the world where they're fed manufactured feed pellets made from a combination of vegetables and fish. Not all farms are the same, and seafood from a farmed source isn't necessarily bad.

Organic. There's probably no other term in today's food world that's more confusing, but primarily it means farmed fish that are certified to have eaten only antibiotic-free organic food. The label is based only on the fish's diet, not its living conditions nor whether the fish farm is pollutant-free.

Wild. These are caught by a boat in the open sea using some combination of methods, including dredging, harpooning, hook and line, traps, and netting. Some of these methods are kinder to the environment than others; the better ones, such as harpooning, catch individual fish only whereas dredging can cause habitat damage. It can be a challenge to know how a wild fish was caught.

Sustainable. The sea is not inexhaustible. "Sustainable seafood" refers to the principle—and practice—of fishing, buying, and eating only fish and shellfish that are from sources that don't exploit or deplete a population or ecosystem. This term applies to both farmed and fished (that is, wild) sources.

Labeling. As of April 4, 2004, all seafood merchants, including fishmongers, supermarkets, and restaurants, are required to know where all unprocessed seafood is from and whether it is farm raised or wild caught. Merchants are required to keep the tags on everything they sell, so you can ask to see this government documentation.

Still confused? Many of us are. One of the best sources for reliable information is SeafoodWatch.org, operated by the Monterey Bay Aquarium in California, which maintains current listings of what's best to buy and what to avoid. The site includes all this information that you can print out on a handy card and carry in your wallet.

Desserts and Other Treats

I think of dessert as a final flourish instead of a milestone, and that is what I've tried to share here.

While I love to bake, especially pies and tarts, I've included few such recipes here. That's partly because our city bakeries do them so well. But their omission is also based on my experience that unless it's a special occasion, people prefer desserts that are lighter and more refreshing. As a result, most of these sweet recipes are made with seasonal fruits or are meant to be eaten in small but still very satisfying bites.

Almond Cream Tart

Classic Apple Crisp

Maryland Peach Cobbler

Stone Fruit Kuchen

Baked Apples Stuffed with Cinnamon Sugar

Roasted Pineapple

Watermelon–Chocolate Chip Sorbet

Pavlova with Seasonal Fruit

Grand Marnier Soufflé

Milk Chocolate Cream Pie

Baked Apricots with Toasted Almonds

Chocolate Shortbread Buttons

Almond Pignoli Cookies

Jan Hagel Cinnamon Cookies

Tangy Lemon Tea Bread

Rhubarb Compote

Cranberry Pecan Conserve

Almond Cream Tart

I learned this recipe in one of the first cooking classes I ever took. I was so intimidated by the prospect of cooking that I chose a class in which nothing was hands-on: the students only watched, learning by looking, not touching. Although this may seem odd, in retrospect it was the perfect way for a twenty-something to get her first exposure to French technique.

Soon after that class I faced my fear and attempted this recipe, with a triumphant result. Over the years I've made it part of my regular repertoire. If you're not interested in making your own pastry dough, it's okay to use a premade pie crust (they're in the frozen food case), but do try to make your own—the flavor is much better.

This tart is intensely almond flavored and not too sweet. A small slice with a dollop of Cognac whipped cream (page 218) and a glass of Cognac is a satisfying way to end a special dinner.

Makes a 10- or 12-inch tart

All-Butter Pastry Dough (recipe follows)

2 cups skin-on sliced almonds (about 12 ounces)

1½ cups heavy cream

3 tablespoons all-purpose flour

3 tablespoons Cognac, good rum, or kirsch

1 teaspoon almond extract

3 tablespoons sugar

Cognac Cream (recipe follows)

Make the pastry dough.

Preheat the oven to 375°F. Position a rack on the lowest level of the oven and a second rack at the upper third.

Remove the pastry dough from the refrigerator and roll to a circle about 1 inch larger than your tart pan and about ¼ inch thick. Using the rolling pin, transfer the pastry dough to the tart pan and press it into place. Trim the edges so that the dough is even to the top of the rim of the pan.

Fill the tart shell with the almonds to just under the top of the rim of the pan.

In a bowl or large measure with a pouring lip, combine the cream, flour, Cognac, almond extract, and sugar. Stir with a fork to dissolve the flour and sugar but don't whip.

Place the tart pan on a rimmed sheet pan to save your oven from any spills during cooking. Pour the cream mixture over the almonds, keeping the liquid below the pan's top. You may have a little liquid left over depending on the size of your pan, the thickness of the pastry dough, and the volume of almonds.

Bake the tart at 375°F on the lowest oven rack for 15 minutes. Lower the oven temperature to 300°F and move the tart to the upper third of the oven. Continue baking until it's fully set and the edges are golden brown, 25 to 35 minutes longer.

Let cool completely. Make the Cognac cream and serve.

All-Butter Pastry Dough

Makes enough for 1 tart shell

1¼ cups all-purpose flour

1 tablespoon sugar

¼ teaspoon salt

½ cup (1 stick) unsalted butter, very cold, cut into ½-inch pieces

3 to 6 tablespoons iced water

Place the flour, sugar, and salt in a food processor fitted with the steel blade and pulse once to combine. Sprinkle the butter over the flour mixture and pulse 4 or 5 times, 1 second for each pulse. The mixture should resemble coarse meal.

Transfer this mixture to a large mixing bowl. Add the iced water, 1 tablespoon at a time, and combine with a fork until large clumps form and the dough starts to hold together. If you need more moisture, sprinkle additional iced water, gradually and in tiny amounts, so that you don't get it too wet. (Although if this happens, don't panic; just gather up the finished dough and pat it with small amounts of extra flour until you achieve a tender, workable consistency.) Adding the iced water by hand and not all at once in the food processor gives you vastly more control and a better, flakier result.

Gather the dough into a ball, flatten into a disc, wrap in plastic wrap, and chill in the refrigerator for about 30 minutes. (You can make the dough up to a day in advance, keeping it in the refrigerator.)

Cognac Cream

1 cup heavy cream, cold

1 tablespoon confectioners' sugar

2 tablespoons Cognac

Whip the cream until soft peaks form.

Add the confectioners' sugar and Cognac and continue to whip until slightly firm peaks form.

Pike Place Market
  Seattle, Washington

Classic Apple Crisp

Nothing pleases me more than this simple apple crisp. I've eaten world-class sweets in very fancy restaurants and patisseries, but this remains my all-time favorite dessert. I love how the grainy, sweet cinnamon topping contrasts with the tang of the soft cooked, sliced apples underneath. The prep takes about a half hour and then it's an hour in the oven. I like this best with Granny Smith apples because they have a bright taste and hold their shape, but it would be good with almost any apple.

Serves 6

6 Granny Smith apples, peeled, cored, and cut into ¼- to ⅜-inch slices

1 cup all-purpose flour

1 cup sugar

1½ teaspoons ground cinnamon

½ teaspoon salt

½ cup (1 stick) unsalted butter, cold, cut into pieces

Optional: ¾ cup small pieces pecans, toasted

Preheat the oven to 350°F. Have ready an 8-inch cake pan or 8- to 10-inch ceramic baking dish. If you use a cake pan, grease it lightly with unsalted butter. A ceramic baking dish won't need to be greased.

Arrange the apple slices in layers in the pan, filling it almost to the top. As the apples cook they will soften and sink a bit, but you still need to leave room for the topping.

Combine the flour, sugar, cinnamon, and salt in a food processor, using the steel blade. Add the butter, and with 4 or 5 quick pulses, process until the mixture resembles coarse meal. You can also combine all the ingredients in a mixing bowl and work them together with a fork.

If you're adding the pecans, stir them into the mixture with a fork.

Press the topping evenly over the apple slices, making sure the entire surface is covered.

Bake until the top is golden brown and the apples are tender, about 1 hour.

Serve warm with ice cream or whipped cream, or plain at room temperature. Leftovers are brilliant for breakfast.

Maryland Peach Cobbler

I first baked this recipe many years ago with my friend Pat at her family home on the Eastern Shore of Maryland. We used local peaches that had a deep yellow flesh and a strong, sweet perfume that became even more intense after baking. This recipe works well with any in-season and flavorful peaches. Make sure they're fully ripe for the best result.

Serves 6

1 teaspoon unsalted butter for the baking dish

⅓ cup plus 2 tablespoons sugar

1 cup plus 2 tablespoons all-purpose flour

½ teaspoon ground cinnamon

6 to 8 large peaches, peeled and cut into ½-inch slices (6 cups)

2 tablespoons unsalted butter, cold

⅓ cup unsalted butter, at room temperature

1 large egg, beaten

1½ teaspoons baking powder

½ teaspoon salt

3 tablespoons milk

Preheat the oven to 350°F.

Butter a 9-inch round or 8-inch square cake pan or baking dish about 2 inches deep. In a large bowl, combine 2 tablespoons sugar, 2 tablespoons flour, and the cinnamon. Add the peaches and stir to coat. Transfer the peaches to the buttered pan and dot with 2 tablespoons cold butter.

In another large bowl, either by hand or using a handheld mixer, cream the softened butter until light and fluffy, about 5 minutes. Add the egg and blend.

Sift 1 cup flour with the remaining ⅓ cup sugar, the baking powder, and salt. Stir the dry ingredients into the butter mixture, alternating with the milk. Do not overmix.

Using a spatula, spread the batter over the peaches as evenly as possible so it covers the fruit.

Bake until the fruit is bubbly and the topping is golden brown, about 30 minutes.

Serve while still warm with whipped or poured heavy cream.

Stone Fruit Kuchen

My friend Karin Giger, a New Orleans city cook, sent me this Giger family recipe. It's a perfect showcase for very ripe summer peaches, apricots, and plums.

Serves 12

2 cups all-purpose flour

¼ teaspoon baking powder

½ teaspoon salt

1 cup sugar

½ cup (1 stick) unsalted butter, at room temperature

6 peaches, 7 plums, or 12 apricots, halved and pitted (peel the peaches first)

1 teaspoon ground cinnamon

2 large egg yolks

1 cup heavy cream

Preheat the oven to 400°F.

Make the shortbread base by sifting together the flour, baking powder, salt, and 2 tablespoons of the sugar into a bowl. Combine with the softened butter using a pastry blender or 2 knives until you have the consistency of coarse meal. If you work quickly, you can also do this with your fingers.

Pat the dough in an 8-by-12-inch Pyrex or ovenproof ceramic dish, covering the bottom and halfway up the sides.

Add the fruit, cut side up, in a single layer.

In a small bowl, combine the cinnamon with the remaining sugar and scatter the mixture over the fruit.

Bake for 15 minutes.

Whisk together the egg yolks and cream and pour over the fruit. Lower the oven temperature to 350°F and bake for an additional 30 to 40 minutes. The shortbread crust should be browned a little, and the custard firm and slightly golden brown.

Serve warm, perhaps with a scoop of vanilla ice cream. It also makes a wonderful breakfast the next day.

Baked Apples Stuffed with Cinnamon Sugar

Baked apples are a homey, sweet dish that can be dessert or part of breakfast or brunch. Everyone seems to love them. Like most of my dinner guests, I generally prefer this simple, fragrant dessert to one that is more elaborate or complex.

In this recipe the apples are filled with the same mixture I use to top my apple crisp. So when I'm making a crisp, I'll make extra topping and freeze it so that I can bake a single apple for myself without having to make a whole batch of topping.

Serves 4

4 Rome apples, rinsed and patted dry

½ cup all-purpose flour

½ cup sugar

¾ teaspoon ground cinnamon

Pinch of salt

4 tablespoons (½ stick) unsalted butter, cold, cut into ½-inch cubes

1 cup apple juice, apple-cranberry juice, or water mixed with ¼ cup brown or granulated sugar

Preheat the oven to 375°F.

Remove the stems from the apples. Using an apple corer, paring knife, or melon baller, scoop out the core from each apple, leaving about ½ inch of the apple intact at the bottom. Do not cut all the way through the apple. Create a cavity about 1 inch wide. Peel each apple halfway so that the top half is peeled and the bottom half remains protected.

In a food processor with the metal blade, combine the flour, sugar, cinnamon, and salt. Scatter the butter on top and pulse until combined and crumbly.

Arrange the apples, peeled side up, in an ovenproof glass or ceramic baking dish. Using a teaspoon, fill the cavities of the apples with the filling, making a small mound of filling at the top. Pour the apple juice into the baking dish. It should come up about ¼ inch around the apples.

Bake uncovered until tender and slightly brown, 45 to 50 minutes.

TIP: Rome apples are perfect for baking. They hold their shape while becoming tender and develop a sweet, full flavor after they've been cooked.

TIP: To make baked apples a fancier dessert, serve with a crème anglaise. An easier alternative is to zap about a cup of good-quality vanilla ice cream in the microwave until it's just melted to a sauce consistency. It will be almost identical to crème anglaise but with a fraction of the effort. Drizzle a few spoonfuls of the melted ice cream over the baked apple, letting it puddle around the bottom of the serving dish.

Roasted Pineapple

This simple method for cooking pineapple brings out its natural, sweet juiciness. Adjust the amount of sugar depending on how sweet and ripe your pineapple is.

Serves 4 to 6

1 ripe large pineapple

4 tablespoons (½ stick) unsalted butter, melted

½ to ¾ cup packed light brown sugar (taste the pineapple for sweetness and use less if possible)

Preheat the oven to 400°F. Line a large rimmed sheet pan with a piece of parchment paper.

Peel the pineapple, removing all of its thick, prickly skin. This is most easily done with a serrated bread knife. Make sure you remove all the brown eyes.

Cut the pineapple lengthwise into 4 wedges. Cut off and discard the thick, fibrous core of each segment. Cut the wedges again into 4 pieces so that you have 16 wedges, each the length of the peeled pineapple and about ½ inch thick.

Place the pieces on the lined sheet pan. Using a pastry brush, coat each piece with melted butter and sprinkle with half the brown sugar.

Roast for 10 minutes. Turn each pineapple piece over, brush with more melted butter, and sprinkle with the remaining brown sugar. Roast until the pieces are bubbling in the pan and the fruit is golden, another 5 to 10 minutes, or about 20 minutes in total.

The Versatility of Roasted Pineapple

A slice of roasted pineapple is sweet and complex on its own, although a scoop of vanilla ice cream adds a cool finish to the warm and tangy fruit.

You can also:

- Serve with a scoop of coconut sorbet (achieving the taste of a piña colada).
- Drizzle with a little butterscotch or caramel sauce.
- Make pineapple shortcakes by buying or making shortcake biscuits and adding a generous spoonful of whipped cream.
- Purée in a food processor or blender, chill, add 1 tablespoon dark rum, and use an ice cream maker to turn it into roasted pineapple sorbet.
- Fold chunks into your favorite coffeecake recipe.
- Top a prebaked tart shell that's been filled with pastry cream or vanilla pudding for a quick roasted pineapple tart.

Watermelon–Chocolate Chip Sorbet

Watermelon sorbet is one of the best summer desserts that's ever been invented. Because the fruit is naturally sweet, you only need to add a little bit of sugar syrup. The chocolate chips add flavor and make the sorbet look like fresh watermelon—complete with seeds.

Makes 1 quart

1 cup sugar

1 cup water

4 to 6 cups cubed watermelon (about ¼ of a midsized watermelon)

1 to 2 tablespoons unflavored vodka

1 cup semisweet chocolate chips or small chunks from a dark chocolate bar

In a saucepan, combine the sugar and water. Bring to a boil over medium-high heat. Cook at a low boil or high simmer, stirring occasionally, until the sugar has completely dissolved, about 10 minutes. Remove the syrup from the heat and let cool completely. This sugar syrup can be made in advance and refrigerated until you're ready to use it.

Prepare your watermelon by cutting the pieces from the inner, darkest part of the melon where it's the sweetest. Make the effort to remove all the seeds, including the little white ones. Place the cubes of melon in a food processor fitted with the steel blade and process until the fruit is completely smooth and liquefied. Pour the puréed fruit through a fine-mesh sieve set over a 4-cup glass measure. Press down on the fruit in the sieve to extract all the juice. Discard the solids.

Add the sugar syrup and stir. You should have about 4 cups of dark pink, very sweet purée that has a strong watermelon flavor. Cover and refrigerate until it's well chilled, at least 1 hour or longer.

When the purée is very cold, add the vodka and stir to combine.

Pour the mixture into your ice cream maker and freeze according to the manufacturer's instructions until fully thickened, slushy, and frozen (this may take 20 minutes or so). Stir in the chocolate chips, transfer to a plastic container, and freeze until it reaches its finished frozen state.

TIP: Ready your ice cream maker by placing the drum in your freezer for at least 24 hours before you plan to make this dessert. Also, try to make this sorbet at least 8 hours before you plan to serve it, so it has time to fully freeze.

TIP: The vodka keeps the sorbet from turning into a solid block of ice after you place it in the freezer, but it adds no discernable taste. If you don't want alcohol in your sorbet, be attentive to how long you freeze the finished mixture or else warm it at room temperature for a bit before serving it so that it can soften.

Pavlova with Seasonal Fruit

Pavlova is a traditional Australian light meringue cake dessert named in honor of the famous Russian ballerina Anna Pavlova. The outside of the meringue is firm but the inside is soft, like marshmallow.

It is important not to rush the meringue's baking; the long cooking at a low temperature means it will become light and crisp but remain pale in color.

Serves 8

4 large egg whites, at room temperature

1 cup superfine sugar

1 teaspoon white vinegar

1½ teaspoons cornstarch

1 cup heavy cream, cold

1½ teaspoons confectioners' sugar

½ teaspoon pure vanilla extract

2 pints raspberries, or 2 cups of sliced strawberries, passion fruit purée, or sliced kiwi fruit

Preheat the oven to 250°F. Position a rack in the middle of the oven. Line a sheet pan with parchment paper.

In the bowl of an electric mixer, whisk the egg whites on medium-high speed until they form soft peaks. Start adding the superfine sugar, 1 tablespoon at a time, and continue beating until the meringue forms very stiff peaks. If the meringue feels gritty, continue to beat as the sugar has not fully dissolved.

Use a spatula to thoroughly fold in the vinegar and cornstarch.

Using the same spatula, spread the meringue in a 12-inch circle on the lined sheet pan. Don't fuss too much as it will spread out a bit during the cooking process.

Bake until the surface is dry and a very pale cream color, about 60 minutes. It needs to cook slowly and should not be brown. Turn off the oven and leave the meringue inside until it is completely cooled.

When you are ready to serve, place the meringue on a serving plate. Whip the cream, adding the confectioners' sugar and vanilla just before the cream is fully whipped into soft but firm peaks.

Spread the whipped cream on top of the meringue and top with the fruit. Use a serrated bread knife to cut into generous wedges.

> **TIP:** To ensure the egg whites whip to the firmest peak, make sure your mixing bowl, beater, and spatula are spectacularly clean—the smallest amount of grease will compromise the whipping process.

> **TIP:** The cooled meringue can be made and stored in a cool dry place, in an airtight container, for a few days or you can leave it in the oven overnight. However, once you add the cream and fruit, you should eat it that day. Leftovers can be put in the fridge, but the meringue will start to soften so it won't taste as interesting as it did on day one.

Grand Marnier Soufflé

Soufflés are surprisingly easy to make, and this recipe for a sweet dessert soufflé will be the center drama of any dinner party. You can make the base a couple of hours in advance, but for the best results, beat the egg whites and assemble the soufflé just before baking. Serving it immediately after you take it out of the oven is essential for the WOW factor and best flavor.

Grand Marnier is a French orange-flavored liqueur that is a mix of Cognac and bitter orange. This classic dessert soufflé is splendid on its own, or you can pass a bowl of whipped cream, vanilla custard sauce, or even some vanilla ice cream that's been melted into a sauce.

Make sure you do not skip the step of preparing the soufflé dish by lining it with a thin layer of butter and a dusting of sugar, since this is essential if the mixture is going to rise up the straight sides of the baking dish.

Serves 6 to 8

3 tablespoons unsalted butter, plus extra to prepare the soufflé dish

6 tablespoons granulated sugar, plus extra to dust the soufflé dish

3 tablespoons all-purpose flour

1 cup heavy cream

5 large egg yolks

5 tablespoons Grand Marnier

6 large egg whites

½ teaspoon cream of tartar

Confectioners' sugar for garnish

Prepare a 2-quart soufflé dish (approximately 8 inches in diameter and 4 inches high) by coating the bottom and sides with butter, dusting with sugar, and shaking out any excess. Set aside in a cool place or refrigerate until ready to fill.

Melt the butter in a large saucepan over low heat or in a heatproof bowl placed over a pan of simmering water. Add the flour and cook, whisking, just until blended, about 1 minute. Keeping the heat low, add the cream and sugar. Stir constantly with a wooden spoon until the sugar has dissolved and the mixture has thickened, 3 to 5 minutes. Remove from the heat and let cool a bit.

In a small bowl, whisk together the egg yolks and Grand Marnier. Add this to the cooked mixture and combine completely. Scrape this mixture into a large mixing bowl. If you're not going to proceed immediately, press a piece of plastic wrap directly onto the surface to prevent it from developing a skin.

Preheat the oven to 375°F.

In a large stainless-steel bowl, use an electric mixer to beat the egg whites and cream of tartar at low speed until the whites become frothy. Increase the speed to high and beat until the peaks are shiny and firm. Be careful not to overbeat or else the whites will become stiff and dry.

Using a rubber spatula, fold one-third of the egg whites into the cooled Grand Marnier mixture so that it is completely combined; fold in the remaining egg whites until just a few streaks remain. Do not overmix.

Gently transfer the mixture to the prepared soufflé dish, filling it about three-quarters full. Place the dish on a rimmed sheet pan. Bake until the soufflé has risen above the rim of the dish and the surface is golden brown, 25 to 30 minutes. Test for doneness by giving the soufflé a very gentle shake; if the top still jiggles, cook for another 1 to 2 minutes until it is completely stable and the surface is puffed and dry.

Dust with confectioners' sugar and serve immediately.

> **TIP:** For individual soufflés, prepare ramekins in the same fashion by buttering and dusting with sugar. Bake the individual soufflés for about 5 minutes less (20 to 25 minutes).

Milk Chocolate Cream Pie

This recipe updates a childhood favorite that my mother would make with a box of My-T-Fine chocolate pudding. In this version I've replaced the boxed mix with an easy and light milk chocolate pudding that uses both cocoa and chunks of milk chocolate but no eggs.

Make the pudding before you bake the crust so the pudding can chill in the refrigerator while the pie crust bakes and cools. The pie is assembled by filling the crust with pudding, topping it with sweetened whipped cream, and decorating with either curls of chocolate or a handful of fresh berries.

This pie begins with a prebaked single pie crust. If you're not a baker or don't have time to make your own pastry, it's fine to bake a store-bought pie crust (they're in the freezer case). But pie crust is simple to make and the difference in flavor and texture makes it worth your time to make your own.

Serves 8

Pie Crust (recipe follows)

2 tablespoons sugar

2 tablespoons cornstarch

2 tablespoons unsweetened cocoa powder

Pinch of salt

2 cups whole milk

4 ounces fine-quality milk chocolate, chopped (not milk chocolate chips, which have stabilizers in them)

1 teaspoon pure vanilla extract

2 teaspoons Kahlúa (coffee liqueur) or rum

Whipped Cream Topping (recipe follows)

Make the dough for the crust but don't roll or bake it.

Sift together the sugar, cornstarch, cocoa, and salt and add to a medium heavy saucepan. Gradually whisk in the milk and bring to a boil over medium-high heat, whisking constantly. Continue to gently boil (making sure the heat isn't too high so that it doesn't burn), still whisking constantly, for about 2 minutes as the mixture becomes thick. Remove from the heat. Immediately add the chocolate and whisk until it melts. Whisk in the vanilla and Kahlúa.

Transfer to a bowl and immediately place a piece of waxed paper or plastic wrap on its surface to prevent a skin from forming.

Refrigerate for at least 2 hours until it's completely chilled. (You can make the pudding in advance and keep it covered and chilled for up to 2 days.) If you are in a hurry, you can place the bowl over a larger bowl containing iced water and stir every couple of minutes until it's completely chilled, about 10 minutes.

Roll out and bake the pie crust.

Remove the pudding from the refrigerator, remove the plastic wrap, and stir the pudding with a wooden spoon or wire whisk to make it soft enough to transfer to the baked pie crust. Use a spatula to smooth its surface. Refrigerate the filled pie for 15 to 30 minutes to let it firm up again.

Make the whipped cream topping. Spread it over the chocolate filling, so it covers the entire surface. Use your spatula to make decorative peaks.

If you're not going to serve the pie immediately, refrigerate it for up to an hour.

> **TIP:** Instead of one big pie, you can make individual tartlets by baking individual tart shells, filling them with chocolate pudding, and covering with whipped cream.

> **TIP:** You can add curls of chocolate as a garnish (pass a vegetable peeler along the surface of a chilled chocolate bar), or you can spoon sliced strawberries or other berries over each plated slice.

Pie Crust

This recipe makes enough dough for a 9-inch pie or tart and combines two fats—butter and shortening. You could also make individual tart shells with this dough. Either way you'll need pie weights—something to fill the crust while it bakes so that the dough doesn't puff up too much. I've used the same container of dried navy beans for many years, but you can also buy metal or ceramic pie weights.

1¼ cups all-purpose flour

1 tablespoon sugar

Pinch of salt

4 tablespoons (½ stick) unsalted butter, very cold, cut into ½-inch pieces

3 tablespoons all-vegetable shortening (Crisco is excellent)

4 to 6 tablespoons iced water

Extra flour for rolling out the dough

Place the flour, sugar, and salt in a food processor fitted with the metal blade and pulse once to combine. Sprinkle the butter over the flour mixture. Pulse 4 or 5 times, 1 second for each pulse. Add the shortening and pulse until the mixture resembles coarse meal. Do not overmix.

Transfer this mixture to a large mixing bowl and add 4 tablespoons iced water. Combine with a fork until large clumps form and the dough starts to hold together. If you need more moisture, sprinkle with additional iced water gradually so that you don't get it too wet. (Although if this happens, don't panic; just gather up the finished dough and pat it with small amounts of extra flour until it achieves a tender, workable consistency.) Adding the iced water by hand and not all at once in the food processor gives you vastly more control and, thus, a better, flakier result.

Gather the dough into a ball, flatten it into a disc, wrap in plastic wrap, and refrigerate for about 30 minutes. (You can store the dough in the refrigerator for up to a day.)

Rolling and Baking the Crust

Remove the dough from the refrigerator and place it on a clean and floured surface. If it's been chilling for more than 30 minutes, let it sit for a few minutes so that it's easier to roll out. Using a rolling pin, roll the dough into a 12-inch circle about ⅛ inch thick. Transfer the dough to a 9-inch pie plate by using your rolling pin. Roll the dough over the pin, lift it over the plate, and roll it into place. If it's off-center just pick up the dough with your hands—it's sturdier than you may think—and center it.

Handling the dough as little as possible, tap it into place in the plate. Using a knife or kitchen scissors, trim the dough so that you have a ½-inch overhang. Flute the edge with your fingers or use a fork to give it a decorative edge. Prick the bottom and sides with the tines of the fork to help keep it from puffing when it bakes. Refrigerate for about 20 minutes before baking.

Preheat the oven to 375°F.

Press a 14-inch length of aluminum foil into the pie plate over the crust. Fill the plate with pie weights (see headnote).

Bake the pie crust in the middle of the oven until the dough begins to dry out, about 15 minutes. Carefully lift the foil and weights out of the crust and bake until the crust is completely cooked and golden brown, 12 to 15 minutes longer.

Cool completely on a rack before filling. You can bake the shell several hours in advance, but it's best the same day; wait longer and it won't be as flaky.

Whipped Cream Topping

1 cup heavy cream, cold

1 heaping tablespoon sugar

Whip the cream until almost soft peaks form. Add the sugar and continue to whip until slightly firm peaks form, about 1 minute total.

Baked Apricots with Toasted Almonds

Fresh apricots are one of summer's best treats, and when baked, their flavor becomes even more intense and luxurious. There's really no need to add a fancy topping, but a little brown sugar and butter help make a sweet syrup as the fruit cooks.

If you want to add some complexity, you can sprinkle them with a little brandy or Cognac before baking or top with a little spoonful of mascarpone or crème fraîche before serving. Save leftovers for breakfast and add them to low-fat Greek yogurt or your favorite cereal.

Serves 4

8 apricots, ripe or almost ripe

2 to 3 tablespoons light brown sugar

2 to 3 tablespoons unsalted butter

Optional: 2 tablespoons brandy or Cognac

¼ cup slivered almonds

Preheat the oven to 400°F.

Cut each apricot in half and remove the stone. (You do not need to peel the fruit as the skin will soften as it cooks). Place the apricot halves cut side up in a shallow baking dish or rimmed sheet pan. It's fine if they crowd together but make sure they're in a single layer. Place about 1 teaspoon brown sugar and a dot of butter on top of each half. If you like, you can also sprinkle them with a little brandy or Cognac but don't add too much—you don't want a pool of liquid in the bottom of the dish. Sprinkle the almonds over the top.

Bake until the fruit is softened and the almonds are toasted golden brown, 15 to 20 minutes.

Serve either warm or at room temperature. If you have leftovers or are cooking the fruit in advance, store covered in the refrigerator until ready to serve.

Chocolate Shortbread Buttons

These cookies are deeply chocolaty and have all the richness of a classic shortbread. But because they're made with cocoa instead of chocolate, they aren't too sweet. I use a small drinking glass to stamp out two-inch discs and then use the prongs of a fork to make two little holes, like the thread holes in a button, making them a cute addition to after-dinner coffee.

Assuming they last that long, these cookies can be stored in an airtight container for up to one week.

Makes about 15 cookies

4 tablespoons (½ stick) unsalted butter, at room temperature

2½ tablespoons sugar, plus more for rolling out the dough

½ teaspoon pure vanilla extract (not vanilla flavoring)

½ cup all-purpose flour

2½ tablespoons unsweetened cocoa powder (either natural or Dutch-processed is fine)

Pinch of fine salt

Preheat the oven to 275°F. Line a sheet pan with parchment paper or a silicone liner.

Using an electric mixer, cream the butter in a mixing bowl until fluffy, about 2 minutes. Add the sugar and vanilla and beat until well blended, about 2 minutes.

Sift together the flour, cocoa, and salt. Add to the butter mixture and mix at medium speed until completely combined and smooth. Using a spatula, transfer the dough to a piece of plastic wrap and refrigerate for about 15 minutes to let the dough rest. (It's okay to refrigerate the dough for longer.)

Sprinkle sugar lightly on a clean counter or cutting board, add the dough, and, using a rolling pin, roll out the dough to form a ⅜-inch-thick circle. Use a 2-inch glass (a shot glass would also work) to stamp out round cookies.

Transfer the discs to the sheet pan, placing the cookies about ½ inch apart (they will not spread). Use the prongs of a fork to make 2 little marks (like on a button) in the center of each disc.

Bake the cookies in the middle of the oven until firm to the touch, 40 to 45 minutes. They will have a rich, chocolate aroma but, as with any shortbread, should not have browned. Let rest for 5 minutes before transferring to a rack to cool completely.

Almond Pignoli Cookies

Pine nuts are the seeds of wild and cultivated pine trees. Because they are labor-intensive to harvest, they can be costly. But used more as an accent than a main ingredient, their rich and satisfying flavor makes them popular in both sweet and savory recipes, including salads, pilafs, and pastries.

In Italy where they're called pignolis, pine nuts add nutty complexity to cookies, especially ones made with almond paste. This recipe was shared with me by Betsy Herold, who would make them for her sister Pat's Christmas holiday gatherings to which I'd be warmly welcomed. I don't know if she knew how many of these cookies would disappear because of me, but they've always been a favorite of mine.

Made with almond paste, sugar, and egg whites, the cookies are finished by rolling them in pignolis so that they look a bit like a porcupine. Unlike most cookies, these include no flour, making them a good choice for those who have a gluten problem.

For the best flavor, try to buy pine nuts that are imported from Europe. They may cost more but they have a far richer, sweeter, and more reliable flavor than those imported from China, which are sometimes thought to leave a bitter, metallic aftertaste.

Makes about 3 dozen cookies (depending upon how large you make them)

1 pound almond paste (not marzipan, which contains sugar)

3 large egg whites

1 cup granulated sugar

2 teaspoons baking powder

1 to 2 cups pine nuts (pignoli)

1 cup confectioners' sugar

Using an electric mixer, combine the almond paste, egg whites, granulated sugar, and baking powder. The dough will be very sticky. Refrigerate for at least 1 hour. The dough can be refrigerated for up to a week, letting you bake cookies in small batches, which can be convenient during the holidays.

Preheat the oven to 350°F.

Roll pieces of the dough into large marble-sized balls (less than 1 inch) and roll in the pine nuts—they will stick to its sticky surface. Place about 1 inch apart on an ungreased sheet pan.

Bake until they are very light brown, about 12 minutes.

Cool on the cookie sheet for 1 minute, then remove to cool completely. When completely cool, dust with confectioners' sugar.

Store for up to a week in an airtight container, so they don't become little sugar-coated rocks.

Jan Hagel Cinnamon Cookies

Many years ago I was invited to attend a country show-horse event at which some very nice tailgating was done. It was a crisp fall day that began with lunches served out of the backs of station wagons and car trunks. My host passed Irish whiskey–spiked coffee along with roast beef sandwiches, paper cups filled with tomato soup, and a basket of these fragrant traditional Dutch cinnamon-almond shortbread cookies. I no longer remember anything about the horses, but this recipe has stayed in my cookie stable all these years.

Makes 30 cookies

1 cup unsalted butter (2 sticks), at room temperature

1 cup sugar

1 large egg, separated

2 cups all-purpose flour

½ teaspoon ground cinnamon

1 tablespoon water

1 cup skin-on sliced almonds

Preheat the oven to 350°F. Lightly butter a small rimmed sheet pan or ovenproof glass baking dish, 9 by 13 inches.

Using an electric mixer, cream together the butter, sugar, and egg yolk until well combined and slightly fluffy, about 2 minutes. Mix together the flour and cinnamon and add to the butter mixture. Mix at medium speed until completely combined.

Pat the dough into an even layer in the prepared pan. The dough can be unwieldy, but pressing it gently with a straight-sided drinking glass or the bottom of a flat measuring cup lightly dusted in flour will help you achieve a flat, even layer.

Using a fork, mix together the egg white and 1 tablespoon water until it's frothy. Brush over the dough and sprinkle with the sliced almonds, covering the surface evenly. Gently press the almond slices onto the dough to help them adhere.

Bake until very lightly browned, about 25 minutes. Be careful not to overcook—don't let the dough or nuts take on more than a little color.

Cut immediately into finger-like bars and let cool completely in the pan.

The Cheese Course

A cheese course can be the centerpiece of a lunch or a luxurious finish to a special dinner. Because it is rich and full flavored, cheese may not be a good choice to follow a heavy meal, but it's a great end to a light menu or in place of a sweet dessert.

- Shop from a good cheese monger for the best selection. Don't hesitate to ask for suggestions.
- Ask to taste each cheese you're about to buy to make sure it's in perfect eat-it-now ripeness.
- Make sure you have at least one each of goat, sheep, and cow's milk cheese, combining hard, soft, runny, and blue.
- Choose flavors ranging from mild to powerful. If the entire plate is full of gentle flavors, it will have less interest; if they're all pungent and stinky, your guests may wish for more variety.
- Buy about one pound total for every four people. Alternatively, plan on three to four tablespoons of each cheese for each person.
- Room temperature is best for both flavor and spreading. If you're serving a cheese course at the end of the meal, take the cheese out of the refrigerator as you sit down for dinner.
- I like to arrange all the cheeses on a single platter or wooden board, with a bunch of grapes in the center. Add a basket of sliced bread and crackers plus small bowls of nuts and dried fruit and ripe fresh pears or apples.
- A classic cheese companion is *membrillo*, a sweet Spanish quince paste sold by many cheese mongers. Other choices could be fig jam, *mostarda* (an Italian preserve that combines fruit jam with a kick of mustard), honey, or an onion confit.
- Place the cheese in a circle or a row ranging from mild to pungent.
- Be prepared to tell your guests what they're having. Write down the name of each cheese and where it's from to prompt your own memory or to make a tabletop cheese menu.
- If there is any cheese left over, wrap it in plastic wrap and then in aluminum foil before returning it to the refrigerator. Otherwise your refrigerator will smell like Gorgonzola, and your Gorgonzola will taste of what's in the refrigerator.

Tangy Lemon Tea Bread

I grew up eating this bread as an after-school snack. Even though it has no yeast, it has a texture that is almost like bread, which makes it fabulous when lightly toasted and served with strawberry jam. The tangy glaze adds even more lemon flavor, plus it keeps the cake from being too sweet and assures its moistness.

Makes 1 loaf

6 tablespoons (¾ stick) unsalted butter

1¼ cups sugar

1½ cups sifted all-purpose flour

1 teaspoon baking powder

1 tablespoon grated lemon zest (a Microplane zester is perfect)

½ teaspoon salt

½ cup chopped walnuts

2 large eggs, lightly beaten

½ cup milk

3 tablespoons fresh lemon juice (1 large or 2 medium lemons)

Preheat the oven to 350°F.

Line a loaf pan (approximately 8½ inches long by 4½ inches wide) with 2 pieces of parchment paper to line the sides and bottom of the pan, leaving about 2 inches of overhang; this will help you remove the cake from the pan once it's baked. You can also use a single piece of paper—if it bunches in the corners, just press it into place.

Using an electric mixer, cream the butter and 1 cup of the sugar together at medium speed until completely combined and slightly fluffy, about 2 minutes.

In a small bowl, whisk together the flour, baking powder, lemon zest, salt, and walnuts so that they're completely mixed.

Add the eggs and milk to the butter mixture and mix at medium speed until just combined. Add the dry ingredients and mix at medium speed until combined, about 1 minute. Your goal is a smooth batter but do not overmix.

Pour the batter into the prepared pan and bake until a cake tester or paring knife inserted into the center comes out clean, about 1 hour.

For the glaze, mix the remaining ¼ cup sugar and the lemon juice in a small bowl.

Remove the cake from the oven and immediately tip it out of the pan. Remove the parchment paper and return the bread to the pan. While the loaf is still hot, pour the glaze over the bread.

Let cool completely in the pan.

Rhubarb Compote

Similar to cranberry sauce, rhubarb compote is a wonderful complement to duck, goose, or roast pork. The sugar in the compote mellows the rhubarb's tart flavor. Because it's sweet, this compote is also delicious when warmed and spooned over ice cream (I prefer it on strawberry ice cream), chilled and mixed with sweetened whipped cream to create a rhubarb fool, or served alongside a slice of plain pound cake.

If you're careful to choose red instead of green rhubarb stalks, the compote will be a pretty pink color.

Makes about 2 cups

6 cups sliced (½ inch) rhubarb

1½ cups sugar

Optional: 1 teaspoon grated lemon or orange zest

In a nonreactive, large saucepan off the heat, combine the rhubarb, sugar, and zest and toss or stir to combine. Let sit until the rhubarb begins to throw off liquid, about 15 minutes. Stir occasionally to help the rhubarb become wetter.

When some sugary rhubarb juice has developed, place the pan over medium-low heat and gently simmer, stirring occasionally, until the rhubarb becomes soft and falls apart, forming a jamlike consistency. This will take 10 to 15 minutes.

Remove from the heat and transfer the compote to a bowl. Let cool.

The compote can be served either warm or cold. It will keep in the refrigerator, covered, for up to 3 days.

> **TIP:** When cooking a highly acidic ingredient like rhubarb or tomatoes, it's best to use a nonreactive pan. Cast-iron, aluminum, and unlined copper are reactive metals; nonreactive materials include stainless steel, glass, and enamelware. When a pan reacts to an ingredient, it can alter the food's flavor and color.

> **TIP:** For a more complex flavor, you can add 1 to 2 tablespoons ruby port or 2 teaspoons orange-flavored liqueur such as Grand Marnier or Cointreau. Use less liqueur than port because the flavor is more concentrated.

Turning Store-Bought into Homemade Desserts

Some home cooks don't like to bake, and others simply don't have time. Take the pressure off by combining store-bought elements to make a satisfying end to dinner. In my experience most people prefer a simple dessert to a fancy bakery-bought pie or cake, and almost everyone loves ice cream. Or just one cookie.

- Bakery-bought brownies, cut into quarters, with good coffee ice cream
- Coconut sorbet with slices of fresh pineapple
- Fresh blueberries with vanilla ice cream
- A large wedge of perfectly ripe Bric and a bowl of green grapes
- A creamy blue cheese such as Fourme d'Ambert with ripe pears
- Fresh raspberries and store-bought lemon cookies
- Ginger cookies and chocolates
- Ice cream sundaes made with *dulce de leche* ice cream and either store-bought or homemade warm caramel sauce
- Shortbread cookies with sliced fresh peaches
- Thick Greek yogurt with honey
- Bakery-bought meringues with fresh berries and just-whipped sweetened cream
- Lemon sorbet with a drizzle of limoncello
- In-season strawberries with separate bowls of sour cream and brown sugar for dipping

Cranberry Pecan Conserve

I have a friend who only likes Thanksgiving dinner because she can have unlimited quantities of cranberry sauce. I understand. But while many of us love cranberry sauce, we sometimes want a little variety, something different than the traditional raw relish or a plain cooked sauce.

A conserve is cooked fruit with a consistency that is more jamlike; it is usually served soon after it's cooked. In this recipe, traditional cranberry flavors are combined with the crunch of toasted pecans, making a flavorful alternative to a traditional cranberry sauce.

There's no reason to only have cranberry flavors during the holidays so buy a few extra bags and keep them in your freezer. They keep nearly forever and usually can go directly into a recipe without thawing.

If your cranberries are frozen, don't bother to defrost them. Just give a quick rinse, pick over them to remove any stems, and put the still-icy berries right into the pot.

Makes about 3 cups

1 cup sugar

½ cup orange juice

¼ cup water

1 tablespoon grated orange zest (a Microplane zester is perfect)

3 cups fresh or frozen cranberries (one 12-ounce bag), rinsed

½ cup coarsely chopped toasted pecans

In a medium saucepan, combine the sugar, orange juice, water, and orange zest. Stir over medium heat until the sugar completely dissolves.

Add the cranberries and stir to combine. Reduce the heat to medium-low and cook, stirring occasionally, until the berries pop. It takes about 5 minutes to cook to a jamlike consistency.

Remove from the heat and stir in the pecans. Pour into a heatproof bowl and let cool.

Refrigerate until you're ready to serve but bring to room temperature for the best flavor. This conserve can be made up to 4 days ahead.

TIP: Toast pecans by spreading them in a single layer in a sheet pan and baking them in a 350°F oven for about 10 minutes. Shake the pan occasionally and watch them closely so that they don't burn. They're usually done when you first detect their toasted aroma.

Matching Dessert to Dinner

I think many home cooks do themselves a disservice when they cook for company by trying to make every course a showstopper. This is a strain not only for the cook but may be as well for the guests. Flavors, quantities, textures, colors, and calories should be balanced over the course of a meal. When deciding on what to serve for dessert, consider the entire repast.

- If a meal has lots of carbs, such as a pasta main course or paella, serve something light, like fruit for dessert.
- If a meal has lots of dairy, such as a cheese sauce on vegetables or tomato and mozzarella salad, don't serve ice cream at the end.
- If you want to make a major dessert like tarte Tatin or chocolate cake, plan the rest of the menu with that in mind. For example, go light on hors d'oeuvres, have a salad to start, and serve fish as the main course, leaving room for the finish.
- Summer meals end well with room-temperature desserts such as fruit pies and cobblers.
- Desserts should be based on the season as much as anything else you cook. Serve berries in the summer, apple pie in the fall, lemon meringue pie in the winter, fresh mangoes in the spring—and chocolate year-round.
- Don't worry about sticking with a single cuisine. It's fun to mix the flavors and ingredients, such as coconut flan for dessert after barbecued pork ribs or shrimp teriyaki.

Buying Great Ingredients: Some of America's Best Urban Markets

While the supermarket is still an urban resource, most American cities have alternatives. Artisanal food is undergoing a resurgence, and there are extraordinary purveyors across the country. Some have been in business for generations, and others are new. All are bringing extraordinary ingredients into our city kitchens.

Today there are butchers, fishmongers, cheese mongers, spice merchants, food halls filled with small shops, and ethnic specialists that let us make authentic recipes of any global cuisine. There are producers who do just one thing (but, wow, do they do it well) like the Natchitoches meat pie shop in New Orleans or the smoked mozzarella specialist in Manhattan's SoHo, plus small grocers that give full-service competition to the mega-markets. And there are bakers who would make anyone's grandmother put her rolling pin into storage.

In addition to the individual merchants listed here, we have hundreds of urban farmers' markets that every day, rain or shine, provide local producers direct contact with urban home cooks. How amazing is that?

I've also listed some of the best online sources for more information about farmers' markets, community supported agriculture, and urban farming.

This list is just a beginning, and I would love nothing more than to have you read it only to pound the table with declarations of all your favorites that I left out. I created this list from my own shopping experience as well as that of friends across the country. Where possible, I've tried to dig deeper than the best-known places (which is the only reason why names like Zabar's aren't included) to put a spotlight on places you might not know.

Some have websites that let you shop long distance, but where possible, I urge you to explore the food merchants in your own city and give them your business. They are an essential part of our food system and a primary reason we can cook the way we do, and as well. Without us, they will disappear.

Baltimore

Lexington Market (food hall)
400 W. Lexington Street
Baltimore, MD 21201
410-685-6169
LexingtonMarket.com

J.W. Faidley Seafood (crab cakes)
203 North Paca Street
Baltimore, MD 21201
410-727-4898
FaidleysCrabCakes.com

Trinacria Macaroni Works (Italian market)
406 North Paca Street
Baltimore, MD 21201
410-685-7285
TrinacriaFoods.com

DiPasquale's Italian Deli & Marketplace
3700 Gough Street
Baltimore, MD 21224
410-276-6787
Dipasquales.com

Prima Foods (Greek and international market)
51 Kane Street
Baltimore, MD 21224
410-633-5500
PrimaFoodsInc.com

Downtown Farmers' Market
On Saratoga Street between Holliday and Gay Streets (under JFX Viaduct)
Sunday, May to December

Other locations in the Baltimore area
mda.state.md.us/md_products/farmers_market_dir.php

Heritage International Food Store (African and Caribbean market)
8727 Liberty Road
Randallstown, MD 21133
410-655-6600

Punjab Groceries and Halal Meat
345 East 33rd Street
Baltimore, MD 21218
410-662-7844

Berger Cookies
2900 Waterview Avenue
Baltimore, MD 21230
410-752-5175
BergerCookies.com

Ostrowski Food Market & Sausage
1801 Bank Street
Baltimore, MD 21231
410-732-1118
OstrowskiofBankStreetSausage.com

Boston

**The North End Fish Market
(Mercato del Mare)**
99 Salem Street, North End
Boston, MA 02113
857-362-7477
NorthEndFish.com

A. Russo & Sons
560 Pleasant Street
Watertown, MA 02472
617-923-1500
Russos.com

Savenor's Market
160 Charles Street
Boston, MA 02114
617-723-6328

92 Kirkland Street
Cambridge, MA 02138
617-576-6328
SavenorsMarket.com

Formaggio Kitchen
244 Huron Avenue
Cambridge, MA 02138
617-354-4750
FormaggioKitchen.com

Boston Public Market
Dewey Square
Tuesday and Thursday, May to November
BostonPublicMarket.org

New Deal Fish Market
622 Cambridge Street
Cambridge, MA 02141
617-876-8227
NewDealFishMarket.com

Dave's Fresh Pasta
81 Holland Street
Somerville, MA 02144
617-623-0867
DavesFreshPasta.com

Don Otto's Natural & Organic Market
577 Tremont Street, South End
Boston, MA 02118
617-778-0360
DonOttosMarket.com

Chicago

Green City Market
South End of Lincoln Park between Clark
and Stockton Drive
Wednesday and Saturday, year-round with
a nearby indoor location for the winter
months
ChicagoGreenCityMarket.org

Conte Di Savoia (Italian grocer)
1438 W. Taylor Street
Chicago, IL 60607
312-666-3471
ConteDiSavoia.com

The Spice House
1512 North Wells Street
Chicago, IL 60610
(locations also in Milwaukee, WI, and
   Evanston and Geneva, IL)
312-274-0378
TheSpiceHouse.com

Fox & Obel
401 E. Illinois
Chicago, IL 60611
312-410-7301
fox-obel.com

Paulina Meat Market
3501 N. Lincoln Avenue
Chicago, IL 60657
773-248-6272
PaulinaMeatMarket.com

Wally's Market (Polish market)
6601 W. Irving Park Road
   (and three other locations)
Chicago, IL 60634
773-427-1616
WallysMarket.com

**Al Khayyam Bakery
   (grocer and bakery)**
4738 N. Kedzie
Chicago, IL 60686
773-583-3077

The Fish Guy
4423 N. Elston Avenue
Chicago, IL 60630
773-283-7400
FishGuy.com

Marion Street Cheese Market
100 S. Marion Street
Oak Park, IL 60302
708-725-7200
MarionStreetCheeseMarket.com

Los Angeles

Hollywood Farmers' Market
1600 Ivar Avenue at Selma Avenue
Hollywood, CA 90028
323-463-3171
Sunday
Farmernet.com

Santa Monica Farmers' Market
Arizona Avenue and 3rd Street
   (and 2 other locations)
Santa Monica, CA 90401
Wednesday, Saturday, and Sunday
www01.smgov.net/farmers_market/
   Wednesday.htm

Studio City Farmers' Market
Ventura Place
Studio City, CA 91604
Sunday
StudioCityFarmersMarket.com

Grand Central Market
317 South Broadway
Los Angeles, CA 90013
213-624-2378
GrandCentralSquare.com

Los Angeles Fish
420 Sanford Avenue
Los Angeles, CA 90744
213-629-1213
LAFishCo.com

Santa Monica Seafood
1000 Wilshire Boulevard
Santa Monica, CA 94101
310-393-5244
SantaMonicaSeafood.com

Artisan Cheese Gallery
12023 Ventura Boulevard
Studio City, CA 91604
818-505-0207
ArtisanCheeseGallery.com

Cheese Store of Silverlake
3926-28 West Sunset Boulevard
Los Angeles, CA 90029
323-644-7511
CheeseStoreSL.com

La Brea Bakery
624 South La Brea Avenue
Los Angeles, CA 90036
323-939-6813
LaBreaBakery.com

Surfas Restaurant & Supply
8777 W. Washington Boulevard
Culver City, CA 90232
310-559-4770
SurfasLosAngeles.com

La Española Meats
25020 Doble Avenue
Harbor City, CA 90710
310-539-0455
LaEspanolaMeats.com

Wally's (wine store)
2107 Westwood Boulevard
Los Angeles, CA 90025
310-475-0606
WallyWine.com

Minneapolis/St. Paul

Kramarczuk's Sausage Company
215 E. Hennepin Avenue
Minneapolis, MN 55414
612-379-3018
Kramarczuk.com

Minneapolis Farmers' Market
312 E. Lyndale Avenue North
Minneapolis, MN 55405
612-333-1718
MplsFarmersMarket.com

St. Paul Farmers' Market
290 E. 5th Street (plus various satellite
    locations)
St. Paul, MN 55101
651-227-8101
Weekends; hours vary by location and
    time of year
StPaulFarmersMarket.com

Coastal Seafoods
2330 Minnehaha Avenue South
Minneapolis, MN 55404
612-724-7425
CoastalSeafoods.com

Rustica Bakery
3220 W. Lake Street
Minneapolis, MN 55416
612-822-1119
RusticaBakery.com

B.T. McElrath Chocolatier
2010 E. Hennepin Avenue #78
Minneapolis, MN 55413
612-331-8800
BTMcElrath.com

Clancey's Meats and Fish
4307 Upton Avenue South
Minneapolis, MN 55410
612-926-0222
ClanceysMeats.com

Golden Fig (specialists in foods from Minnesota and Wisconsin)
790 Grand Avenue
St. Paul, MN 55105
651-602-0144
GoldenFig.com

New Orleans

Charlie's Seafood (Natchitoches meat pies)
8311 Jefferson Highway
Harahan, LA 70123
504-737-3700
CharliesSeafoodRestaurant.com

Johnny's Seafood (jumbo lump crabmeat)
5104 Lapalco Boulevard
Marrero, LA 70772
504-349-3500
JohnnysSeafood.net

Hong Kong Food Market (Vietnamese market)
925 Behrman Highway
Terrytown, LA 70056
504-394-7075

Nor-Joe Importing Co. (Italian market)
505 Frisco Avenue
Metairie, LA 70005
504-833-9240
Norjoe.com

Creole Country Sausage Factory
512 David Street
New Orleans, LA 70119
504-488-1263

Flour Power Bakery
2101 Paris Road
Charlmette, LA 70043
504-276-9095
FlourPowerNola.com

Vietnamese Farmers' Market
14401 Alcee Fortier Boulevard, 1 block north of Chef Menteur Highway
New Orleans, LA
Saturdays

Crescent City Farmers' Market
Downtown New Orleans, 700 Magazine
    Street at Girod Street, Saturday
Uptown New Orleans, 200 Broadway
    Street at the River, Tuesday
Mid-City New Orleans, 3700 Orleans
    Avenue at the Bayou, Thursday
CrescentCityFarmersMarket.org

Langenstein's Market
1330 Arabella Street
New Orleans, LA 70115
504-899-9283

800 Metairie Road
Metairie, LA 70005
504-831-6682
Langensteins.com

Dorignac's
710 Veterans Boulevard
Metairie, LA 70005
504-834-8216
Dorignacs.com

New York

Blue Apron Foods (grocer)
814 Union Street
Brooklyn, NY 11215
718-230-3180

Dorian's Seafood
1580 York Avenue
New York, NY 10028
212-535-2256
DoriansSeafood.com

Kalustyan's (spice market)
123 Lexington Avenue
New York, NY 10016
212-685-3451
Kalustyans.com

Sahadi's (Far and Middle East market)
187 Atlantic Avenue
Brooklyn, NY 11201
718-624-4550
Sahadis.com

A Cook's Companion (cookware)
197 Atlantic Avenue
Brooklyn, NY 11201
718-852-6901
ACooksCompanion.com

Joe's Dairy (mozzarella)
156 Sullivan Street
New York, NY 10012
212-677-8780

DiPalo Dairy (Italian market)
200 Grand Street
New York, NY 10013
212-226-1033
DiPaloSelects.com

Greenmarket Farmers' Markets
Launched in 1976, today New York has
the nation's largest network of farmers'
markets, with more than fifty seasonal
and year-round locations featuring local
farmers and producers.
GrowNYC.org/greenmarket

Dickson's Farmstand Meats
Chelsea Market
75 Ninth Avenue
New York, NY 10011
212-242-2630
DicksonsFarmstand.com

Saxelby Cheesemonger
Essex Street Market
120 Essex Street
New York, NY 10002
212-228-8204
SaxelbyCheese.com

**Murray's Cheese and
  Murray's Real Salami**
254 Bleecker Street
New York, NY 10014
212-243-3289

Grand Central Market
Lexington Avenue at E. 43rd Street
New York, NY 10017
212-922-1540
MurraysCheese.com

The Lobster Place
Chelsea Market
75 Ninth Avenue
New York, NY 10011
212-255-5672

252 Bleecker Street
New York, NY 10014
212-352-8063
LobsterPlace.com

Schatzie's Prime Meats
555 Amsterdam Avenue
New York, NY 10024
212-410-1555

Esposito's Pork Store
500 Ninth Avenue
New York, NY 10018
212-279-3298

Borgatti's Ravioli & Egg Noodles
632 E. 187th Street
Bronx, NY 10458
718-367-3799
Borgattis.com

**Flying Pigs Farm (rare heritage breed
  pork and poultry)**
Greenmarket at Union Square
  on Saturday
Broadway at W. 16th Street
New York, NY 10003

Greenmarket at Grand Army Plaza
  on Saturday
Brooklyn, NY 11215
518-854-3844
FlyingPigsFarm.com

Titan Foods (Greek market)
25-56 31st Street
Astoria, NY 11102
718-626-7771
TitanFoods.com

Philadelphia

The Market at Talula's Table
102 West State Street
Kennett Square, PA 19348
610-444-8255
TalulasTable.com/market.shtml

Headhouse Farmers' Market
2nd and Lombard Street
Philadelphia, PA 19147
Saturday and Sunday, May to December
TheFoodTrust.org/php/headhouse

Reading Terminal Market
(indoor, year-round, 7 days)
12th and Arch Streets
Philadelphia, PA 19107
215-922-2317
ReadingTerminalMarket.org

Downtown Cheese
Reading Terminal Market
12th and Arch Streets
Philadelphia, PA 19107
215-351-7412

D'Angelo Bros. (meats, game, sausage)
909 South 9th Street
Philadelphia, PA 19147
215-923-5637
DangeloBros.com

Portland, OR

Portland Farmers Market
At Portland State University in South
    Park Blocks between SW Harrison
    and SW Montgomery and 5 other
    locations
Days and months vary by location
PortlandFarmersMarket.org

Foster & Dobbs (cheese)
2518 NE 15th Avenue
Portland, OR 97212
503-284-1157
FosterAndDobbs.com

Newman's Fish Company
Portland City Market
735 NW 21st Avenue
(and 2 other locations)
Portland, OR 97209
503-227-2700
NewmansFish.com

Chop Butchery and Charcuterie
Portland City Market
735 NW 21st Avenue
Portland, OR 97209
503-221-3012
ChopButchery.com

New Seasons Market
Arbor Lodge (and 7 other locations)
6400 N. Interstate Avenue
Portland, OR 97217
503-467-4777
NewSeasonsMarket.com

Pastaworks
3735 SE Hawthorne Boulevard (and 3
    other locations)
Portland, OR 97214
503-232-1010
Pastaworks.com

San Francisco

Cowgirl Creamery
1 Ferry Building #17 (also in
    Washington, DC, and Point Reyes, CA)
San Francisco, CA 94111
415-362-9355
CowgirlCreamery.com

Anthony's Cookies
1417 Valencia Street
San Francisco, CA 94110
415-655-9834
AnthonysCookies.com

Bryan's and Bryan's Quality Meats
3445 California Street
San Francisco, CA 94118
415-752-0179

Ferry Plaza Farmers Market
1 Ferry Building
San Francisco, CA 94111
415-291-3276
Tuesday, Thursday, Saturday
FerryBuildingMarketplace.com/farmers
    _market.php

Far West Fungi (mushrooms)
1 Ferry Building, #34
San Francisco, CA 94111
415-989-9090
FarwestFungi.com

**Bi-Rite Creamery & Bakeshop
    (ice cream)**
3692 18th Street
San Francisco, CA 94110
415-626-5600
BiRiteCreamery.com

Alemany Farmers' Market
100 Alemany Boulevard
San Francisco, CA 94110
Saturday year-round
sfgov.org/site/alemany_index.asp

Drewes Bros. Meat
1706 Church Street
San Francisco, CA 94131
415-821-0515
DrewesBros.com

Seattle

**Pike Place Market
    (year-round indoor food market)**
Pike Street at First Avenue
Seattle, WA 98101
PikePlaceMarket.org

Salumi Artisan Cured Meats
309 Third Avenue South
Seattle, WA 98104
206-621-8772
SalumiCuredMeats.com

Uwajimaya (Asian grocery)
600 5th Avenue South
Seattle, WA 98104 (and 3 other locations,
    including Oregon and Virginia)
206-624-6248
Uwajimaya.com

**CasCioppo Brothers Italian Meat
    Market**
2364 Northwest 80th Street
Seattle, WA 98117
206-784-6121
cascioppomeats.com

The Fresh Fish Company
8002 24th Avenue NW
Seattle, WA 98107
206-782-1632

Ballard Sunday Farmers Market
Ballard Avenue at 22nd
Seattle, WA 98107
Sunday, year-round
206-781-6776
FremontMarket.com/Ballard

Mount Townsend Creamery
338 Sherman Street
Port Townsend, WA 98368
Cheeses sold at Seattle area farmers'
    markets and online
360-379-0895
MtTownsendCreamery.com/team.html

World Spice Merchants
1509 Western Avenue
Seattle, WA 98101
206-682-7274
WorldSpice.com

Uli's Famous Sausage
Pike Place Market (also available online
    and at Seattle-area markets)
206-839-1000
UlisFamousSausage.com

Beecher's Handmade Cheese
1600 Pike Place
Seattle, WA 98101
206-956-1964
BeechersHandmadeCheese.com

Washington, DC

Maine Avenue Fish Market
1100 Maine Avenue SW
Washington, DC 20024
202-484-2722

Dupont Circle FreshFarm Market
1500 Block of 20th Street
Washington, DC 20015
202-362-8889
Sunday, year-round
FreshfarmMarket.org/markets/dupont
    _circle.html

Wagshal's (delicatessen and market)
4845 Massachusetts Avenue NW
Washington, DC 20016
203-363-0777
Wagshals.com

Web Merchants

Gustiamo.com
Imported Italian food products, especially from small specialty producers

Penzeys.com
Spice merchants

RussAndDaughters.com
Smoked fish, caviar, Jewish foods and grocery

NimanRanch.com
Beef, pork, lamb, and charcuterie, humanely and sustainably raised

MrChocolate.com
Chocolates by Jacques Torres

Peets.com
Coffee, tea, and the equipment to make them

DespanaBrandFoods.com
Spanish imported foods and ingredients, including Iberico hams

HHBagels.com
New York's best bagels shipped worldwide

DArtagnan.com
Game, pâtés, foie gras, cured meats, truffles, and poultry

iGourmet.com
Specialty grocery, cheeses, charcuterie, hard-to-find imports

NutsOnLine.com
Nuts, chocolates, coffees, teas

KingArthurFlour.com
All types of baking supplies and tools, including gluten-free ingredients

HomeCanning.com
Jars, lids, canning kits and cookbooks, pectin, and pickling salt

Tienda.com
Spanish ingredients, spices, charcuterie

PickleGuys.com
From Manhattan's Lower East Side, all things pickled

Zingermans.com
Large and resourceful specialty food store—cheese, bread, imported groceries, American regional specialties

Other Information Sources

These are some of the best-regarded and most useful organizations and sources of information about farmers' markets, community supported agriculture (CSA), urban farming, and the overall quality of our food supply.

LocalHarvest.org
For information about farmers' markets and CSAs in your area

SustainableTable.org
Information about buying healthy ingredients

GreenPeople.org
An online directory of eco-friendly products and services. They sell no products.

CommunityGarden.org
For information about urban and community gardening

GreenerChoices.org
An initiative of *Consumer Reports* to educate about "environmentally-friendly products and practices"

CooperativeGrocer.coop/coops/
Cooperative Grocers' Food Co-op directory

Ncga.coop
National Cooperative Grocers Association, to help find a food co-op in your area

JustFood.org
A New York leader in promoting sustainable food through CSAs, city farming, and education

EatWellGuide.org
Help in finding local, sustainable, and organic food in your area

OrganicConsumers.org
A nonprofit grassroots organization that promotes environmental sustainability and free trade

SlowFood.com
An international organization devoted to "good, clean and fair food"

SeafoodWatch.org
Monterey Bay Aquarium's Seafood Watch Program

AMS.usda.gov/AMSv1.0/NOP
United States Department of Agriculture's National Organic Program

Glossary—
Today's Food Language

A friend told me about an adventure he had trying to buy an organic turkey for Thanksgiving dinner. He went to a small neighborhood butcher shop and asked if they could order one for him. "Are you sure? Organic?" they asked. "Absolutely," he insisted and they arranged for him to pick up his fresh, organic bird the day before the holiday. On Thanksgiving morning he unwrapped his fresh turkey, which had been carefully packaged in a large plastic bag—only to stagger back in shock to find that while dead and plucked, the turkey was fully intact. With head, feet, and guts still in place. For that butcher shop, this was "organic."

You've got to ask what the words mean. And you can never be sure the definitions will stay true from place to place, food to food, producer to producer.

Given the state of the food supply in America today, most of us could use a grocery GPS. Unfortunately we're on our own to investigate and vet the foods we buy to cook in our own kitchens. Reading labels is always an essential step, but today's food terminology is at best fluid and at worst imprecise and misleading. Just because our food has one of these labels doesn't necessarily mean it's healthier or tastes better. Or that your holiday turkey has been beheaded.

I wish I could give you precise definitions. I can't because they don't really exist. But these are generally what these words mean and how they should guide your grocery shopping choices. The most important thing you can do to be an educated food shopper is to read labels, be skeptical, ask questions, and try to buy from trusted merchants.

Fair trade. A trade policy without government interference that lets prices freely determine resource allocation. In theory this means the consumer gets to pay the producer, without the bureaucracy or cost of middlemen, so that more of the income goes to the producer. The term is most commonly applied to coffee.

Farmed. A term that's usually used in counterpoint to "wild." For instance, farmed salmon is raised in pens with a controlled diet, while wild salmon is caught in its natural habitat. Farmed isn't necessarily bad, but you need to know the quality and conditions of the farm. All organic fish is farm raised since you can't call it organic unless you've controlled what it eats. In my opinion, wild fish is generally superior to farmed, including organic farmed.

Free-range. A term used primarily to describe how poultry is raised, "free-range" suggests that the chicken and other poultry are not living in a confining coop. In fact the USDA lets a bird be labeled free-range as long as its cage has access to the outdoors. A window or open door a few minutes a day is enough. So to say something was raised free-range is no guarantee of anything.

Foodie. A pathetic word that trivializes anyone who takes a serious interest in what they're eating. This is the only time this word will appear in this book.

Heritage and heirloom. These terms are used to describe both animals and plants that have not been subject to the kind of horticultural and/or breeding corrections made by agribusiness for commercial and mass production. These terms are often used with (heritage) pork and (heirloom) tomatoes.

Local. Food that has been grown or produced within a relatively short distance from where it's sold. Some define local as less than fifty miles, but others think anything that's a day's truck distance still qualifies. Essentially it describes food that is grown as close to home as possible.

Locavore. Someone who is dedicated to eating all or mostly locally grown and produced food.

Natural. This is a marketing term that has no consistent meaning and is not regulated. A product may be labeled "natural" and still contain artificial ingredients.

Organic. This term is generally used when animals and fish are raised without hormones or antibiotics in their feed and when fruits and vegetables are grown without pesticides. Within that broad cast, the criteria are frequently adjusted by the USDA, which also oversees the rules and documentation required for a product to be labeled as organic.

Just because something is called organic doesn't necessarily mean it's superior to its nonorganic (often called "conventional") counterpart. For example, a small sheep farm could produce an artisanal cheese using a higher standard for quality than the USDA's but not be able to keep the records and file all the paperwork required to label its cheese organic. At the same time, a huge cheese company could hire a staff to fill out the USDA paperwork for its factory-produced but certified organic cheddar.

Slow Food. A movement that began in Italy in 1989 as a response to the prevalence of fast food. Using the concept of "eco-gastronomy" as its core principle, the Slow Food organization works to protect the heritage and traditions of food, the world's food supply, and the pleasures of eating.

Sustainable. A term used to describe the philosophy and practice of harvesting crops or seafood without causing the land or species to be depleted. This term is often used in association with seafood and farmland.

Vegan. A diet that excludes all animal and animal-derived products, including honey, eggs, and dairy products. Veganism extends to lifestyle and forbids the use of any animal-derived products in clothing, furniture, or any other item.

Vegetarian. A diet of plant-based foods that omits meat, fish, and poultry. Some vegetarians eat dairy products, some eat eggs, some eat both, and some eat neither. Still other forms of "semi-vegetarianism" may include fish or poultry.

Wild. A term used often to describe seafood that has been caught in its natural habitat rather than raised in a controlled farm condition.

Metric Equivalencies

Liquid and Dry Measure Equivalencies

Customary	Metric
¼ teaspoon	1.25 milliliters
½ teaspoon	2.5 milliliters
1 teaspoon	5 milliliters
1 tablespoon	15 milliliters
1 fluid ounce	30 milliliters
¼ cup	60 milliliters
⅓ cup	80 milliliters
½ cup	120 milliliters
1 cup	240 milliliters
1 pint (*2 cups*)	480 milliliters
1 quart (*4 cups, 32 ounces*)	960 milliliters (*.96 liter*)
1 gallon (*4 quarts*)	3.84 liters
1 ounce (*by weight*)	28 grams
¼ pound (*4 ounces*)	114 grams
1 pound (*16 ounces*)	454 grams
2.2 pounds	1 kilogram (*1000 grams*)

Oven Temperature Equivalencies

Description	°Fahrenheit	°Celsius
Cool	200	90
Very slow	250	120
Slow	300–325	150–160
Moderately slow	325–350	160–180
Moderate	350–375	180–190
Moderately hot	375–400	190–200
Hot	400–450	200–230
Very hot	450–500	230–260

Acknowledgments

So much about both writing and cooking is solitary. But it took a community of cooks, book lovers, food merchants, and friends to make my dream for *The City Cook* come true.

At Simon & Schuster, Sydny Miner first brought me into the family, but as she took her own journey, she made sure I was put into the steady hands of Michelle Rorke, whose meticulous care and love of both writing and cooking (in her own small city kitchen) made her my perfect editor. Nancy Inglis and Nancy Singer transformed my manuscript into a volume I am so very proud to call mine. And Michelle Jasmine made sure anyone interested in the changing world of urban home cooking would know about *The City Cook*.

I've cooked from enough cookbooks to know that when a recipe leaves its author's kitchen it must work in everyone else's. To be sure mine would perform in any city kitchen I recruited a company of friends and fellow cooks who tested and retested every single recipe: Arthur White, Karin Giger, Maureen O'Toole, Meile Rockefeller, David Neibart, and Lorrie Stuart. This book is certainly better because of you.

Teigh Thompson, Dave Overbeck, Jerome Vitucci, Arthur White, and Gautam Choudhury extended our camera's reach into urban markets across the country. A special tribute to photographer Ivan Henry who generously shared his lifetime of looking through the lens to guide and coach the photographic ambition for this book. Ivan, you have a standing invitation for dinner any time you want.

Greg Socha, Karin Giger, Betsy Herold, Emma Murphy, Dorian Mecir, and Clayton Smith shared treasured and practiced recipes and stories so that city cooks everywhere could sit at their virtual dinner tables.

This book can't leave my hands and be held in yours without remembering my beloved friend and fellow cook Patricia Herold Nielsen, who not only taught me how to bake a Peach and Bourbon Ham but also encouraged my passion for cooking and my dream for *The City Cook*. I miss you constantly.

Friends across the country helped make sure that *The City Cook* crossed the Hudson River, especially Bill Thorness in Seattle, Dan and Ellen Kolsrud in Los Angeles, Brent

Marmo in Minneapolis, and Sherman Spritz in Boston. And here in New York, my friend Irene Miller gave me unconditional support that was both a gift and an assurance.

For both inspiration and hard facts, the extraordinary people at Just Food have always encouraged The City Cook's mission and been generous with their expertise. And the marketing and culinary specialists at Fresh Direct helped me understand the shifting demographics and grocery preferences of today's urban households.

My time spent in kitchens and classrooms at The French Culinary Institute changed my life. But I'm particularly grateful for the tough love received in a food writing class from the much published and much decorated Alan Richman, who taught me that the last word that any great food writer ever uses is "delicious."

New York City's extraordinary food merchants inspire me every day not just to write but also to cook. Among them a special thanks goes to Fairway's Steven Jenkins, who was among the first to give The City Cook his support and believed in my dream to create this book.

When you write a website and put your work out into cyberspace, you never know who may be watching and reading. Soon after I launched TheCityCook.com I discovered my newsletter subscribers included legendary editor Judith Jones and the extraordinary cookbook writer Barbara Kafka. You both will never know how much your attention to my work and your encouragement let my voice remain my own.

This book stands on the shoulders of TheCityCook.com, and so I offer boundless appreciation to its readers whose passion for cooking and eating well motivate me every day. Jacqueline Broner, a designer of gigantic talent, created our witty and bold skyline logo. And to the people of Animus Rex, who have become family, thank you for listening to me when I brought you my nascent idea for TheCityCook.com and turning it into a place of constant imagination and utility: Bev Anderson, Roger Zuniga, Bernado Zuniga, Charles Loflin, and the mighty Todd Rengel. I love you all.

Finally, I will never forget the day that Janis Donnaud stepped through my computer screen and into my life. As a brilliant literary agent, she is advocating, smart, and creative. But she became a friend who inspired me to do my best while also making me laugh. I am so very grateful to know you.

And to my husband, Mark—thanks for never asking, "What's for dinner?"

Index

About the Author

Kate McDonough is the editor of TheCityCook.com, which she launched in 2007 after a successful career in corporate communications. She attended The French Culinary Institute and is a graduate of the Graduate School of Design at Harvard University from which she received a master's degree in city planning. She lives and cooks in Manhattan with her husband, Mark Dichter.

About the Photographer

Mark Dichter is a documentary filmmaker and recording engineer. He is also the photographer for TheCityCook.com and sometimes refers to himself as The City Dishwasher.

Printed in the United States
By Bookmasters